AN INTRODUCTION TO THE STUDY OF SOCIETY

By the Same Author

1. Sri Aurobindo and the Future of Mankind,
   Calcutta University Press, 1934.
2. Negative Fact, Negation and Truth,
   Calcutta University Press, 1942.
3. An Introduction to Logic, Vols. 1 and II,
   Kamala Book Depot, Calcutta, 1949.
4. Sri Aurobindo and Some Modern Problems,
   General Printers, Calcutta, 1958.
5. A Commentary on the life and Teaching of Sri Ramakrishna,
   General Printers, Calcutta, 1958.
6. Parapsychology and Religion,
   General Printers, 1959.
7. Studies in Philosophy,
   Firma K. L. Mukhopadhyay,
   Calcutta, 1962.

An Introduction To The Study of Society

A. C. DAS, M.A., Ph. D.,
Premchand Raychand Scholar,
Former Head of the Department of Philosophy,
University College of Arts,
Calcutta University

MOTILAL BANARSIDASS
DELHI :: VARANASI :: PATNA

Indological Publishers & Booksellers
Head Office : BUNGALOW ROAD, JAWAHAR NAGAR, DELHI-7
Branches : 1. CHOWK, VARANASI-1 (U.P.)
2. ASHOK RAJPATH, PATNA-4 (BIHAR)

First Edition
1972

Printed in India
BY SHANTILAL JAIN, AT SHRI JAINENDRA PRESS, BUNGALOW ROAD, JAWAHAR NAGAR, DELHI-7 AND PUBLISHED BY SUNDARLAL JAIN, MOTILAL BANARSIDASS, BUNGALOW ROAD, JAWAHAR NAGAR, DELHI-7

Dedicated

To

The Hallowed Memory Of

Raja Ram Mohun Roy

The Maker of Modern India

PREFACE

This book is meant to be an Introduction to the Study of Society. The analysis given in it is designed to cover the area in which the problems regarding society and social life fall. At the very outset, the issue whether there is anything like social philosophy, which is to be distinguished from sociology, has been discussed and an attempt made to settle the question : Is there a general science of society as against the special social sciences? Some, following Herbert Spencer, hold that philosophy is unification of the sciences, in the sense that philosophy as a speculative study arises by way of synthesizing the results of the sciences. In the field of social studies also a similar view of sociology in relation to the special social sciences has been developed. We are told that the former is only a body of generalizations on the basis of the results of the special social sciences. But the analogy between philosophy and sociology breaks down in view of the fact that philosophy is an abstract study as it proceeds by speculation, whereas sociology is an empirical study, though it is the general science of society. The point is that sociology is not quite based on the special social sciences, though the latter supply much material to the former. There is nevertheless an intimate relation between sociology as the general science of society and social philosophy. If we do not identify sociology with social philosophy—there is no reason why we should—we have to note that the former tends to merge into the latter.

The term "philosophy" is a controversial one. It is rather paradoxical to say that after three thousand years of philosophy, the present-day philosophers are debating among themselves what philosophy is about. This is unfortunate indeed. Though the conceptions of philosophy are not as many as there are philosophers, the conception of it varied from age to age. In the beginning, it was occupied with the physical world, then it turned from matter to mind. Now it turns round man. The latest school of philosophy takes man as the subject matter of philosophy. But man in the concrete is a being who lives in society. So the study of man as apart from that of society is abstract. This brings out the importance of the social studies. Society is, indeed, the matrix of our life and existence. The study of society is therefore one of first importance. The University Grants Commission and UNESCO are obviously right in emphasizing humanistic studies like ethics, sociology *cum* social philosophy, and comparative religion. It is important to consider how philosophy is taught in the Indian Universities. Generally, students are introduced to the subject through history of philosophy. But history of philosophy is taken only in the sense of a succession of systems of thought and is taught without reference to the history of the relevant periods with the result that students do not know what philosophers belonged to what periods. That way they only gather some ideas torn from the flow of events in which they were rooted. It would doubtless be rational to teach philosophy by the help of history, including as it does the study of society in its origin and development. From this point of view also the study of society appears to be of paramount importance. That without social studies the education of our boys and girls remains incomplete has been recognized by the Educationl Authorities all over the world. They have therefore made provision for the teaching of the subject at the primary, secondary, and higher stages of education. This is one bright feature of the prevailing system of education, which, however, needs to be overhauled.

Here I should express my indebtedness to some former pupils of mine, especially to Sri Dhananjay Nath of the Ramakrishna Mission Multi-purpose School, Midnapore, and Sri Pijus Das, Lecturer, Kakdwip, College, who constantly encouraged me to make the book ready for publication. I also express my gratitude to Motilal Banarsidass for so kindly undertaking publication of the book at a time when the cost of paper and printing is very high.

Calcutta
October 1. 1972.

A. C. Das

CONTENTS

I. SOCIAL PHILOSOPHY : MEANING AND SCOPE

Philosophy and Science ; Social Philosophy and Social Science ; What is society ? Is there any animal society ? Special social sciences ; Special Social sciences enumerated ; Need for a general social science ; Sociology as a general social science ; Sociology as the science of society ; Sociology as the study of the generalizations of the special social sciences ; Sociology as the study of the postulates of the special social sciences ; Politics as the study of the State presupposes society ; Archaeology presupposes society ; Comparative Philology posits society ; Comparative religion postulates society; Society defined; Dynamic and Static Sociology ; Relation of sociology to some sciences ; Social Philosophy

II. RELATION BETWEEN SOCIAL PHILOSOPHY AND SOME OTHER STUDIES 13

Auguste Comte founded the science of sociology ; Social Philosophy dependent upon social sciences ; Social Philosophy and Psychology ; Difference between Social Philosophy and Psychology ; Social Philosophy and Politics ; Political Philosophy not a branch of social philosophy ; Social philosophy and ethics—ethics a normative science ; In ancient times social philosophy included ethics ; Social philosophy and philosophy ; Philosophy as understanding the universe; Social philosophy is a departmental study; Social philosophy and philosophy of history; Spencer's philosophy of the world; Marx's view

III. SOME SOCIAL CONCEPTS 25

Community ; MacIver's view, Ginsberg's view ; Cole on community, examples of community ; McDougall on the origin of cities ; Relation of Community to Society ; A caste no community ; Is a religious group a community? Common use of the word "Community", World Community ; Association—definition, examples ; Institution—definition, examples ; Relation between Association and Institution ; Is a school an institution ? Custom—Custom and institution; Custom and law; Custom and moral law ; Divine law ; Folkways—definition and examples ; Cross-Cousin Marriage—definition, illustrations ; Propinquity ; Incest ; Social Composition ; Social Constitution

IV. THE METHOD OF THE SOCIAL STUDY 44

Empirical method in science—What is observation? What is experiment ? Observation and experiment constitute one method ; Objective method in the study of society ; Environment and society ; The view that the environment determines society ; Criticism of this view ; Social adaptation is creative ; Subjective-objective method ; Experimental method in the absolute sense cannot be used in the study of society ; Historical method to be supplemented by the teleological method ; Mechanical explanation. Teleological explanation

V. THE SOCIAL NATURE OF MAN 56

Social nature based on instinct ; Social nature and parental instinct ; Criticism ; Social nature and herding instinct ; Social nature and consciousness of kind ; Criticism ; Social nature and intelligence ; Social nature and the sense of utility ; Social nature based on contract ; Hobbes, Locke and Rousseau ; Social nature and imitation ;

Mutual-aid theory ; Social nature intrinsic in man ; Social nature based on self or spirit.

VI. THE FAMILY 80

Is the Family an association? Earliest form of the family ; Consanguine Family ; Punaluan Family ; Syndyasmian Family ; Patriarchal Family ; Monogamian Family ; Basis of the power of the father in the family ; *Paterfamilias* ; Patria potestas ; Matriarchal form of the family ; Patriarchal and modern family ; Basis of the family ; Mackenzie's view considered and criticized ; Economic condition of the family ; Marx and Engels ; Women in ancient society ; Modern family ; Family and free love ; Family and late marriage ; Religion and modern family ; Facts or factors tending to disrupt the family

VII. MARRIAGE 113

Is marriage all sex? Marriage is rooted in family ; Westermarck's view ; Marriage as the means of getting an assistant in domestic work ; Different aspects of marriage, physical, psychological, ethical, and spiritual ; Marriage as an institution ; Forms of marriage; Totemism and *gotra*; Forms of Hindu marriage; The ideal form of marriage

VIII. VARṆĀŚRAMA DHARMA 139

Four colours for four classes ; Fourfold organization of Vedic society ; Training and discipline for the classes ; Origin of the four castes ; Relationship between the castes ; Stages of life and their duties ; Forms of marriage ; Castes and sub-castes ; Gotra

IX. INDIVIDUAL AND SOCIETY

Atomistic conception of society ; Mechanistic theory ; Organic conception of society ; A double relation between individual and society; Society and social reformers; Society as an organization

X. EDUCATION AND EDUCATIONAL INSTITUTIONS 170

Plato's theory of education; Gymnastic for the body and music for the soul; Aristotle's theory of education; Education in ancient Rome; Education in the Middle Ages; Locke's theory; Rousseau's theory; Education in ancient India; Education in India of the Christian era; Theories of Tagore, Aurobindo, and Gandhi; Basic and Primary Education; Modern systems of Education; Kindergarten; Nursery School; Montessori; Higher education; Co-education; Religious education

XI. SOCIAL MIND 209

Social Mind as collective consciousness; Espinas, Durkheim, and Wündt; Social Mind as group mind; Social Mind and General Will; Five senses of "General Will"; Ginsberg on General Will; Social Mind as social harmony; Giddings on social Mind; Different aspects of the social Mind; Tradition, Primary, Secondary and Tertiary

INDEX 231

Chapter I

SOCIAL PHILOSOPHY : MEANING AND SCOPE

Before we proceed to discuss the nature and scope of Social Philosophy, we have to consider the distinction, if any, between Social Philosophy and Social Science. And for this purpose we should explain how, generally, philosophy is distinguished from science.

Philosophy and Science : Science, as we know, is the study of positive facts, and as there are different kinds of facts, there are different sciences to deal with them. These sciences are called the special sciences because each of them is concerned with one department of Nature, i.e. one kind of facts. There are thus sciences like physics, chemistry, biology, psychology, and so on. Physics studies physical things, chemistry deals with chemical phenomena, biology with animal life, and psychology with mental phenomena. The sciences investigate facts and events in their respective spheres, and make generalizations and formulate laws about them.

According to some, there is an intimate relation between philosophy and science, or the special sciences, as they are called. Philosophy as a study arises, they say, by way of considering the generalizations of the sciences, and arriving at further generalizations on the basis of them all. Herbert Spencer, for example, says, "Science is *partially*-unified knowledge ; Philosophy is completely-unified knowledge."[1] That is to say, philosophy is the unification of the special sciences through reflection on the generalizations they make. If we accept this definition of philosophy, it ought to be clear that philosophy for its origin is dependent upon science or the sciences. We shall briefly consider here the difficulties involved in this view of the relation between science and philosophy.

1 *The Synthetic Philosophy of Herbert Spencer,* **Ed. F. H. Collins, Williams & Norgate, London, 1901, p. 18.**

If Philosophy is really dependent upon science, there could be no philosophy without science. But there was philosophy in ancient times when there was no science in the strict sense. And philosophy was just investigation of the universe as a whole, including facts and values. When, however, science was developed, philosophy derived much material from it and thus enriched its content. But to say this is not to say that philosophy is dependent upon science. Philosophy, even today, may proceed in its own way without considering the results of the sciences. As Bosanquet puts it, "The inquiry into reality as such may begin anywhere."[2] So philosophy is not necessarily to be founded upon science. But we should recognize the fact that some sociologists utilize the view that Philosophy is the unification of the special sciences in forming their conception of Social Philosophy in relation to the special Social Sciences.

Social Philosophy and Social Science : Like physics or chemistry, social science is a positive science. It studies society as a phenomenon, its structure, laws, institutions, and so forth. But there is an important difference between social science and any other science. Sciences like physics, chemistry, and biology each study individual things of a kind or class, which exist in isolation from each other. But social science deals with society which is a group-phenomenon in the sense that it is a whole made up of individuals or individual minds.

What is society? It is common knowledge that some animals in their wild state live in groups. They are : cows, buffaloes, elephants, etc. They live in groups and move in groups. Every cow in a locality, in the jungles, for instance, instinctively feels its kinship with every other cow, and in this way they hang together. So also do buffaloes, elephants, and the rest. They are for this reason called gregarious animals. Now coming to the human world, we find that men also live in groups in their characteristic way. And what is called society is nothing but a group of human beings living together for all purposes in mutual help and co-operation. A

2 *Science and Philosophy*, George Allen and Unwin, Ltd., London, 1927, p. 22.

large number of men living in a territory, speaking a common language and having a common way of life constitute society.[3]

Is there any animal society? Some sociologists, however, take the word "society" in a wide sense; they speak of human and animal society.[4] They recognize "the remarkable social organizations" of some insects, such as ants, bees, and hornets. Really, we are amazed by the behaviour of these insects among themselves. The ants, as we observe, live and move together. But we cannot say that they simply herd together. On the contrary, they exhibit activities that seem to be sympathetic and co-operative. When, for example, some ants of a group attack a fly, others or all the others come up and join forces with them. When they build an ant-hill they each carrying a particle of earth in their tiny mouths resemble day-labourers carrying bricks to a building under construction. The co-operative activities of the bees and hornets are more elaborate, and among the bees especially there is a sort of division of labour. But this group-life is based on and is determined by instinct; there is no tinge of intelligence around it. The behaviour of the insects we have mentioned remains constant. There is no development or deterioration of it, showing that it is more or less mechanical. Human society, whatever be its origin, grows and develops. And this is because of the fact that human society consists of individual minds who come together on the basis of their recognition of each other and of their awareness of a common end or interest. So to avoid confusion we should confine society to men.*

As there are different groups of this type, there are different societies. All this goes to justify the conception that social science, unlike a physical science, studies a group-phenomenon or some group phenomena. Social science is

3 F. H. Giddings, *Inductive Sociology*, Macmillan Co. Ltd., 1914, London, pp. 5-6.

4 MacIver and Page, *Society*, Macmillan and Co. Ltd., London, 1957, p. 6.

*F. Howard Collins, *The Synthetic Philosophy of Herbert* Spencer, Williams And Norgate, London, 1901, p. 351.

therefore of its own kind in so far as its subject matter is concerned. Social science is, in short, concerned with groupings of men, not with individual men isolated from one another. But generally social science is divided into general and special. We can develop our conception of Social Philosophy only by way of considering the nature and scope of the general social science as well as of the special social science or sciences. Therefore, we propose to consider these under three sub-heads.

1. Special social sciences

Special social sciences are enumerated. There are in fact several special social sciences such as politics, economics, comparative philology, comparative religion, and archaeology. McDougall mentions as the social sciences ethics, economics, political science, philosophy of history, sociology, and cultural anthropology, and the more special social sciences—the science of religion, of law, of education, and of art.[5] Since these sciences study the special aspects of society, they are called the special social sciences. Thus politics considers the nature and structure of the State, its origin and development; economics explains wealth, its production and distribution; comparative philology analyzes and compares the different languages; comparative religion makes a comparative study of the religions; while archaeology deals with the remains of the past that have been dug out of the earth.

Need for a general social science. Now, if there are some sciences to investigate the different aspects of society, it seems that there is no need for a general science. Some sociologists, however, posit a general social science and call it sociology. But what is it like? There is a difference of opinion on the nature and status of sociology in relation to the special social sciences. Here we may consider the theories developed by Auguste Comte, Herbert Spencer, F. H. Giddings, and others.

5 *Introduction to Social Psychology*, Methuen and Co. Ltd. London, 1913, p. 1

2. Sociology as a general social science and its relation to the special social sciences.

Sociology as the science of society considered as a whole. Auguste Comte maintains that the special social sciences are no sciences in the strict sense. Each of these sciences, in his opinion, studies one definite aspect of the social whole, and studies it in abstraction from the whole. But an abstraction is an abstraction and is by itself no fact.[6] Suppose that a table is brown. The colour brown is in the table. But if we fix on this colour in abstraction, i. e., as apart, from the table, the colour does not represent any colour of the table. This colour is a quality of the table only when it is considered to be in the table. This colour or any other colour is a fact only when it attaches to an object. A colour does not exist by itself. So it is no fact when it is taken out of relation to an object. Similarly any limb of an animal or a plant organism, say, hand, eye, tongue, leaf or bough, when severed from the whole to which it belongs, does not remain to be a fact; it withers away altogether. Comte presses this analogy in the case of society and its different aspects. He points out that the State, wealth, language, etc. are only some aspects of society and are intelligible only with reference to it. Therefore, the special sciences, abstracting as they do these different aspects from the social whole, do not, says Comte, deal with any concrete facts. Obviously, no one of the special sciences is a science since a science is the study of a concrete fact or facts. Society is a concrete fact or phenomenon, and sociology is the only science that studies it systematically. For Comte the social science is just the science of society, and is not divided into general and special.

Sociology as a collective description of the special social sciences. According to Spencer, we can well speak of sociology as the general science of society. But sociology as a general science, he points out, is only the summation of the special social

6 *Cf.* Giddings, *The Principles of Sociology*, The Macmillan Company, New York, 1920, p. 28.

sciences;[7] sociology is the body of knowledge of which the special social sciences are only parts. In Spencer's opinion, sociology is only a generic name which is employed in order to make a collective description of the special social sciences. In other words, sociology as a general science is no study distinct from the special studies of the social whole. Sociology is only a collective name of the special social sciences.

Sociology as the study of the generalizations of the special social sciences. Some may suggest that sociology as the general science of society accepts the generalizations of the special social sciences and proceeds on the basis of these to wider generalizations.[8] *This view of the relation between sociology and the special social sciences is parallel to the view of the relation between philosophy and the special sciences, which we have considered above.* Clearly, this view makes sociology wholly dependent upon the special social sciences. For data the former entirely depends upon the latter. And the development of the general science, i. e., sociology, hinges upon the development of the special social sciences. In that case, sociology becomes only a secondary science in the sense that it only manipulates the results of the special social sciences.

Sociology as the study of the postulates of the special social sciences. According to F. H. Giddings, sociology is a general science and as such studies the basic presuppositions of the special social sciences.[9] Economics, as we know, is the science of wealth; it deals with production and distribution of wealth. But why is there wealth at all? Men produce and possess wealth because it is considered the means of fulfilling their desires. Behind wealth there is, then, a volume of desires—desires of all men. The economist, however, does not investigate desire, its nature and origin. He only takes it for granted and proceeds to deal with his subject matter, namely, wealth. But production and distribution of wealth

7 *Ibid.*

8 *Cf.* J. S. Mackenzie, *Outlines of Sociology*, George Allen Unwin Ltd., London, 1956, p. 13.

9 *The Principles of Sociology*, p. 31.

presupposes a number of human individuals living in social relationships, who realize and can realize their desires only through co-operation, i. e., in society. Therefore, the study of human desires falls within the scope of sociology.

Politics as the study of the State presupposes society. Politics investigates the State in its nature and origin. The State is a group of men, generally, speaking one and the same language, living in a territory with a government of their own without allegiance to any other territory. Every State has its constitution, which means the form of government such as monarchy, oligarchy democracy, etc. There are different States in the world, and the constitution varies from State to State, or some States have or may have the same constitution as against the other States. It is quite clear that there cannot be a bare State, i. e., a State without constitution. A State without constitution is an abstraction, a mere idea, while a State in actual existence is embodied in a definite form of government. That is to say, the State is always with or within a constitution. But a government is for a people. So the people living together in co-operation, mutual help and sympathy are the necessary presupposition of the State. A number of people living together in mutual relationships in a geographical area constitute what we call society. The State, in short, posits society and is based on society. Politics as a science is concerned with the State and not with society. Politics, however, takes society for granted. Hence there is need for a science to study society. This science is sociology.

Archaeology deals with the relics of the past and takes society for granted. Archaeology, as we have seen before, deals with the relics of the past. Archaeologists have to date carried out excavations all over the world—at Mahenjo-daro and Harappa, for instance, in undivided India and at other places in Europe, Africa, America—and dug up instruments, implements, ornaments, artistic creations, ruins of towns, cities, etc. which some past generations made and used. They study all these and try to determine the kind of life they lived. But such a study presupposes society, that those people were social beings in that they had social relationships between them. Nevertheless, archaeology does not investigate society as such. It leaves the study of society to a different science, namely, sociology.

Comparative philology posits society. Comparative philology is concerned with some different languages. It analyzes the major languages, old and new, and explains their origin and development. By comparing them with each other it traces some languages to the same root, or makes groupings of them according to their origin and growth. But language is a social product. As we know, even the lower animals have a language of their own—a language of inarticulate signs and sounds. Through this language they express their inner feelings and experiences. For example, a dog wags its tail when it is glad, barks when it is frightened; a cat mews to express its varied feelings; a horse neighs; a lion roars; and so on. These expressions are rather instinctive and are not determined by intelligence or free choice. Hence they are inarticulate.

It is indeed true that there was little difference between the lower animals and the earliest men. The latter also had a language of inarticulate signs and sounds, which presumably varied from individual to individual. It was only much later, when they had developed social relationships among themselves, that human speech originated. It came into the articulate form by some stages. When primitive men formed into an aggregation they came very close to each other. Naturally, there arose in them the desire for communication. At first, as has been indicated above, they communicated with each other somewhat like the lower animals. But that mode of communication gradually changed along with social development, with the development of intelligence and thought in men. Then the signs and sounds used for the purpose of communication were conventionalized; in other words, the signs and sounds were given fixed meanings. That way indeed there arose in due course what we today call language. Language is therefore a social product. It is not found anywhere outside society.

We are now in a position to see that the study of language or the languages presupposes society. The philologist for his part reckons with society. But he does not study it himself. With him society or social life is a postulate.

Comparative religion postulates society. Comparative religion likewise posits society. It is well known that there are different forms of religion. There are primitive and organized religions. There are again some different forms of primitive religion itself. But religion, like language, is a social product. Religion is not mere belief; it is belief *plus* practice. And religious practice broadly consists of worship, rites and rituals. The form or framework of religious practice is determined by the collective experience and aspiration of the group of people concerned. Religion, therefore, takes its rise and develops in society. There is or can be no religion outside the social *milieu.* Comparative religion, being concerned with a comparative study of the religions of the world, presupposses society.

Thus we see that with each of the special social sciences society is a postulate. So society remains a phenomenon to be studied. The study of society would obviously be independent of the special social sciences. Therefore, sociology as the general science of society should not be confounded with any of the special social sciences or with the totality of such sciences.

Sociology Defined. "Sociology" derives from a combination of the Latin word *Socius* and the Greek *Logos,* meaning respectively society and knowledge. Sociology is, then, knowledge of society.

We can now define sociology. And we define it as follows:—

Sociology is the general science of society as a phenomenon with its laws and principles. Sociology is the general science of society as a phenomenon with its structure, laws and principles.[10] As Giddings puts it, "Sociology is then an attempt to account for the origin, growth, structure and activities of society."[10] Blackmar mentions some different definitions of sociology : (i) "Sociology is the science of

10 Giddings, *The Principles of Sociology,* p. 8; Blackmar *Outlines of Sociology,* Macmillan Company, New York, p. 13.

society" (Ward); (ii) "Sociology is the science of social phenomena" (Ross); (iii) "Sociology is the study of men considered as affecting and as affected by association" (Small); and some others. In spite of the different wordings, these definitions mean somewhat the same thing and more or less agree with the definition given by Giddings.

Dynamic and Static sociology. Some sociologists speak of dynamic and static sociology[11]. Sociology is considered dynamic as it studies society in its origin and development. As society in its growth is a changing phenomenon, its study is conceived to be dynamic. Sociology is static when it studies society as it exists now with its laws, customs and institutions. Here the terms "dynamic" and "static" are derived from the science of mechanics. This science has two branches—statics and dynamics. Statics deals with bodies that are at rest and without change, while dynamics deals with bodies that are in motion and are ever changing. By comparison, static sociology is concerned with society at rest, whereas dynamic sociology is concerned with society changing from age to age. Some sociologists call the static study descriptive sociology and the dynamic study historical sociology.[12] Some, again, employ the phrases "social kinetics" and "social statics".

There is, however, no opposition between static and dynamic sociology. They only represent two points of view from which society is studied. In studying society as it exists at the present time we analyze and describe its structure, laws, customs and institutions. But society has come to its present state of existence by gradual development from a small beginning. There is, in short, history of society. And from the historical point of view we investigate how society originated in the distant past and developed over the centuries. So static and dynamic sociology, as they are

11 Auguste Comte, *The Positive Polity*, tr. by H. Martineau, Vol. II, George Bell and Sons, London, 1886, p. 218. James P. Lichtenberger, *Development of Social Theory*, George Allen and Unwin Ltd. London, 1924, p. 314.

12 F. H. Giddings, *Descriptive and Historical Sociology*.

called, together constitute the complete study of society as a fact.

Relation of sociology to some sciences. Sociology derives its material from several sciences—psychology, geology, anthropology, and biology. Society is an association of minds, and the sociologist deals with minds and their operation in relation to each other. Psychology being the science of mind, the sociologist must be a psychologist. He must know how the human mind works. He has to understand the laws that determine mental phenomena in their origin and growth. In society individual minds come together and function in co-operation and mutual help and produce a structure through which they realize themselves. Therein the minds are creative, and the laws, customs, and institutions which they create reflect their inner necessities and common interests. So the sociologist must have a thorough knowledge of the mind and its working in order properly to analyze social phenomena. It is obvious that sociology is very intimately related to psychology. Geology is the science of the strata of the earth. Men live on the earth, and they appeared there at a particular stage of its development. Therefore, the history of the earth throws much light upon the history of man. The sociologist indeed derives much help from geology. Anthropology is the science of man and in fact studies his bodily, mental and cultural development. It shows how from a very low level of existence man developed from a near-beast into a rational being. It also studies how the human organism itself was modified by environmental conditions, and how the bodily growth of man was followed by higher and higher degrees of intelligence. The anthropologist traces the history of culture and civilization. He studies how man developed ideas and ideals and how in his endeavour to realize them changed the environments to his needs and desires. Society, as we know, exists in a physical environment, in a geographical area. So a knowledge of the environments of man in the different periods, and of their mutual relations is necessary for the understanding of the origin and development of society. Anthropology, again, is concerned with group-life and groups of men called races. Sociology, as we have seen, investigates group-life and groupings of men. There is evidently a very close connection between anthropology and sociology as the study of society. Biology is the science of animal organism. It traces the existing species of animals to some simple forms of life. Biology, therefore, has much to say about the origin and development of man. The sociologist has to reckon with biology. In short, he must be a historian, psychologist, geologist, anthropologist and biologist.

3 Social Philosophy :

We shall now consider the definition of Social Philosophy as against sociology. But some use the terms "social philosophy" and "sociology" indiscriminately. According to them, there is, or there should be, no distinction between social philosophy and sociology. Such a view Giddings suggests when he says, "So it turns out that every social philosopher creates a sociology in the image of his professional speciality." But, really, social philosophy is different from sociology. Social philosophy, as the term indicates, is the philosophy of society, i.e., an interpretation of society. "Social philosophy deals with analysis, criticisms of conceptions and categories and with the problem of values."[13] But sociology is the general science of society. It only describes society as it is and its development. Sociology as such is an empirical science and does not concern itself with social or moral values, which are the primary concern of social philosophy as the speculative study of society.

13 M. Ginsberg, *Reason and Unreason in Society*, Longmans Green and Co., 1948, p. 51.

CHAPTER II

RELATION BETWEEN SOCIAL PHILOSOPHY AND SOME OTHER STUDIES

Social Philosophy and Sociology :

As we have seen before, sociology is an empirical study. It analyzes and describes society in its structure, generalizes about its function, and traces its origin and development. Social philosophy, on the other hand, only interprets social phenomena as well as the data gathered by sociology and the special social sciences. Social philosophy seeks to determine the ultimate conditions of society and the ideal that guides the course of its development. But to say that the function of social philosophy is different from that of sociology is not to say that they are apart from each other. There is in fact a very close connection between them; sociology supplies much material for social philosophy.

From the historical point of view, however, social philosophy precedes sociology and the special social sciences. Plato (born in 427 B.C.) and Aristotle (born in 384 B. C.) developed their respective social philosophies, though there was in their time no sociology as a distinct science, nor was there any special social science in the strict sense. In ancient Greece there were small States called City-States. Every city was a State with a population of 3000,00 to 4000,00, and in the Greek conception of the City-State, society was not distinguished from the State. So the intellectuals of that time discussed social and political problems together, and their theory of the State was social philosophy as well. The situation in which Plato lived suggested to his mind the problem of justice, which he solved or tried to solve in one of his major Dialogues, the *Republic*. He worked out his conception of the ideal State or society in which alone, he pointed out, justice was to be found. In the remote past,

Plato thus developed his social philosophy in some of his Dialogues, and Aristotle his in the *Politics*. But in the middle ages society was clearly distinguished from the State, and the distinction came to stay. But the study of society during this period and long later was fragmentary. In the eighteenth and nineteenth centuries indeed the social study became intensive and assumed a new form. Social philosophy was now identified with history of society.

Auguste Comte founded the science of sociology. On the other hand, during the first half of the nineteenth century Auguste Comte in France laid the foundation of the science of sociology. Since then sociology as a positive science has been developed by the thinkers influenced by the theory of evolution propounded by Charles Darwin in his book *The Origin of Species* published in 1859. For a few past decades of the present century a great many thinkers in Europe as well as in America have been developing three kinds of social studies, namely, sociology, the special social sciences, and social philosophy.

So we have to recognize the fact that social philosophy, as it is, does not quite depend upon a science like sociology, or upon the special social sciences. Social philosophy, as indicated above, was in the past developed independently of any social science, and was indeed the study of the ultimate source or conditions of society and of its ultimate end or ideal. Social philosophy was speculative investigation of society in its origin and development, particularly of how best it could be organized in the light of the ideal it seeks to realize.

Social philosophy derives some help from social science. At the present stage of culture, however, social philosophy has to reckon with the general science as well as the special sciences of society. Social philosophy, needless to say, derives much material from them. But to say this is not to say that social philosophy is wholly dependent upon the science or sciences of society. The relation of social philosophy to social science is somewhat similar to that of philosophy to science. As we have seen at the outset, philosophy originated independently of science. But now philosophy draws much material from science itself. So also social philosophy developed in the past without the help of social science, general or special, although social science or sciences now supply social philosophy with a good deal of material.

Social philosophy and psychology : Psychology etymologically means the science of the psyche or soul. Psychology indeed originated and developed as the study of mind and mental phenomena like thinking, feeling, and willing. But in modern times there has been psychology without soul. There is, for instance, the school of Behaviourism, according to which there is nothing like mind or soul in the usual sense, and psychology as a science is concerned only with the organism and its behaviour. The behaviour of an organism is just a response to a stimulus or stimuli coming from outside, and this response has nothing to do with what we call mind or soul. Psychology is thus brought to the level of a science like physics or chemistry in which precision in the result of the study in question is attained by quantitative measurement. Generally, however, psychology is regarded as the science of the mind or soul and mental phenomena. Psychology in this basic sense studies individual minds and their operations, and by systematic observation as well as by experiment, makes generalizations about the working of the minds. That is to say, psychology studies mental phenomena and proceeds to laws that regulate them. As McDougall puts it :

> "It is, then, a remarkable fact that psychology, the science which claims to formulate the body of ascertained truths about the constitution and working of the mind, and which endeavours to refine and add to this knowledge, has not been generally and practically recognized as the essential common foundation on which all the social sciences—ethics, economics, political science, philosophy of history, sociology, and cultural anthropology, and the more special social sciences, such as the sciences of religion, of law, of education, and art—must be built up."[14]

14 *An Introduction to Social Psychology*, Methuen and Co. Ltd., London, 1913, p. 1.

Social philosophy deals with society and, for that reason, with individual minds in their mutual relationships. Therefore, in his investigation the social philosopher has much to do with psychology. He, in short, must be a trained psychologist. There is indeed an intimate relation between psychology and social philosophy. Psychology is an aid to social philosophy.

Difference between psychology and social philosophy. There is nevertheless difference between social philosophy and psychology, and we may note two points of distinction between them.

(i) First, psychology deals with individual minds, and determines how they function or work. But social philosophy does not deal with minds severally; it deals with them in their collective function, i. e., in so far as they function in association with each other. Psychology is the study of individual minds, of how they evolve with their diverse states. Social philosophy, on the other hand, considers how minds in relation with each other react upon their environment, and brings out by analysis the implications of their mutual relationships, and seeks to determine what it is in human nature that is in fact responsible for the origin and growth of society.

(ii) Second, psychology regards mental phenomena as effects produced by external things or forces. The psychologist studies how stimuli from outside act upon minds and bodies, excite states and modify those that are already there in the minds. But social philosophy reverses this process and point of view. It regards minds as active agents and mental phenomena as dynamic forces. The social philosopher investigates how individual minds come together, function together and produce changes in the external world.[15] Society is a phenomenon that exists in a geographical area. It has its nature and structure. But it did not originate spontaneously. It was definitely produced by individual minds working together. While psychology regards minds as being acted upon and mental states as effects produced by external causes, social philosophy regards minds as creative and mental

15 Auguste Comte, *Positive Polity*, Bhon's Philosophical Library, Vol. II, George Bell and Sons, London, 1896, p. 266.

states as dynamic causes that brought into existence the phenomenon of society.

Social Philosophy and Politics :

Politics presupposes society. As we have seen before, politics is one of the special social sciences. It deals with the State which is an aspect of society. The State is, in short, the machinery wherewith law and order is maintained in society, or the anti-socials are restrained or brought to book. But there was a time when there was nothing like State; there was simply society—a large number of human beings living in a locality in mutual relationships. In the course of development of social life, however, the State came into existence as a social necessity. Politics as a science studies the State in its structure, origin and development. Politics, however, takes society for granted as an aggregation of individuals, from which the State took its rise. For politics, therefore, society is an assumption or a postulate. But society as a whole is the subject matter of social philosophy. So we see that social philosophy studies what is a presupposition for politics.

Political philosophy is not a brcnch of social philosophy. Generally, nevertheless, politics is called political philosophy, and is taken to mean not merely an empirical study based on observation and analysis, but the speculative investigation of the State. Political philosophy as such, then, investigates the ultimate source or condition as well as the ultimate end of the State. Social philosophy, on the other hand, is the speculative study of society, which seeks to interpret social evolution in the light of some basic idea or ideal. It may seem that as it deals with one aspect of the social whole, political philosophy is a branch of the philosophy of this whole, i. e., social philosophy. But a little reflection will show that political philosophy in the strict sense cannot be regarded as a branch of social philosophy.

As has been indicated above, the State is only an aspect of society, and the relation between society and an aspect of it is similar to, or identical with, the relation between whole and part. But the relation between whole and part is such that the ultimate explanation of a part of a whole is not possible without the ultimate explanation of the whole. The final explanation of a limb of an organism, say, the heart or liver, is feasible only in and through the final explanation of the organism in its structure and function. Social philosophy purports to be the ultimate explanation of society as a whole. Political philosophy, if anything, is no branch of social philosophy, particularly because the philosophy of the State cannot be worked out apart from the philosophy of society. In other words, political philosophy in the strict sense of the term cannot be a study distinct from social philosophy. But there is no denying that politics as a special social science stands, although it depends upon social philosophy for clarification of its postulate, namely, society.

Social Philosophy and Ethics :

Ethics, as is well known, is the study of moral consciousness, which is the consciousness of moral value. Our actions can be considered under three heads. Some of our actions are moral, some immoral, and the rest non-moral. The involuntary, reflex and ideo-motor actions are excluded from moral judgment because these actions are automatic and not deliberate. Actions that are going on in an organism, for instance, the functionings of the lungs, liver, kidneys, stomach, etc., are not dependent upon our will or choice. They are just involuntary. Automatic reactions or responses of the body or a bodily organ are reflex actions. Shrinking from a heated thing, blinking against something coming straight at the face[16] are two reflex actions. They take place independently "of the consciousness or intelligence of human beings"; we perform them without thought. An ideo-motor action, on the other hand, is one which proceeds from a mere idea and is done without desire or decision. One performs such an action when, for example, he only thinks of going out of the room where he is and goes out. He goes out even without wanting to do so. All such actions as

16 L. T. Hobhouse, *Mind in Evolution*, Macmillan and Co. Ltd., 1915, p. 42.

are described above are excluded from moral consideration; they are neither moral nor immoral. They are just non-moral.

Actions that are moral or immoral are deliberate, however. They are the results of a process in mind, which involves several steps. Of these steps decision is the most important. This process is called willing, which takes place through conscious reflection and choice. We are therefore responsible for our deliberate actions. They are subject to moral judgment and are either moral or immoral If a deliberate action conforms to the moral law or standard, it is moral or morally good; if it does not conform to the law or standard, it is immoral. The moral law is there. But more often we do not obey the law, though we feel that we ought to obey it. Hence ethics investigates the "ought", i. e., what we ought to do, and to this end tries to determine the moral law or standard and the moral ideal by reference to which the moral quality of an action is determined. Ethics, being thus concerned with a norm or value, is called a normative science.

Ethics is a normative science. Ethics as a normative science is distinguished from a positive one. A normative science, as we have just stated, is concerned with a norm or ideal, while a positive science is concerned with facts of a kind as they exist. The latter explains the origin of the facts in question and discovers the laws that determine their occurrence. The former, however, in addition to doing what a positive science does, seeks to determine the ideal that guides our actions or experiences. Psychology is a positive science and as such investigates mental phenomena in their growth and development but does not deal with the question whether any ideal functions around our mental life. Psychology is a descriptive science and deals with mental phenomena as they occur. Ethics, on the other hand, is partly descriptive; it describes and analyzes moral life and moral consciousness. But ethics is mainly *prescriptive* because it describes and analyzes moral consciousness only to find out the law and ideal that function therein. Ethics prescribes the moral law or ideal for us to follow.

So *ethics comes close to social philosophy* which is concerned with an interpretation of society or social phenomena. Social philosophy studies how society or social organization is ultimately determined by human values, moral, economic, and spiritual. Obviously, social philosophy is dependent upon ethics in so far as the analysis of moral value is concerned. The social philosopher must be a moral philosopher as well.

On the other hand, moral life is lived only in society. Moral consciousness in the individuals grows and develops in the course of the development of social life. We may even say that moral consciousness is a social product, for moral consciousness is not found outside society. So the study of moral life and consciousness is not complete apart from social philosophy which deals with the ultimate basis of society. The *study of moral consciousness and moral value, i. e., ethics, is, then, dependent upon social philosophy for the ultimate explanation of its subject matter.* Society or social life is a presupposition or postulate for ethics but is the main concern of social philosophy.

In ancient times social philosophy included ethics. In ancient times, nevertheless, ethics was not a study distinct from social philosophy. In the time of Plato (5th-4th century B. C.) the three studies—ethics, politics, and social philosophy—were not clearly marked off from each other; ethical, political and social problems mingled up and were discussed together in the course of discussion of the affairs of the Greek City-States. Aristotle, of course, developed ethics as a distinct study but mixed up politics with social philosophy. Despite the difference between Plato and Aristotle regarding ethics in relation to social philosophy, the mixing-up points to the fact that there is a close relation between moral, social and political problems. Though today ethics, politics and social philosophy are studies distinct from each other, the fact remains that they are intimately related to each other.

Social Philosophy and Philosophy :

Philosophy is understanding the universe as a whole. Though it is not true to say that there are as many definitions of philosophy as there are philosophers, yet most philosophers differ from one another on what exactly is meant by the term "philosophy." But I think we are not far wrong in defining philosophy as understanding the universe as a whole, including facts and values. So nothing is excluded from the scope of philosophy. But the world exhibits multitudinous facts or phenomena, or diverse departments of facts. One may fix upon a fact or phenomenon, or a department of Nature, and investigate its ultimate conditions. So a study which seeks an ultimate or a final explanation of its subject matter may be called a philosophy, for philosophy is the study of the ultimate. Thus political philosophy is the philosophy of the State, scientific philosophy is the philosophy of science; social philosophy is the philosophy of society. But it is to be noted that each of these is departmental philosophy and for its method depends upon philosophy as a general study in the sense that it deals with the world as a whole.

Social philosophy as a departmental study assumes a basic relation between society and the world. Nevertheless, each of the departmental philosophies is a philosophy within limits. It takes for granted something which it cannot investigate. Scientific philosophy, for instance, begins with the assumption that science or scientific knowledge falls within a whole. But what exactly is the ultimate nature of this whole, i. e., the world, scientific philosophy does not or cannot determine independently of philosophy. In like manner, social philosophy assumes that there is a basic relation between society and the world. But this assumption or postulate is considered by general philosophy. Each of the departmental philosophies is therefore incomplete and can attain completeness only by expanding itself, i. e., merging into general philosophy.

Social philosophy and philosophy of history. As a matter of fact, according to some, social philosophy is only a phase of general philosophy which is in its turn taken to be just the philosophy of history. Some philosophers of history, again, identify social philosophy with the philosophy of History itself. Hegel, for example, maintains that Absolute Spirit is the ultimate reality and that the world with its things and beings comes about by way of manifestation of the Spirit in external forms. "Spirit.............may be defined as that which has its centre in itself. It has not a unity outside itself, but has already found it; it exists *in* and *with* itself......... Spirit realizes itself and makes itself actually that which it is *potentially*."[17] So it may be said of Universal History that it is the exhibition of Spirit in the process of working out the knowledge of that which it is potentially. Hegel amplifies this idea when he says, "Universal History exhibits the *gradation* in the development of that principle whose substantial purport is the consciousness of Freedom. The analysis of the successive grades in their abstract form, belongs to Logic, in their concrete aspect to the philosophy of Spirit."[17] Hegel means to say that social philosophy is only a phase of the philosophy of Spirit, as the former investigates society which is one of the grades of the manifestations of Spirit.[18]

H. Spencer's philosophy of the world. As we have mentioned before, Darwin propounded the biological theory that the existing species of animals, far from being created at one time in the past, gradually developed out of some pre-existing simple forms of animal life. This theory was called the Theory of Evolution. Applying this new-fangled notion of evolution, Herbert Spencer in the nineteenth century developed his theory that the world with its different levels of existence evolved out of matter—the original stuff in its nebulous state. According to him, human beings and human society fit into his general scheme of evolution with the twin principles of integration of matter and differentiation of form. Herbert Spencer distinguishes between three kinds of evolution, namely, the Inorganic, the Organic and the Super-Organic. According to him, the sociologist or social philosopher restricts himself "to that form of Super-Organic Evolution which human societies exhibit." Therefore, social philosophy, in Spencer's

17 Hegel, *Philosophy of History*, G. Bell and Sons, London, 1890, p. 18.

18 *Op. cit.*, pp. 58-59; G. D. H. Cole, *A History of Social Thought*, Vol. II, Macmillan Co. Ltd., London, 1954, p. 17.

opinion, only represents an aspect of the philosophy of the world.[19]

Marx's view of philosophy. In this connection, we shall do well to consider another great philosopher, Karl Marx, according to whom, philosophy is the philosophy of history of the world, including the history of man or human society. Emile Burns says, "Marxism is a general theory of the world in which we live, and of human society as a part of the world. It takes its name from Karl Marx (1819-1883), who together with Friedrich Engels (1820-1895), worked out the theory during the middle and latter half of the last century."[20]

According to some, social philosophy is a part of general philosophy; according to others, social philosophy is identical with the philosophy of history. Thus we see that some take social philosophy as a part of their general philosophical theory, i. e., their theory of the world, while others take philosophy in a narrow sense, in the sense of philosophy of history, and identify social philosophy with the philosophy of history. Giambattista Vico, "the profound creator of the philosophy of history" (166 '-1744), for example, made man the criterion of the Universe. According to him, "History is the development of human nature."[21] In Herder (1744-1803) there was "a positive hatred of all metaphysics and metaphysical categories". He was himself a poet and viewed history in a poetic way. He, like Vico, made an approach to history through the study of poetry, art, language, and law.[22] Vico and Herder, like some present-day existentialists, emphasized the study of man, and seemed to suggest that philosophy worth the name was philosophy of history and that the philosophy of history was just social philosophy.

Generally, however, philosophy is taken to mean metaphysical investigation into the ultimate reality. And social philosophy is regarded as the speculative study of society and

19 Collins, *Synthetic Philosophy of Herbert Spencer*, 1901, pp. 63, 351.

20 *Vide*, R. Falckenberg, *History of Modern Philosophy*, Henry Holt And Company, New York, 1893, pp. 548-49.

21 Hegel, *Philosophy of History*, George Bell and Sons, London, 1884, Preface, XVI.

22 *Ibid.*

social values. In other words, social philosophy is viewed as the application of the philosophical technique to the interpretation of society and social phenomena, just as the philosophy of history is considered to be taking advantage of the philosophical discipline in the matter of interpretation of history.

We may thus distinguish between general philosophy, the philosophy of history, and social philosophy. While general philosophy investigates the universe as a whole, the philosophy of history is confined to the history of man and his culture, and social philosophy to society. But we cannot say that social philosophy is apart from or independent of the philosophy of history. As we have seen before, in our study of society we consider the question of its origin and development. For this the social philosopher depends upon the philosophy of history. He needs the help of the latter study, especially when he comes to deal with the problem of social progress and social ideal. He can solve this problem only in the light of the data the philosopher of history collects and interprets. Social philosophy is obviously dependent upon the philosophy of history for some material as well as for general guidance, and upon general philosophy for the intellectual discipline it follows in the study of society and social phenomena.

CHAPTER III

SOME SOCIAL CONCEPTS

Before we proceed to deal with the basic social problems we should explain and clarify the words and concepts that are employed in the social study. We consider them one by one as follows:

Community : *MacIver's View.* According to MacIver, a community is any group of human beings, large or small, who live together and share all the basic conditions of life.[1] He, however, goes on to say that a community is "an area of social living" and has some degree of "social coherence". But we become confused about the relation between community and society. From the account given above, short though it is, one may be led to think that "community" and "society" mean much the same thing. It is indeed true that MacIver and Page emphasize territory as the physical basis, and the sentiment of "belonging together" as the necessary psychological condition, of a community. But these two features are also found in society. Society, as we say, does not hang in a vacuum, but exists in a geographical area and consists of individuals who have a common way of life. It is therefore necessary to consider more details about community.

Ginsberg's View. Ginsberg clearly says that society is not to be identified with community, since the latter involves relationships that remain formless in the sense that they are not yet embodied in any associations or institutions. He suggests that society is just the sum total of associations and institutions.[2] The idea is that society is a complex whole formed by social individuals and rendered definite or determinate by different forms of group life, while community is a simple

1 *Society*, Macmillan and Co. Ltd., London, 1949, pp. 8-9; MacIver, *Community*,...........

2 M. Ginsberg, *psychology of Society*, Methuen and Co. Ltd., London, 1933, p. 127.

form of collective life and as such is the source of society as a complex organization. Community is, in short, a less-organized whole than society.

Cole on Community. The conception that behind society there stands community is clarified by Cole when he says that community gives rise to an organized society. As he puts it, "By a 'Community' I mean a complex of social life, a complex including a number of human beings living together by a common, however constantly changing, stock of conventions, customs, traditions, and conscious to some extent of common social objects and interests."[3]

From the accounts of Community given above it appears that there is no clear line of distinction between Community and society. The idea is, however, conveyed to us that the former is only a rudimentary form or stage of the latter.

Examples of Community. Some sociologists, including MacIver and Page, regard a village, a city, a town, a tribe, a nation, each as a community, and also speak of a world community. I think we are not far wrong when we say that a village is a community in the sense of a social group. But a village in a developed country is a miniature society, since in it there are some social classes with their respective functions representing some broad features of the wider society of which it is only a unit. In a village there are priests, cultivators, artisans, traders, and others. They together maintain the life of the individuals who live in the village more or less independently of any outside organization. But a city or town is not like a village. It will be clear to us if we consider the origin and development of a city or town.

McDougall on the origin of cities. According to McDougall, a city or town is to be traced to the gregarious instinct.[4] In a city or town there are congestion, high rates, dirt, disease, smoke, and squalor. Still, people come in large numbers and settle down there. It is because of the herd instinct functioning in them, says McDougall. But if we reflect a

3 *Social Theory*, Methuen and Co. Ltd., London, 1920, p. 25.

4 *An Introduction to Social Psychology*, Methuen and Co. Ltd. London 1913, pp. 296-297.

little, we shall find that the reasons for crowding in a city or town are partly economic and partly personal. In the first place, most of the people who settle down in a city or town have their respective work there—in Government offices, mercantile firms, industrial concerns, schools, colleges, universities, etc. Even the day-labourers cluster round railway stations, market-places and other areas only for a living. Again, McDougall's description would hold of cities and towns of the undeveloped or underdeveloped countries. But those of the developed countries are, as we know, neat and clean, free from dirt and foul disease, and are full of modern amenities of life. These are indeed attractions for those who can afford to come and live there. If the herd instinct is really responsible for town or city life, we cannot see why people should leave their villages and make for cities and towns. A village after all represents group life. Therein a large or small number of people live together from their birth in co-operation and mutual help. And they hold together by a natural impulse. So it is off the point to say that a town or city grows because of the herd instinct. Secondly, there is no cohesion in the aggregation in a town or city. As the people have different motives behind their lives there, there is no immediate reason why they should come together, though they exist together. In a city or town families living in the different flats even on the same premises do not, for example, know each other.

A city or town is no community in the basic sense. Groupings none the less occur there. But they occur mostly according to profession, friendship, ideology, caste and creed. But they do not inspire any physical groupings, however. The persons concerned remain scattered over the city or town. It is then abundantly clear that there the population, considered as a group, is only a loose sort of aggregation without pervasive mutual relationships. A city or town therefore does not quite answer to the definition of Community as the primary group out of which organized society takes its rise, though we can consider a city or town to be a community in the sense of a social group. On the other hand, a city or town has its institutions and associations, which, far from being confined to it, extends beyond it. A city or town is indeed an organization which arises out of organized society and is not in itself an island of group life. The point is that a village or a city or a town, considered a community, is included in a wider whole called society.

The conception of a nation or tribe as a community is an absurdity. A tribe embraces a whole society, and a nation, generally speaking, comprises several organized societies. The Santals, for instance, are a tribe. But the Santal tribe is identical with the Santal society. So if this tribe is at all a community, we must be slow to consider a nation to be a community as defined above. The Santal society may be considered to be a community representing a simple form of group life. But a nation is far too complex to be a community. The Indian nation, for example, covers many societies, such as Bengali society, Bihari society, Madrasi society, and so on. So, if a nation is a community, the latter is wider than society.

Three conceptions of the relation of Community to Society. Thus we have three conceptions of relation of Community to Society, namely, that community as a small group of men living together in co-operation is included in society, that community is identical with society, and that community consists of several societies. But these conceptions are extremely confusing to us.

A Caste is no community in the strict sense. Sometimes the word "Community" is applied to a caste or a special social class. Thus "Brahmin" means a Hindu caste; so also does each of "fisherman", "weaver", and "blacksmith". And in Hindu society the castes form a hierarchy with the highest and the lowest caste. But individuals belonging to a caste generally do not live in the same locality. They remain rather scattered over a territory amongst other people, sharing with them a common way of life. Whatever be the origin of caste, a caste does not fulfil the main condition of community, which is "living together" and "the feeling of being together." The castes, as they are, are social classes which are more or less exclusive of each other. The highest caste has only negative relations to the lower ones in the matter of interdining, intermarriage, etc. The higher castes likewise have negative relations to the lower and the lowest. The lowest caste is the most excluded class. Originally, there were, as we know, social classes determined by different professions people followed. But they were later hardened into castes when they became exclusive of each other.

Is a religious group a Community? The term "Community" is applied also to religious groups such as Hindus, Christians, and so forth. And one is regarded as communal when he tries to promote the cause of his group even at the expense of the other groups. This attitude or practice is called communalism.

But the point is that in either case (a caste or a religious group) community denotes only a section of the population and connotes only similarity in some social attitude between some individuals. In conceiving Hindus and Christians, as two communities, for example, we in each case only think of a number of individuals grouped according to the religion they profess. But similarity in one respect between some individuals, however large their number, cannot make them into a community, for community, if anything, must involve a common way of life.

The common use of the word "Community". We should, however, note that the word "Community" in its common use means society or a social group. In presenting to Parliament the budget for 1963-64, Sri Morarji Desai, then Finance Minister, Government of India, said, "Our requirements are so massive that we cannot possibly meet them without expecting a contribution even from the poorer section of the community."[5] By community he obviously meant society. But when we speak of the student community or the business community we mean a social group. We also use the word to mean a caste as when we speak of the backward communities of West Bengal, for instance.

Nevertheless, if we, in the study of society, use the word "Community", we have to use it with a fixed meaning in order to avoid confusion. At all events, the view Ginsberg

5 *The Statesman*, March, 1963, p. 6.

and Cole hold in common—we have already considered this view—regarding the relation between community and society is most rational. To repeat; according to them, a community is a sort of unorganized group life out of which society takes its rise.

World Community : Some sociologists and social philosophers speak of World Community, and maintain that it is going to be the highest achievement of the present time. Needless to say, the technique of modern civilization derives from science. The easy and quick means of transport have brought the peoples of the world much closer than ever before. Between the nations contact is occurring at different levels—political, economic, and cultural. Often, again, there occur clashes between one nation and another, or between one group of nations and another. And in consequence, particularly because of the armament race between the great nations there is tension all over the world. Some great thinkers, however, envisage a new World Order arising out of the chaos of the present time. Scientific civilization, as we see, has come to such a pass that the world is now faced with two alternatives—total annihilation by nuclear war or world harmony based on the recognition of the deepest values of human life. And we believe that to avoid the ultimate catastrophe the United Nations would in future evolve into a World State. But the idea is not that to this end there would first be a World Community. We cannot here press the analogy of community in relation to organized society. As we have seen above, society is an organized body of institutions and associations presumably developed out of a simple or primary form of group life called community. We must bear in mind the fact that a community needs a region or geographical area and involves the sense of living together and sharing a common way of life. It may, however, be pointed out that World Community would have the earth as the requisite area and that the peoples of the world would recognize the fact that they all alike inhabit the earth. Perhaps they do so even now. Still, they are separated from each other by the differences of race, religion, ideology and colour. And the sense of difference between nation and nation has really been accentuated by the fact that they inhabit the same earth. They have not yet the sense that they live and have to live together. How to reconcile the differences and instil into all men the sense of common interests and a common goal is now the major problem before us. This problem would indeed be solved when and only when an effective world organization has been brought into existence to control and guide the affairs of men. It would not grow spontaneously, but would come about through co-operative thinking, planning and acting by the nations. If it is at all actualized, it may be called World Community or World Society or World State. But, strictly speaking, these words would be applied there only in a figurative sense. Neither of these words would by definition apply to the world organization in question.

Association : Association is generally defined as a teleological group, i.e., a group which is organized to realize some purpose or purposes. And there is a clear distinction between Community and Association. A community is far wider than an association, in the sense that an association falls within or is organized in a community. Community is indeed the presupposition of Association. If people do not have a common life or a common way of life, there is no question of any association. It is only against the general background of common life that an association is established for some specific purpose. While a community comprises all interests and covers all conditions of life, an association is based on a specific purpose.[6] A trade-union, a cricket-club, a Philosophical Congress, a Mathematical Society, an Insurance Company, etc., are associations.

We have to note two points about an association. An Association has a common interest or interests and has some rules to guide or regulate the activities of its members so as to enable them to realize their common interest or purpose. Suppose that some villages organize a collective farm for the purpose of producing food grain on a large scale. But they cannot proceed at haphazard. They have to proceed

6 M. Ginsberg, *Psychology of Society*, p. 121.

methodically. So they frame a set of rules to guide their co-operative activities in the pursuit of their purpose. So also in regard to an Insurance Company or any other association.

From the definition of Association it is clear that an association is an organization deliberately formed for a purpose. An association, again, may be a multipurpose body; it may have several purposes to fulfil. Thus a students' Home may be an association which gives shelter to poor and needy students, also oral and physical training to them. A teachers' Association may have for its objects the improvement of their financial condition, reform in education, and the welfare of the student community at large.

Institution : What is an institution? An institution is not a group or an association, though it may be embodied in an association, and function through a group of human beings.[7] An institution is, in fact, a mode of relationship or behaving recognized and sanctioned by society. Cole defines institution "as a recognised custom or form of social tradition or idea, manifested in and through human beings either in their personal conduct and relationships or through organized groups or associations."[8] Marriage, monarchy, religion, property, government, etc. are institutions. They arise to fulfil some social needs. Marriage is a form of union between a male and a female recognized and sanctioned by society at large, which fulfils the necessity of regulating sexual relations. This institution obviously operates through social beings. Monarchy is a form of government recognized by the people, and as such functions through the king or queen. Religion is the form of worship adopted by a people, and is an institution in the sense that it satisfies the spiritual hankering of men. Religion is, however, embodied in the relevant church which is an association formed for furthering the spiritual well-being of the social individuals. An individual from his very nature

7 Cole, *Social Theory*, *p*. 45.

8 *Cf*. *Encyclopaedia of the Social Sciences*, Ed. Edwin R. A. Seligman and Alvin Johnson, Vol. VIII, The Macmillan Company, New York, 1932, pp. 84-89.

seeks to realize himself by appropriating things from outside. So he possesses or wants to possess necessary things. He needs food, clothing, housing, and the rest. This idea of possession is indeed crystallized into the idea of property. Property is an institution, since it supplies the basic physical needs of men.

Institution and Association : Though an institution is not an association, yet it may well be embodied in an association. But to say this is not to say that an institution as such is embodied in an association. It is indeed true that an association involves this or that institution. As we have seen before, religion is an institution which is embodied in a church, which is an association of the believers. But most institutions stand and function by themselves and do not need to be encased in associations. The idea of spiritual value is such an institution.

We should in any case distinguish between the ideal and the material side of an institution. Thus there is the idea of marriage, i. e., the idea of union between a male and a female as sanctioned by society. But the idea itself is abstract, for there is no union in the abstract. Such union would indeed have a form. So the idea is embodied in the form which represents the concrete side of marriage. So also is the idea of government embodied in the form of government; and so on. And the form of an institution varies from time to time and from society to society. But, more often than not, only the form of an institution changes. As we know, the form of marriage changed over the centuries, and no less did the form of government.

Is a School, College or University an Institution or an Association? We must here clear up one confusion. We often use the word "institution" in a loose sense; we apply it to a school or a college, even to a university. Thus we say, for instance, "The Scottish Church College is a great institution", "The Mitra Institution is a famous school," "The University of Calcutta is a century-old institution." Here the school, the college, and the university are each an association in our sense of the term. Each of them, however different in size from one another, is an organized body set up for the purpose of imparting instruction to youths, and the university especially is pledged to the advancement of learning. But, as we have seen before, there is a clear distinction between Institution and Association, though an institution might be embodied in an association. And in the examples cited above all three,—the school, the college, and the university—embody an institution, namely, *teaching*. The only justification for any of these being called an institution is that they are the concrete embodiments of an institution. This is nevertheless a loose use of the term, which should not minimize the distinction between Institution and Association.

Custom : A custom is a kind of social behaviour which has settled in society by way of long practice. Imitation is the dynamic condition of a custom. A certain behaviour of an individual could spread to other individuals only through the agency of imitation. By imitating one another individuals in society in the long run standardized a certain behaviour. Such a standardized behaviour—a settled mode of behaving—is a custom. Some call a custom a social habit. Indeed a custom is to society what a habit is to an individual. As we know, a habit is an outcome of a series of uniform voluntary actions. Suppose that a person begins to learn smoking. First he practises it by efforts, and gradually he gets used to it, and he now smokes without any voluntary act or effort. Smoking becomes a habit with him, so we say. He does it without much thought about it. In like manner, a mode of behaviour in some individuals which was originally based on voluntary action and a conscious purpose becomes automatic with them in the long run. They now perform it without reflection, as a matter of course. It then spreads to others through imitation that functions in society. When a person adopts a course of action, others probably follow it by suggestion; they follow it because they feel that they should follow it. Or some interest, vague or articulate, impels them to adopt the course. And when they all have repeatedly performed the action in question it becomes a habit with them, in the sense that they do it without reflection or deliberate consideration. An action thus becomes a custom. As Thomas E. Holland puts it, "Before a custom is formed there is no juristic reason for its taking one direction rather than another, though doubtless there was some ground of expediency, of religious scruple, or of accidental suggestion ....There can in fact be no doubt that customary rules existed among peoples long before nations or states had come into being."[9]

Every society had or has its customs. Bengali Hindus, for example, observe the son-in-law Day—the day of entertaining the son-in-law. In some societies a new-born baby is greeted by its relatives each with a piece of gold. In some Indian societies, the bridegroom's father holds a reception in his house after his son's marriage, at which invitees give presents to the bride. In the Western countries, a newly-married couple spend honeymoon at a place away from their home. And so on.

Custom and Institution : One may break a custom but cannot violate an institution without being punished. There is a sharp distinction between Custom and Institution. As we have seen, an institution is an idea or a mode of relationship which is recognized and sanctioned by society. An institution is indeed regarded as a social value since it regulates some relationship between individual and individual in a social group so as to promote ethical development in them. Thus marriage is an institution in that it means a settled emotional and physical relationship between two individuals of opposite sexes. This relationship leads to ordered sex-life and self-development in the individuals concerned. A custom, on the other hand, is a constant mode of behaviour social individuals adopt by way of imitating one another without the least idea that it would serve some social need or purpose. Thus it is a custom that a widowed woman among the upper-class Hindus renounces her ornaments. If, however, a widowed woman there does otherwise, she is not deterred from doing so or denounced; her people only feel that she is not quite observing the custom. But if one infringes an institution, society comes down upon him. Sexual connection between a

9 Thomas E. Holland, *Elements of Jurisprudence*, Thirteenth Edition, Progressive Publishers, Calcutta, p. 57.

male and a female outside marriage, for example, is not only disapproved, but is also socially punished.

A custom changes more rapidly than an institution. There is difference between Custom and Institution from yet another point of view. An institution is in fact rooted in society. It lasts out its use; it continues as long as it serves the social need. And if it changes, it changes in the course of development of society itself. There is evidently a tendency in the social individual to conserve an institution. As a custom is not quite an outcome of a social need, it changes more rapidly than an institution. Indian women in the nineteenth century, for example, kept indoors and did not by themselves stir out of their homes. But today they move about freely. Some customs nevertheless persist. Dressing in *sarees* on the part of Indian women has come to stay. Many educated male Indians adopted European costume. But the women clung and still cling to their *sarees* as tenaciously as their counterpart in the West cling to their frocks and gowns.

Custom and Law : Physical Law. The word Law is used in some different senses. Firstly, Law means order or method in the phenomena of Nature. Thus we find order in co-existence and also in succession between phenomena. "The phenomena of nature exist," says John Stuart Mill, "in two distinct relations to one another; that of simultaneity and that of succession. Every phenomenon is related, in a uniform manner, to some phenomena that co-exist with it, and to some that have preceded it and will follow it".[10] Mill really means to say that there are two kinds of Law—the law of simultaneity and the law of succession. And these are natural laws in the sense that they are intrinsic to the phenomena. That is to say, the phenomena of Nature happen and exist according to these laws. There is order or regularity in the relation of succession between phenomena, and this relation, which cannot be reversed, is formulated as the law of causation, meaning that every event has a cause. Thus a rise in the river follows a heavy downpour, a peal of thunder

10 *A System of Logic*, Longmans, London, 1959, p. 211.

follows a clash of clouds, the melting of butter follows its being placed on the fire, and so on. The order in simultaneity or co-existence is illustrated in "Men with narrow foreheads possess low intelligence," "Yellow flowers are sweet-scented", etc.

Moral Law. There is, again, the moral law. Whatever be the source of this law, there is a clear distinction between it and a natural law. The moral law as a law is to determine men's actions. But it does not by itself determine them. The law of causality, on the other hand, determines a phenomenon in the sense that it does not or cannot happen without conforming to the law. But men's actions may not conform to the moral law. This law implies an "ought", that we ought to follow the law in our actions. More often, however, we do not obey the moral law than we do, although we feel that we ought to follow it. And when we follow it we do so out of reverence for it. In that case, only the idea of the moral law, not the law itself, determines our actions.[11] In other words, in moral actions we make our will conform to the moral law. There is obviously no such necessity around the moral law as we find around a natural law.

Law as Rule of Action. There is a third sense in which "law" is taken. It is taken to mean a "rule of action."[12] In Holland's words, "The term Law is employed in Jurisprudence not in the sense of the abstract idea of order, but in that of the abstract idea of rules of conduct."[13] Laws as rules of actions are external to them, and are established by a determinate human authority. Here we consider law only as a rule of conduct and try to determine whether there is any relation between custom and law.

Divine Law. Some speak of divine laws, and they hold that the divine laws express or embody the divine will. God often reveals Himself to men, some believe, and imposes His Will upon them by commanding them to follow a course or

11 *Cf.* Kant's Theory of the Moral Law.

12 Holland, *Elements of Jurisprudence*, p. 20.

13 *Op. cit.* p. 21.

some courses of action. Thus God revealing Himself in Jesus Christ, they say, commanded : "Love thy neighbour as thyself." This is a divine law. A human law, however, expresses the will of a human authority—the people, the monarch, the State or government. A divine law, like a human law, prescribes or prohibits a course of action. "Love God with all thy heart" is prescriptive like the human law "Ornaments must be made only of 14 carat gold", and "Do not covet another's wife" is prohibitive like "one must not steal another man's things." The infringement of a divine law is punished by God just as that of a human law is punished by the relevant human authority.

The distinction between a divine and a human law is only the distinction between the sources of the two kinds of law. A divine Being is the source of a divine law, while a human authority is the source of a human law. Those who disobey a divine law commit sin and suffer consequently. But the difficulty is that with the majority of men God is problematic and that His dispensation of justice occurs in the future, on the Day of Judgment—after death—which is really all dark to us. So we leave the divine realm with its laws, if any, alone. Human laws are, however, tangible and are concerned with the affairs of the present life. Human laws are the rules of actions enacted and enforced by a *human authority for order and harmony in society.* And law in Jurisprudence means such rules of human actions.

It is to be noted that there is no law without the State.[14] There was beyond question a stage of society when there was no State. There were nevertheless moral conceptions and customs, which were the source of whatever order there was then in social life. But these had no binding force upon the people. When the State evolved, the political authority gave sanction to some conceptions and customs. They were thus raised to the status of law. And the sanction consisted in the fact that if actions did not conform to the moral conceptions or customs, the authority would interfere and punish the infringement. According to

14 Holland, *Elements of Jurisprudence*, p. 56.

needs, the authority later framed new rules of conduct. In this way there arose the juridical or legalistic tradition in society.

An intimate connection between Custom and Law : Clearly there is an intimate connection between Custom and Law. A custom, as we have seen, is based on the repetition of a mode of action in the social individuals. A custom nevertheless assumes a legalistic aspect when the political authority gives sanction to it. Law in the sense of the rule of action in fact evolved out of Custom. We may therefore consider a custom as a law in the making. At the earliest stage of society order in life was indeed maintained by means of custom. Law aims at and enforces uniformity of behaviour in citizens, while Custom means a uniform behaviour people have adopted though a repetition of the same or similar acts. The political authority therefore took advantage of this aspect of Custom and maintained order in society by giving sanction to customs. Clearly, then, a custom was distinct from a judicial sentence and preceded the latter. A custom nevertheless became a law when it was taken as the norm or standard by which the acts of men were judged. In the evolution of law there was an epoch of Customary Law, and "the period of Customary Law" led up to "the era of Codes". The Twelve Tables of Rome were the most famous of the ancient codes which include the Laws of Manu. Now customary laws were framed in the shape of rules. A decemvirate or a council of ten in authority drew up the Twelve Tables of ancient Roman Law. And "the Roman Code was merely an enunciation in the words of the existing customs of the Roman people."[15] This codification of customs was indeed made possible by the art of writing. Later, of course, new laws were added, and law-making became an articulate process. What was true of one country in this respect was more or less true of another. So in jurisprudence, i.e., philosophy of Law the emphasis is laid upon Custom. Even today local customs supplement Law in the matter of deciding a case in court. We are told that

15 *Maine, Ancient Law*, John Murray, London, 1870, p. 18.

in many cases decided by the Supreme Court and lower courts in India Custom overrode Law.[16]

Folkways : The folkways are the modes of behaving in some social beings which correspond more or less to the instinctive activities of animals.[17] The former are direct and and immediate and are based on past experience. They are preserved by tradition and are handed down from generation to generation. Social conventions and forms of etiquette fall among them. Thus wearing a turban or a necktie or a *chaddar* is a folkway. Shaking hands or making an obeisance with folded hands as a respectful way of greeting is another.[18]

Mores : When the folkways are regarded as regulators of social conduct and not mere patterns of behaving they become *mores*. The *mores* are folkways themselves and bring out only the functional aspect of the latter. The Mores are folkways considered "instruments of control" of social behaviour. They are both positive and negative. A positive More compels or controls behaviour, while a negative one only forbids a specific mode of behaving. The Mores in their negative form are taboos.

A taboo means a prohibition as well as the thing or person the prohibition is aimed at. In early society, the king or the priest was often considered an incarnation of a god and possessed of supernatural powers.[19] As the king or the priest was apart from ordinary men, restrictions were imposed on the behaviour of the latter towards the former. These restrictions were taboos. People were told, and they thought, that if they did not obey the restrictions some evil consequence would befall them. Such being the case, the king and priest themselves became taboos. They were the object of the restrictions themselves. So some "don'ts" regarding them were to be observed, such as "Do not touch and

16 D.H. Mulla, *Principles of Hindu Law* N. M. Tripathi Private Limited, Bombay, 1959, Introduction, p. 64.

17 *Vide* MacIver, *Society* p. 19.

18 W. G. Sumner and A.C. Keller, *Science of Society* I, New Haven, 1927, p. 120.

19 J.G. Frazer, *The Golden Bough, Third Edition,* Part II, *Taboo and the Perils of the Soul*, p. 1.

eat of the dishes of the king or priest", "Do not wear the clothes of the king or priest." If anybody ate the food of the king or priest, or out of "the sacred dishes"[20] his throat would become swollen. If anybody wore their clothes, his body would become inflamed. And so on.[21] In some societies, savage and civilized, a woman at menstruation or at child-birth is a taboo And people are to observe the prohibition "Don't touch her", the idea being that they would risk some evil consequence if they do not obey it.

There are indeed different kinds of taboos, and they are or can be interpreted differently. Some taboos are based on superstitious beliefs, some on dread of incest. Some, however, have wholesome motives behind them and are designed to serve some social or hygienic purposes. Whatever might be the source of a taboo, it is definitely a prohibition which is to guide the behaviour of social individuals towards certain things and persons, and which the former observe with the idea that if they do not observe it some evil consequence would happen to them.

Cross-Cousin Marriage : The children of brother and sister are called cross-cousins. In cross-cousin marriages, therefore, a man marries the daughter of his mother's brother, or the daughter of his father's sister. It prevails in the Fiji Islands, the Southern New Hebrides, South India, and in some parts of Melanesia. Mohammedans, to be sure, practised cross-cousin marriage. They marry the daughter of the mother's brother and also the daughter of the father's sister.

Propinquity : It means blood-relationship between two or more groups of men through intermarriage, who live in the same geographical area. Propinquity between the Vedic Aryans and some aborigines of India represents a certain stage of social evolution in India.

Incest : Incest is sexual connection between individuals who are related by blood, such as father, daughter, mother,

20 *Op. cit.*, p. 131.

21 W.H.R. Rivers, *Kinship and Social Organization*, Constable and Co. Ltd., London, 1914, p. 23.

son, brother, and sister. In societies, ancient and modern, incest is looked upon with horror. It was strictly forbidden in Vedic times,[22] and was banned by Plato. He says, "Then I fancy that when the men and women have passed the age of having children we shall, of course, leave them at liberty to associate with whomsoever they please; except that a man must not associate with his daughter or his mother, or his grand-daughter or grandmother; and the women we shall allow to associate with any one but a son or a father, or grandson or grandfather."[23] Plato speaks of "the unwritten law" against incestuous connection. He in the Republic does not, however, bring under incest the union between brother and sister. "The law may allow the union of brothers and sisters", he says, "if the lot fall in that way, and the priests of Apollo approve."[24] In the *Laws*, however, he says, "No open or secret connection takes place between sisters and brothers; incestuous connection is infamous."[25]

Social Composition : Whatever else we may say regarding the beginning of society, we can safely say that the physical aggregation was the foundation of social life in the remote past. And two distinct forms of organization arose out of the social population, namely, *Social Composition and Social Constitution.*

Social Composition is the combination of individuals of both sexes into groups, and of such groups into higher groups and of the higher groups into still higher groups. Thus a man and a woman enter into a specific social relationship and form a family. A number of families form a village or clan, several villages or clans a tribe, some tribes a nation, and so forth. This process starts with individuals and continues in the progression of grouping. This sort of progressive grouping is obviously based on near or distant

22. *The History and Culture of the Vedic People*, Vol. I, Ed. R.C. Majumdar, George Allen and Unwin Ltd. London, 1957, p. 389.

23 *Republic*, tr. by Lindsay, J. M. Dent and Sons Ltd. London, 1923, V, 461 p. 172.

24 The *Dialogues of Plato*, Jowett, Vol. V—Laws 838, p. 220.

25 Laws, 838.

blood-relationships, and as a result entails a basic sense of kinship or "Consciousness of kind" on the part of the individuals of the group in question.

Social Constitution : Social Constitution, on the other hand, means a division of the social population into classes on a *functional basis*. When one definite function is assigned to one group of people who have the requisite skill for the function, according to different functions, there come about different groups of people. Thus there are farmers, weavers, traders, builders, smiths, teachers, and so on, each group with its distinctive function.

Thus we see that Social Composition is ultimately based on the family. Therein the family is the unit, which progressively expands and increases in size. In Social Constitution, however, there is a population, large or small, to begin with, and a social organization is effected on the basis of division of labour.

These two forms of social organization are not exclusive of each other. Rather every society exhibits these two modes. They indeed interpenetrate each other.

Chapter IV

THE METHOD OF THE SOCIAL STUDY

In Chapter II we have considered three studies namely, sociology, special social science, and social philosophy. We have seen that these studies are distinct, though they are related to each other. In this chapter we propose to discuss the method of social philosophy. And we can determine it when we have understood the method sociology as the general science of society employs.

The Empirical Method in Science. As we know, a science in the ordinary sense of the term follows the method of empirical study, which consists of observation and experiment.

What is Observation? Observation is regulated perception. We are said to observe something when we perceive it with an end in view. Whenever we, in our normal life, open our eyes we perceive something, provided the eyes are in working order and there is something to see. But such perception is not observation. When we investigate anything we concentrate on it and do not consider irrelevant facts. "Such close and purposive perception is observation."[1] For instance, we come on some wax melting in the sun, and presently we are seized with the problem whether the sun-rays are the cause of the melting of the wax. With this end in view we then perceive some further pieces of wax placed in the sun at the same time or on different occasions. Such regulated perception of a fact or facts under investigation is called observation.

What is Experiment? Experiment is only a kind of observation. In it we observe some fact or facts under artificial conditions. There we in our way create a situation in which we study the phenomenon in question. Take a plant for the purpose of an experiment, to see whether it reacts like an animal

1 *Cf.* A. C. Das, *An Introduction to Logic,* Vol. II, Kamala Book Depot, Calcutta, 1949, p. 54.

organism to an irritant as well as a healing balm applied to it. First of all, we eliminate all known elements from the place where the plant is put. Then we pour some irritant upon its leaves to see that they droop. Thereafter we pour some medicine upon the affected leaves, whereupon the latter at once regain their original state. All this constitute an experiment because here we observe a phenomenon under artificial conditions.

Observation and Experiment Constitute one method. Observation and experiment together constitute the method of the sciences like physics and chemistry, which indeed involves some steps, namely, analysis, comparison, hypothesis, and verification. In the scientific explanation of a phenomenon we are concerned with the cause or law which determines it. And in our procedure we follow the steps just mentioned. In the first instance, we minutely observe the phenomenon as it occurs in Nature, then analyze it and compare the circumstances in which it occurs. We now frame a hypothesis as to its possible cause or law. Last of all, we verify the hypothesis—determine whether it is true or not, and the verification is just observation of what the hypothesis posits. We often use an experiment for the purpose of verification. Dr. Ross, as we know, discovered the cause of malaria. According to him, the bite of the anopheles mosquito is the cause. But how did he discover it ? He first observed cases of malarial fever, analyzed its symptoms, and then framed some alternative hypotheses. Finally, he tested them one by one and found the hypothesis about the anopheles mosquito to be true.

The Objective Method in the Study of Society. According to some—Aristotle, Bodin and Montesquieu especially—society as a phenomenon originated and grew in a physical environment. Therefore, in our explanation of society, they contend, we have to adopt the objective method, i. e., the method of explaining with reference to the objective conditions alone—the nature of the soil, climate, food-supply, etc. In the application of this objective method in the study of society there is beyond doubt ample scope for the method of a physical science. Pareto, the Italian sociologist, regards sociology as "a logico-experimental science" based on the observation of and experiment with the social facts and forces.[2]

The Environment and Society. The emphasis on the objective method in the study of society is linked to the view that human society is dependent upon the physical environment. Life as such, as we see, is possible only within an appropriate environment. A seed, for instance, sprouts forth and a plant gradually develops out of it under some physical conditions—light, air, moisture, etc.[3] And there are some different kinds of plants which grow only in their different environments. Some grow in marshy places, some on dry land, some still on hilly tracts. Again, the plants and creepers of the tropical countries are a good deal different from those of cold climates. It has been observed that if they are grown in a region different from their native one, very important changes occur in them. Similarly human beings for their life and growth are dependent upon their environment. But different groups of men live under different conditions and develop their respective peculiar characteristics according to their different environments. Thus those who live in mountainous regions are far more robust and hardy than those who live on plains ; the inhabitants of hot countries are generally slothful and sluggish in their habits, while those of cold countries are ever energetic and adventurous. Human beings nevertheless have some common conditions of life, namely, air, light, water, and food-supply from the surroundings. Without them, or any one of them, human beings cannot live. Scientists, as we know, are still speculating whether there are human beings on Mars. They say that human beings could be there only if there were the same sort of atmosphere as is there around the earth. If air could be eliminated from our environment, we would have perished

2 Sorokin, *Contemporary Sociological Theories*, Harper and Brothers, New York, 1928, p. 40; Ginsberg, *Reason and Unreason in Society*, Longmans, Green and Co., London, 1948, pp. 84-85.

3 MacIver and Page, *Society*, p. 73.

in a moment. All this shows how intimate is the relation between us and our physical environment. But how about society? Can we say that society as well was determined by the physical conditions under which men lived ?

There is the view that the environment determines the constitution of society. According to some sociologists, the relation between the environment and society is a causal one. The physical conditions, in their view, under which a group of men live, determine the structure of their society. Thus the customs and way of life of the people of one region of a country are different from the customs and way of life of the people of another region, let alone those of the peoples of the different countries. And this difference in their social behaviour, they say, is due to the different physical conditions under which they live. Thus the customs and social norms of West Bengal are different from those of, say, East Punjab and Kashmir. If people leave their native land and settle down in a new country, they, it is contended, change and must change in certain respects. A nineteenth-century French sociologist, Frederic Le Play, traced society to local conditions. Through his influence there has developed what is known as the geographical theory of society, which means that society is based on geographical conditions. Some American sociologists, R. E. Park, E. W. Burgess and R. D. McKenzie especially, emphasizing the intimate relation that is there between the environment and society, have developed a new branch of sociology, namely, social *ecology*, which is mainly concerned with the relation of society to the environment.

Criticism : too much emphasis is laid on the environment. Those who maintain that the environment determines the constitution of society make much of the former. It is true to say that a man is not a pure spirit hovering in an ethereal realm; he has a body which is sustained by physical means. Human beings therefore very much live in a physical environment. But to say that they could not live without the environmental conditions is not to say that human society was wholly dependent upon the latter.* Considering plant-life, we find that we cannot quite say that a plant in its origin and growth is absolutely determined by some physical conditions. As we see in the same environment different kinds of plants grow and thrive. There are the same soil, the same light, and the same moisture. How, then, could there be different plants? To this question there is only one answer. It is that there are different seeds, to begin with. Obviously, the difference between the different plants is explained by the difference between the seeds themselves. So even in the plant world the physical conditions cannot by themselves constitute the cause of a plant; the seed has much to contribute to it.

Social adaptation is Creative. Coming to human society, we find that it began as an association of minds, and that there is much difference between the biologico-psychological and sociological points of view. From the biological as well as the psychological point of view the environment is regarded as the cause and the changes in the body and mind as effects. But from the sociological point of view the relation between the environment and the mind is reversed. The latter is now regarded as the cause which acts upon the former. Some may point out that the mind as it exists and grows must adapt itself to the environment and that in adapting to the environment the mind inevitably changes. But, if the mind changes there, the environment is clearly the cause of the change. The point, however, is that the adaptation in the social context is *creative*. Therein the mind adjusts itself to the environment by changing or modifying it. As MacIver puts it, "Social adaptation........always involves some standard of value."[4] In social life we endeavour to realize some value. That is to say, therein we seek to realize our desires, or rather some common desires, and for this purpose we change the environment according to needs and create a structure through which we try to realize our

**Cf. The Essays of Bhudev Mukhopadhyaya* (in Bengali), Ed. by Pramathanath Bisi, Mitra and Ghosh, Calcutta, 1364 B. S., p. 30.

4 *Society*, p. 77.

ideas and ideals. Society is, in short, a phenomenon which a group of individuals brings into existence in their common efforts to realize themselves, of course, on the basis of the environment. So, properly speaking, in the social context the environment is made to conform to the desires of men and men are never absolutely moulded by the environment. Such being the case, we cannot seek for the explanation of society in the environment itself. In the study of society we have indeed to take into consideration the function of the geographical conditions. But we cannot explain society absolutely in terms of these conditions, important as they are as its external basis.

The Subjective-objective Method. We, then, cannot explain society wholly in objective or physical terms, for it consists of individuals or individual minds. Some sociologists, for this reason, insist on the subjective method. They point out that we shall have to explain society strictly in subjective terms, with reference to some subjective fact or facts. Hume, Kant, and Hegel belong to this group. The fact, however, remains that though society comprises individual minds, it does not hang in a vacuum; it exists in a geographical area. So, as Giddings points out, in our study of society we have to combine the subjective and the objective method. That is to say, we have to explain society with reference to both mind and physical conditions.

The experimental method cannot be used in the study of society. It is to be noted nevertheless that the experimental part of the physical method is hardly applicable in the case of society since no aspect of the social whole nor its physical conditions can be studied in an artificially created sphere without harm to the individuals who together constitute the whole. Indeed some experiments were made in the past to ascertain the effect of social life upon the nature and growth of an individual. In one case a child was long confined in a place outside society, and it was found that it did not quite grow to be a human being despite its human birth and human body. MacIver and Page mention the case of Anna, an illegitimate American child who was isolated from social environs when she was only six months old. When she was discovered after five years or so it was found that she was not growing as a normal child. She could not speak or walk.[5] So in the study of society we cannot make any experiment, in the ordinary sense of the term, upon individuals without detriment to them. Nor can we change the physical environment of society to see how the individuals behave under the changed conditions. We cannot, for instance, change at will the climate of a region, or interfere with the waterways there. We may, however, improve the quality of this or that physical condition of society in the light of its normal working. We can, for example, use fertilizers to improve the soil and to increase its yield. But there is in no case a study of the conditions of society in a situation of isolation or elimination. Such a study is not only undesirable but is impracticable in view of the fact that the relation between society and its physical conditions is somewhat organic.

The Historical Method in the Study of Society. The social scientist investigates social phenomena as they occur and exist. By observation, analysis and comparison he determines or seeks to determine their causes and laws. But he cannot possibly confine his attention to society as it exists now. As we have indicated before, society, consisting as it does of individual minds, grows and in fact originated in the past and has come to its present state of existence by some stages. So we have to reckon with the history of society. The study of the history of society is very important, for it would supply us with sufficient data, which in their turn would throw light upon the nature and structure of society as it exists today. The present is not atomic, but is, to be sure, linked to the past. As Sri Aurobindo puts it, "The past is our foundation, the present our material, the future our aim and summit."[6] Truly, we cannot break with the past. Past, present and future indeed form a causal nexus. So we may say that the causes or reasons of the present-day social laws, customs and institutions lie buried in the past. The sociologist has to

5 *Society*, Macmillan and Co. Ltd., London, 1957, p. 45.

6 A. C. Das, *Sri Aurobindo and Some Modern Problems*, General Printers, Calcutta. 1958, p. 129.

dig them up and utilize them in his study of society and social phenomena. Referring to the historical method to be employed in the social study, Auguste Comte says:

> "When the method has been used long enough to disclose its properties, I am disposed to think that it will be regarded as so very marked a modification of positive research as to deserve a separate place; so that in addition to observation, properly so called, Experiment and Comparison, we shall have the Historical Method as a fourth and final mode of the art of observing."[7]

And also:

> "Though abstract science must hold the first place, as Bacon so plainly foresaw, the direct construction of concrete science is one of the chief offices of the new philosophical spirit, exercised under historical guidance, which can alone afford the necessary knowledge of the successive states of everything that exists."[8]

Comte, as we see, speaks of a *fourth method* by which the sociologist has to supplement the three methods of observation, experiment and comparison. The fourth method is the historical method which consists in collecting relevant historical data for sociological investigation. It is indeed the mode of observing past facts and events. As society grows and, as such, is a living thing, the historical method is peculiarly suited to sociology. But the question is whether social philosophy follows the same method or methods as sociology as the general science of society does.

Some sociologists propose and practise the statistical method. The twentieth-century development of social thought lays emphasis on sociology as a social science and also on experimental methods in the study of social facts or phenomena. There has been a shift from speculative to empirical research, which recognizes the importance of the statistical

7 *Positive Polity*, Vol. II,
Bohn's Philosophical Library,
George Bell and Sons, London, 1896, p. 256.

8 *Op. cit.*, Vol. III, p. 403.

method leading only to probable knowledge. Thus Weber, the German sociologist, and the American sociological societies conceive sociology as the science of social behaviour.[9] The statistical method is a device to study facts in terms of number. By applying this method in the case of social facts or forces sociologists try to determine the nature of the connection of a trait or some traits with a certain group of social facts, or to determine their relative value in the social context. And this method necessitates a correct counting of facts and the study of their recurrence within a given time or sphere. This method is specially used in social surveys.[10]

The historical method has to be supplemented by the teleological method which may be regarded as the sixth method of social studies. As we have seen before, there is a distinction between sociology and social philosophy. Sociology is a positive science; it describes society, analyzes its structure, laws, institutions and the empirical processes of their development. But social philosophy is the speculative study of society. It, of course, considers the social phenomena as well as the data supplied by sociology and by some other sciences. But the function of social philosophy is different from that of sociology. Social philosophy proceeds by way of analysis and criticism, and evaluates social phenomena. It particularly studies the values human individuals seek to realize through social life, and determines the ideal that guides social development. In this function of interpretation social philosophy takes advantage of teleological explanation.

Mechanical explanation. Ordinary scientific explanation is mechanical explanation. It is mainly determined by the conception of causality. The principle or law of causality means that every event has a cause and that there is nothing uncaused in the world. There is no spontaneous origination. Whatever happens is determined by a cause. The things and events of the world are causes and effects in relation to each

9 *Encyclopaedia Britannica,* Vol. 20, 1959, pp. 913-14.

10 Blackmar, *Outlines of Sociology,* Macmillan Company, New York, p. 532.

other. They indeed form a causal nexus. In a physical science the explanation of a thing is therefore mechanical in the sense that it is traced to its cause which precedes it. In a causal explanation there is a backward reference and in it we explain the present by the past. If things and events are units that belong to the physical world, mechanical explanation is appropriate to them. Thus we explain a rise in the river by a heavy downpour, the devastation of an area by a flood or fire or an earthquake or any other event. Causation is obviously connected with change. When there is a change in a thing we look for its cause. But mechanical explanation fails in the case of a process of growth, which is more than change. If butter is held to the fire, it melts ; here the melting means that the butter placed on the fire becomes ghee. Sometimes one thing replaces another. We often change our dress. The chameleon, as we know, assumes different colours at different moments. A boy sits now on a table, now beneath the table. These are cases of change of substance, quality and relation. Change, then, implies transformation or replacement. But growth implies and involves much more than this ; it means change towards a goal or a plan which might be only an unconscious plan of Nature. If we observe the process of growth that proceeds out of a seed, we find that the whole process is planned towards the production of a plant of a definite kind. If we try to explain the process of growth by what stands at the beginning of the process, it becomes unintelligible to us.

Teleological explanation. As we know, a tree grows out of a seed. The seed is at the beginning of the process. An oak, for instance, comes out of an acorn only by some stages, not all at once. Now can the seed by itself explain the tree ? If one says that it can, we fail to understand how such a tiny thing could ever be the cause of so big a tree. To understand the process of growth, we have to consider its different stages, especially the final stage, which throws light upon the whole process. The Greek word "telos" means end and "logos" discourse. So the word "teleology, deriving as it does from a combination of these words, means the view or theory that every thing and every event in the world has an end or a design behind it, and that no causal or mechanical explanation is complete without a final cause. Now, as regards the process of development of a tree out of a seed, we find that only one kind of thing develops out of one kind of seed. This is true not only of the seeds of plants, but of all seeds. A human being grows out of the human seed, and the other animals—cow, horse, mule, etc.—come out of their respective kinds of animal seed or sperm. But a seed is not the whole cause. A plant seed, as we see, cannot by itself produce a tree. If it falls on a stone, it dries up. When, however, it is in contact with soil, light, moisture, etc., it begins to sprout and a process of development starts. The seed nevertheless remains the basic condition, the other conditions being only auxiliary to the process, for the nature or structure of the effect is evidently determined by the seed. But what is meant when we say this ? Only that the effect, the tree in question, was in some way, present in the seed, obviously as an end to achieve. Were the tree physically present in the seed, there would be no need for a process. Still in some sense the tree was there in the seed; in some sense, again, it was not there in the seed. However, the point to be noted is this, that the physical presence of a tree, which is a big thing, in a small thing like a seed is an impossibility. When we cut open a seed we do not find any tree there. Nor do we find the tree there as an end when we look into it. The end in the seed, if any, is rather revealed by the process of development, especially by the last term or stage of the process. When, for example, an oak has developed out of an acorn we read back the process and take the oak as the end of the acorn as well as of the process of growth. In teleological explanation therefore we explain by the last term, while in mechanical explanation we explain by the first term.

Social philosophy adopts teleological explanation. Society is a living whole; it grows and develops. It has indeed come to its present state of existence through development over the centuries, and is still growing. Being concerned with an interpretation of society and social phenomena, social philosophy has to look into the whole process of social growth. It has to analyze the latest, or to be more precise, the highest social achievements represented by political, moral and religious life. The social philosopher has to make a proper assessment of the values individuals in society have been trying to realize through co-operation at the present time, and interpret the history of society in the light of the values that have evolved in human consciousness. While the sociologist utilizes the knowledge of history, the social philosopher interprets history—the history of society especially. Social philosophy as the philosophy of society adopts and emphasizes teleological explanation, although it takes advantage of the method which comprises observation, analysis, comparison, and historical study, even of the statistical method.

CHAPTER V

THE SOCIAL NATURE OF MAN

There are different theories regarding the social nature of man. According to some, it is based on an instinct in man ; according to some, again, it is based on utility, while, according to others, it is just natural to man. In Marx's view, however, social nature is determined by the production of wealth. Let us consider these views one by one.

I. *Social nature is based on instinct.* (a) *Society and the sex instinct.* David Hume (1711-1776) deals with the problem of social nature in his own way. According to him, society originates from the sex instinct. The family, in his opinion, is based on the sex relation between a male and a female, and it is from the family that man's social nature derives. Hume points out that the sex instinct together with the sentiment of sympathy, which is also innate, gives rise to social feelings and relations. As he puts it,

> "But in order to form society, 'tis requisite not only that it be advantageous, but also that men must be sensible of these advantages ; ....
> Most fortunately, therefore, there is conjoined to these necessities, whose remedies are remote and obscure, another necessity, which, having a present and more obvious remedy, may justly be regarded as the first and original principle of society. This necessity is no other than that natural appetite betwixt the sexes, which unites them together, and preserves their union, till a new tie takes place in their concern for their common offspring."[1]

1 *Cf.* E. S. Bogardus, *A History of Social Thought,* J. R. Miller, Los Angeles, 1928, p. 188;
Philosophical Works of David Hume, Vol. 11, Adam Black, Edinburgh, pp. 254-55.

But the difficulty is that we cannot see how all our other-regarding feelings and attitudes are motivated by sex. Sex is indeed the source of our bodies. But worthy feelings and sentiments like parental affection and filial piety cannot proceed from mere sex. On the other hand, sex as sanctioned by society is the basis of the family. So sex involved in the marriage-relation presupposes society. If we grant that at the earliest stage of human existence sex-relations were irregular, it remains a problem how out of sexual chaos ordered life evolved. Social relations, again, are not confined to the family, and all relations in the family itself are not sexual. Social relations cover even those who come to a group as strangers, or who are not sexually related with each other. Most of the individuals who are members of one society do not bear, even remotely, sexual relations with each other. So sex is not quite relevant to the question of the source of the social nature of man. As G. D. H. Cole puts it, "In the past, some social theorists have based their whole theory upon the analogy of the family, and have striven to explain all wider phenomena of association and community in its light. Any such explanation seems to-day so obviously misleading that it need not detain us at all."[2]

We, then, see that we cannot make much of sex in the context of social life. Sex is an instinct in the lower animals also. In every species a male and a female come together through the functioning of this instinct in the proper season, and though the sex-relation pervades the animal world, there is no society in that world in the human sense of the term. So we must be slow to accept Hume's theory.

(*b*) *Social nature and parental instinct.* According to some psychologists, there is in many species of animals the parental instinct with an attendant tender emotion. And the parental instinct is specially the maternal instinct, which "compels the mother to protect and cherish her young." This instinct is, however, present in the father also, and is discernible in the lower animals as well. Tortoises, fishes, and birds, for example, lay eggs. The female, often together with the male, takes good

2 *Social Theory*, Methuen & Co. Ltd., London, 1920, p. 13.

care of the eggs. They protect or seek to protect them against predatory beasts and birds. It is observable that when a fish lays eggs she with her male partner watches over the eggs as if they are very anxious for them, until of course, they are prevented from the course by some hostile circumstances. When the eggs are hatched the parents accompany their young as they move from place to place in the water. As we know, a tortoise lays eggs on land. But as she moves about in the water she ever remembers the eggs and their place and very often returns to them. Many species of birds—sparrows, pigeons, swans, bees and the like—incubate their eggs and literally rear their young. As regards the animals which give birth to their young alive, one species of monkeys especially exhibits the parental instinct. The female monkey holds the young in her arms in all her wanderings, showing how attached she is to her offspring. In these animals the parental instinct expresses itself in some specific behaviour. But in man this instinct is surrounded by awareness and feeling. The human mother, the father also in normal cases, forgoes all comfort for the sake of their child ; they even suffer infinite pain in their effort to protect and nurse it. In McDougall's opinion, this emotion gives rise to all altruistic feelings.[3] As he points out, there occurs "a vast extension of the field of application of the maternal instinct." When a mother or father sees a child of another person, she or he would naturally have the same or somewhat similar emotion towards the child as they have towards their own. The extension is based on the similarity of the object in question to the primary object—one's own child. The helplessness of the child excites the parental instinct and a tender emotion in its mother or father, or in both. Now, then, occurs a further extension of the tender emotion. If any adult is in distress, his state of helplessness would provoke the protective instinct and evoke the tender feeling. McDougall, therefore, concludes that the parental instinct and the attendant tender emotion really render human nature social.

3 *An Introduction to Social Psychology*, p. 71.

Criticism. Morris Ginsberg brings some objections against McDougall's position. In the first place, he points out that there is no reason why we should regard social feelings or impulses as derivative. He contends that they might originally be there and be of their kind. If men are self-regarding absolutely, there is no way of positing social nature, in the true sense, in them. The attempt to explain social impulses by the analogy of parental or family affection is misleading since social relations are not confined to blood relations, but cover even those individuals who belong to different stocks. Social emotion is of its own kind and cannot be affiliated to any family emotion. Secondly, Ginsberg tells us that psychologically the two types of feelings—the self-regarding and the other-regarding impulses—are fundamental or primary in men.[4]

Ginsberg's objections have doubtless much force. We indeed cannot explain the social impulse or feeling only with the help of an analogy. That way we only point up similarity between the social feeling and the parental emotion but cannot explain the former. McDougall obviously makes much of the state of distress one may be in. He in so many words says that the origin of the social nature of man is tragic to the extent that it is occasioned by one's sufferings, and that we in our social relations simply act the part of the parents in relation to their offspring. The fact, however, remains that if the distress of a person excites sympathy and sympathetic reactions in others, they are already possessed of social nature.

(*c*) *Social nature and the herding instinct.* In his explanation of the social nature of man McDougall, again, draws upon the gregarious instinct. "We may briefly sum up", he says, "the social operation of the gregarious instinct by saying that, in early times when population was scanty, it must have played an important part in social evolution by keeping men together and thereby occasioning the need for social laws and institutions."[5] But he thereby fails to improve his position. He puts minimum meaning in the phrase "the

4 Morris Ginsberg, *Psychology of Society*, Methuen & Co. Ltd., London, 1933, p. 16.

5 *An Introduction to Social Psychology*, p. 301.

gregarious instinct." He takes it to mean only "the impulse to herd together."[6] But social nature cannot be reduced to the herding impulse. It is, of course, true that some animals live in groups of their own. Thus cows, elephants, buffaloes, and some other kinds of animals in their wild state graze together and move together. This mode of living has, however, no social implication. Furthermore, the groupings of the gregarious animals are not at all explained by the herding instinct. This instinct only means that some animals have the impulse to live in a group. The gregarious instinct is then the herding instinct. On the other hand, if the emphasis is laid on living in a group, we may ask : What group ? There may be groups consisting of animals that belong to different species. There are no such natural groups, however. Such hybrid groups are only made by men. There such a group comes about when, say, some cows, some goats and some buffaloes are put together, and we have the word "cattle" for such a group of animals. And such a group, we say, might perfectly well satisfy the herding instinct in these animals. But the point is that the gregarious animals, in their natural state live in their respective *Species* groups. That is to say, cows live with cows, horses with horses, elephants with elephants, and so on. This fact evidently the herding instinct cannot explain. Far less can it explain the social nature of men who are self-conscious beings. That men herd with men, not with any lower animals show that men's social nature cannot be explained by the herding instinct, even if it functions in men. Again, an aggregation is only the physical condition of social life in the sense that without it social life is not possible. But an aggregation by itself is no society. It is only the foundation of society. So the mere fact of herding together cannot give us any idea what social nature is like. The original aggregation of men in the pre-social stage might have occurred in different ways. It might have been just accidental, or individual primitive men might have been thrust together by a natural

6 *Op. cit.*, p. 296.

calamity—a flood or an earthquake or a storm. It might also be that individuals were roaming in search of a fertile territory and that when they found one they settled down there. The gregarious animals lived in groups for a long time, but they have not yet developed among them any social life. If the human beings,like the gregarious animals, at first simply herded together, they could not possibly develop social life. For the seed of social life, then, we have to look into the very aggregation they formed in the remote past.

Trotter nevertheless takes gregariousness very seriously. He maintains that the gregarious impulse makes each member of the herd sensitive to the behaviour of his fellows, and impels him to remain with the herd.[7] The impulse makes for "a profound transformation of the mental make-up of the members of the herd." Trotter in fact tries to deduce everything, social and moral, from the relationships of the herding members.

Here we may repeat the criticisms we have urged against McDougall's position. And we may add that Trotter makes overmuch of gregariousness. All that he says in regard to the effects of the herding instinct relates precisely to the human herd, and not to the gregarious animals as they are. If we consider the human herd, as we may call it, and compare it to any species of gregarious animals, we notice a marked difference between them. The difference lies in the fact that the human herd is much more than a mere aggregation and, unlike an animal group, is just society wherein a large number of individuals live in mutual relationships, acting and reacting upon each other. As we cannot attribute a mental process like recognition or reflective consciousness to the lower animals, the gregariousness of the gregarious animals is to be explained only by a peculiar sort of instinctive behaviour they have towards each other in groups of like members. It is indeed a far cry from the herding instinct of the gregarious animals to the social consciousness of men.

7 Trotter, *Instincts of Herd in Peace and War*, Fisher Unwin, London 1920.

II. Social Nature is based on the Consciousness of Kind.

The Consciousness of Kind. F.H. Giddings develops in his own way a significant theory. Though he is not impressed by the instinctive theory of society, yet he tries to explain the social nature of man by a basic psychological state which he calls the consciousness of kind. According to him, the consciousness of kind is the primordial social fact with which the study of society must start.[8] He points out that this state is the state of immediate awareness in an individual that he is of kindred nature with some other individual or individuals. This consciousness is more feeling than knowledge, and functions even in the animal world. And Giddings seeks to explain the group life of the gregarious animals by the consciousness of kind. Some animals in their wild state always live together in groups, he says, because of the consciousness of kind which functions in them. Thus cows, goats, elephants, etc. live and move in groups. Such groups are homogeneous in the sense that cows go with cows, goats with goats, and so on. A gregarious group is never a mixed group consisting of animals of different kinds, say, some cows, some goats, and some elephants. As animals of one species group live together, it, in Giddings's opinion, is clear that the behaviour of these animals in relation to each other is determined by their innate sense of kinship with each other. According to him, primitive men were very much like the gregarious animals in their mode of existence. They came together and lived together under the sense that they were alike. Though this sense of kinship was not articulate in the beginning, it nonetheless functioned in them, and in the long run created social nature in them. From this account of social nature it appears that the organization and development of society was just the process of articulating and deepening the consciousness of kind.

Criticism. If we reflect a little, we shall find that Giddings really deals with the problem of the herding

8 F. H. Giddings, *The Principles of Sociology*, Macmillan Company, New York, 1920, pp. 17-18.

instinct, and tries to settle it by his notion of consciousness of kind. And his position is somewhat like this; to say that the gregarious animals swarm together because of a sense of kinship among them is to say that we understand the herding instinct more clearly than when we say that the animals herd together because of an instinct. But we do not quite know whether there is any consciousness of kind in the gregarious animals. If we emphasize the fact that this consciousness is innate in the animals in question, we only mean that it is of the nature of an instinct. And the theory of the consciousness of kind is only the theory of the herding instinct in a new form. If we on the other hand regard this state really as a state of consciousness, it involves and must involve analysis and comparison among individuals concerned. In this sense there can obviously be no consciousness of kind in any lower animals; it is to be confined to men who are self-conscious rational beings. If we take the phrase "the consciousness of kind" in either of the senses, we fail to see how this could be the source of the social nature of man. If the innate sense of kinship determined the behaviour of gregarious animals in their groups, it determines their behaviour down to this day. But they could not yet develop social life among them. This shows that there is no germ of social life in the consciousness of kind, as it is called. If, on the other hand, the consciousness of kind is a complex process and involves reflection and analysis, it is not the innate sense of kinship. We, however, find something common to men and the lower animals. It is a matter of ordinary experience that when some oxen or dogs meet for the first time they appear hostile to each other, although they each belong to a kind. The oxen belong to the class "ox", and the dogs to the class "dog". But their initial behaviour towards each other is not ruled by any sense of kinship. We cannot make much of the analogy of the gregarious animals in the context of social consciousness. The analogy in fact breaks down because of the fact that when individual human beings first meet together as strangers, they, far from being guided by a sense of kinship, become impressed by the differences between them. If they find any likeness between them, they find it only later by mutual analysis, comparison, and communication with each other. Therefore, we have to say that Giddings's theory of the consciousness of kind oversimplified the fact of social consciousness.

III. *Social Nature is based on intelligence.*

We distinguish between some forms of this theory and would discuss them one by one.

(a) *Social Nature and the Sense of utility.* Plato was perhaps the earliest social philosopher to develop the theory that social organization was possible through human intelligence. For him indeed there was no distinction between society and the State, or the City State, as it was in Greece in his time. His theory is therefore applicable to society as it is involved in the State. As Plato pointed out, when individual men found that they could live their lives and have their needs fulfilled only by co-operation they organized themselves by way of division of labour into what later came to be called society. One group of people was entrusted with one kind of work for which they had skill and capacity, another group with another kind of work, and so on. And as a result there arose some different groups or classes with their respcctive functions.

As Plato put it :

> "The origin of a city is, in my opinion, due to the fact that no one of us is sufficient for himself, but in need of many things."[9]

He meant to say that society was "the outcome of our need". There were some basic needs such as food, clothing, and "a dwelling place". In the beginning, therefore, when people settled down together they allotted one kind of work to one group of people and another to another group for which they were best fitted, in order to supply the needs. The organization was established because the people perceived its utility. Thus agriculturists, weavers, builders, carpe-

9 *Republic*, tr. by A. D. Lindsay, J. M. Dent and Sons, Ltd., London ,1923, p. 54.

nters, smiths, traders and labourers, rulers and soldiers came up. They in fact constituted the original social classes. Thus society originated from a deliberate choice and a course of activity the pre-social individuals adopted. In other words, society was the outcome of intelligence in primitive men. They were quite aware of themselves and their needs and also of their surroundings, and thought out how best they could live and live together. This view influenced Herbert Spencer and some others in the nineteenth century.[10]

Here one comment may be made on Plato's theory. It seems that Plato did not clearly distinguish between the origin of the principle of division of labour, on the one hand, and the origin of society, on the other. His account of the social classes is beyond doubt relevant to the question of dlvision of labour. It is true to say that people distributed diverse functions among different groups according to their aptitudes when they found that no one man could fulfil all his needs. But we cannot say that division of labour marked the beginning of society. If we could say so, social nature was imposed upon men by the purpose of fulfilling their needs of life. And the implication is that social nature in men was only an accident and that it is not intrinsic in them. Furthermore, the view Plato propounded presupposed what he sought to explain. People could think of allotting different kinds of work to different appropriate groups if and only if they had lived together. But a large number of individuals living together in co-operaticn and sympathy without apparent division of labour among them represented a primitive form of society. Again a large number of individuals was not necessary for the purpose of forming society. Even a small number of individuals in association with each other might have made the beginning of society.

The Vedic people may be cited as an example here. At one stage of their history every individual, especially the head of the family, had to perform multifarious duties : he

10 F. Howard Collins, *The Synthetic Philosophy of Herbert Spencer*, Villiams & Norgate, London, 1901, pp. 399-408.

maintained the family and family tradition, he acquired the food-supply, perhaps with the assistance of the other members of his family, tilled the land, wove the clothes, built houses, shared in the defence of the territory, and peformed family worship. Later, however, the duties were considered too much for one man, and this awareness in the end led to a great social change, namely, the adoption of the principle of division of labour. As a result of it, as we know, there arose four main classes in society—the priests, the warriors, the producers and traders, and the labourers. One specific function was given to each of these classes. Pursuit of knowledge, defence, production of wealth, and service were their respective duties. This functional organization of society represents only a stage of social evolution and points to the pre-existence of society.

Obviously we cannot explain the social nature of man unless we have understood how society as earliest co-operative life among individual human beings originated and whether society as such was determined by some external circumstances, or whether it was the outcome of human nature itself.

(*b*) *Social nature is based on contract.* The Epicurean theory of society anticipated in a significant way the modern contract theories of society. Epicurus, the Greek materialist (341-270 B. C.), maintained that society exists for individuals and was created by individuals. In order to resolve the difficulties of the pre-social existence they entered into a contract among themselves whereby they established some mutual relationships between themselves so that they might live in peace.[11]

As we have seen above, Plato also sought to explain social organization by the perception of its utility. This theory was obviously reoriented or reformulated in the seventeenth and eighteenth centuries.

Thomas Hobbes (1588-1679) was opposed to the idea of society growing from a small beginning. In his opinion,

11 James P. Lichtenberger, *Development of Social Theory*, George Allen & Unwin Ltd., London, 1924, p. 62.

society had never begun as an organization of individuals and developed by some stages, but had an arbitrary beginning. According to him, in the pre-social days primitive men were in a state of "war of all against all". Their minds were ruled by base passions, greed for gain and self-interest ; they were equal to each other in their bodily strength and mental powers. In consequence, they were involved in a fierce competition. They seized the person, wives, children, and possessions of each other, and they knew no rest or peace of mind. Weary of such an unsettled and uncertain state of existence, particularly in order to find conditions of peaceful life, they entered into a form of covenant whereby society was brought into existence.

As Hobbes put it,

> "Hereby it is manifest, that during the time men live without a common Power to keep them all in awe, they are in that condition which is called Warre; and such a warre, as is of every man, against every man....
>
> ....
>
> "The Passions that incline men to Peace, are Feare of Death; Desire of such things as are necessary to commodious living; and a Hope by their Industry to obtain them. And Reason suggesteth convenient Articles of Peace, upon which men may be drawn to agreement."[12]

This Hobbesian idea was accepted by Spinoza. He says that in the state of Nature every individual sought what was useful to him. Consequently there was a ceaseless strife among primitive men. That was an intolerable state of existence. So they came to form a contract among themselves that they would respect the rights of each other. They in this way brought order out of chaos by establishing society wherein they controlled their passions and desires in order to live. Human beings are rational, So in their strivings in life they realize themselves as rational beings. When they recognized that the end they sought to realize was their rational nature, they came to perceive that that was a common end to themselves. As Spinoza says, it was under the sense of a common

12 *Op. cit.*, 187.
Leviathan, Ed. A. R. Waller, Cambridge, 1904, pp. 83 & 86.

end they were trying to realize that they came together and lived in mutual relationship. This was indeed the origin of society, says Spinoza.

According to Locke (1632-1704), however, the state of Nature prior to the origin of social life was a state of freedom and equality, although this state was far inferior to the state of organized society. But the former was not a state of war. In that state men had unlimited liberty as regards their person and possessions. They disposed of them in any way they liked. They, however, never destroyed themselves. Nevertheless, there was, according to Locke, a law of Nature to control that state, which prompted individual men to respect the rights of others, and produced in them a sense of obligation, i.e., the feeling that as they were equal to and independent of each other, they were not to do any harm to anyone. The state of Nature was, in Locke's view, governed by the law of Nature, which in fact proceeded from man's nature.[13]

To quote Locke,

> "A State also of equality, wherein all the power and jurisdiction is reciprocal, no one having more than another; there being nothing more evident than that creatures of the same species and rank, promiscuously born to all the same advantages of nature, and the use of the same faculties, should also be equal one amongst another without subordination or subjection unless the lord and master of them all should, by any manifest declaration of his will, set one above another, and confer on him, by an evident and clear appointment, an undoubted right to dominion and sovereignty.[14]
>
> "The state of nature has a law of nature to govern it, which obliges every one; and reason, which is that law, teaches all mankind who will but consult it, that, being all equal and independent, on one ought to harm another in his life, health, liberty or possessions."[15]

13 *Social Contract*, The World's Classics, Ed. E. Barker, p. 5.

14 *Op. cit.*, p. 5.

15 John Locke, *The Second Treatise of Government*, Basil Blackwell, Oxford, 1956, p. 5.

Jean Jacques Rousseau (1712-78), however, regarded the state of Nature as an ideal state of existence and the state of social life as a degenerate state of man. "Man is born free", said Rousseau, "and he is everywhere in chains." He drew a sharp contrast between the pre-social state and the state of social life. In his view, in the former state men were free, well adapted to the environment, and enjoyed perfect health and happiness. They were strong and robust like animals in their wild state. But in society men lived under restrictions and cramping conditions; therein they suffered from sickness, became weak in body, diffident and mean in mind. In the state of Nature, they were led by instincts which functioned with a flair for the right things or right ends to achieve. They had only physical wants which were satisfied by things gathered from the surroundings. But as they entered upon social life they created artificial wants which were difficult or impossible to fulfil; they came to know of disease and death which always cast them down.[16]

As Rousseau puts it, "I assume for the sake of argument, that a point was reached in the history of mankind when the obstacles to continuing in a state of Nature were stronger than the forces which each individual could employ to the end of continuing in it. The original state of Nature, therefore, could no longer endure, and the human race would have perished had it not changed its manner of existence."[17] "Some form of association must be found as a result of which the whole strength of the community will be enlisted for the protection of the person and property of each constituent member, in such a way that each, when united to his fellows, renders obedience to his own will, and remains, as free as he was before. That is the basic problem of which the Social Contract provides the solution."[18]

Criticism. The contract theories of society have one capital point in common. It is this, that society came into existence by a deliberate choice on the part of primitive men. They passed from the state of Nature to the state of social

16 *Social Contract*, Introduction by E. Barker, p. xxxix, xli.

17 *Social Contract*, Chap. VI.

18 *Ibid.*

life by free choice and mutual agreement, the implication being that society or social life was originally based on reason or intelligence. But the theories have their difficulties.

In regard to Hobbes's theory, we should like to point out that the assumption that men in the state of Nature were equal in body and mind is gratuitous. Individuals in society, as we see, differ from one another in this or that respect or in many respects—in bodily and mental powers, and they are born different from one another. If individuals were originally equal, we cannot understand how they could become different when tbey formed into society. Furthermore, if it is that in the state of war of all against all men seized the possessions of each other, there was obviously some sort of organization around their lives, though there was no machinery to control their lower passions. That might have been a rudimentary sort of society but that was society nevertheless. Hobbes's position only shows that social development was effected by a conscious act of thought or reason. But this leaves the problem of the social nature of man where it was. In this view we find no explanation whatever of the origin of society. Clashes between individuals do not necessarily negate social life; they rather posit it. They could come into clash with each other because they were in some way mutually related with each other. Clash and coercion are two of the different aspects of society. Why they occur is another matter. We cannot enter into it here.

Now, if we reflect on Locke's view of the state of Nature, we shall find that he only spoke of the state as a simple form of social life in contrast to the state of more organized society. This interpretation of Locke's view is confirmed by the fact that he recognized a law that governed the state of Nature and that the law proceeded from human reason. It ought to be clear, then, that in Locke's view the state of Nature was only less organized than developed society. But the difficulty is whether individual men who formed into society were men with intelligence or reason developed to the extent that they could frame laws or rules to control their mutual relationships. It is a patent fact that both body and mind developed along with, and through the medium of, social evolution.[19] Locke's theory therefore presupposes society, and does not explain it.

As regards Rousseau's view, it is to be noted that the state of Nature was an ideal state, while the state of social life is an artificial one. If it be so, reason or intelligence is responsible for the degradation of man. Social nature, then, represents deterioration of man, while the state of Nature is all perfect. But this view reverses the ordinary conception of man. Whereas man is ordinarily conceived to be a rational being, reason being essential to him, according to Rousseau, reason should be an accident to man, which indeed degrades him, his nature being conceived in terms of instinct. In that case, we fail to understand how reason was tacked on to human nature and by whom. Even granted that reason was there in man, we cannot see why reason should interfere with the ideal life of instincts, and bring about an organization like society wherein life is ruled or sought to be ruled by intelligence. Rousseau's view of society in relaiion to the state of Nature is in a certain respect similar to Freud's view of social life. According to Freud, natural life is dominated by the sex instinct. The sexual impulse or urge is, in his opinion, the ultimate source of human activities. But social life with its rules and restrictions runs counter to natural life, and as a result the sex impulse in its natural functioning is controlled and repressed by social life. Freud suggests that society owes its origin to the repression of sex. This repression, he tells us, makes havoc of the human mind. The impulse, being thwarted in its natural working, follows a tortuous way of expression and satisfaction, leading to the formation of complexes in mind, which in their turn become symptomatic of neurosis, i.e., abnormality or nervous disorder. Freud's view, in short, means that the life of the unobstructed sex instinct is normal life and that social life, regulating as it does sexual relations between men and women, is a deviation from normalcy. Freud, however, does not say why people took to repression of sex. If society

19 *Cf.* MacIver and Page, *Society*, Macmillan & Co. Ltd., London, 1957, p. 62.

represses sex, the latter does not explain social life, but presupposes it. In any case, though Rousseau's view of society is not quite the same as Freud's, yet both in a way agree that social life is a sort of degradation from the natural state.

In some contexts, however, Rousseau expresses a view of the state of Nature which is opposed to the view which is generally attributed to him. "The passage from the state of nature to the civil state," he says, "produces a truly remarkable change in the individual. It substitutes justice for instinct in his behaviour, and gives to his actions a moral basis which formerly was lacking......By dint of being exercised, his faculties will develop, his ideas take on a wider scope, his sentiments become ennobled, and his whole soul be so elevated, that, but for the fact that misuse of the new conditions still, at times, degrades him to a point below from which he has emerged, he would increasingly bless the day which freed him for ever from his ancient state, and turned him from a limited and stupid animal into an intelligent being and a Man."[20] Here, obviously, Rousseau maintains that the state of social life came about as a development from the state of Nature. He in so many words says that in the state of Nature a man was only a being of instincts, or rather an animal and that life in society is life of reason. He clearly reverses his original view that the state of Nature was an ideal state and that civil life was only a state of degradation from it.

We have considered above separately some different forms of the contract theory of the origin of society. We think we can urge one broad criticism against all the different forms of the theory. It is this, that the exponents of the theory did not quite grasp the distinction between society and the State. It is now a sociological common sense that in the earliest stage of society there was no State and that the State originated later by way of a social necessity. So while they sought to explain the origin of the State, though their theory as the theory of the State is open to

20 *Social Contract*, Ed. E. Barker, Chapter VIII.

debate, they thought they explained the origin of society. That was indeed an illusion on their part.

(c) *Social nature is based on imitation.* This theory was first propounded by Bagehot and was later developed by Tarde. According to the former, imitation was a great force in primitive society and is even now "the most fundamental of social prineiples." There is indeed the process of imitation in every sphere of life. Common dress and diet, common habits, a common speech, in short, a common way of life came about through imitation. Suppose that a certain person starts a fashion in dress; then another person imitates him, and a third imitates the imitator, and so on. In this way the fashion becomes widespread in society. So also in regard to diet, habits, speech, etc. According to Bagehot, however, imitation is involuntary and unconscious, and belief is the seat of "the imitative part of our nature." People imitate beliefs and ideas more readily than anything else. And this imitative tendency in men make them ridiculously credulous. Thus belief in ghosts, witchcraft, the efficiency of magical rites, etc. become infectious[21].

Tarde worked out his theory of imitation independently of Bagehot. According to the former, the social process "consists in the mental interaction between the members of a group." This interaction functions in three forms, namely, repetition, opposition, and adaptation.[22] Repetition has its physical form in undulation, or wavy motion as in sound passing through air, its biological form in heredity which consists in some essential characteristics of the organism being transmitted from generation to generation; and its essential form is found in imitation on which society is based.

Criticism. There are some difficulties in the way of accepting the view that the social nature of man is based on imitation. In the first instance, imitation is not confined

21 Walter Bagehot, *Physics and Politics*, Kegan Paul Trench Trūbner & Co. Ltd., London, 1873, pp. 92-94.

22 *Vide* M. Ginsberg, *Psychology of Society*, Methuen & Co. Ltd., London, pp. 22-23.

to human beings; it functions in the sub-human world also. Some birds imitate the call of others. The cat-bird, for instance, as Giddings tells us, imitates the call of the robin. But this fact of imitation does not make for any social relationship between them. Secondly, imitation is involved even in conflicts in the human as well as in the animal world. When two individuals quarrel or fight each copies the words or blows of the other. When two dogs are about to fight, if the one growls, the other also growls; if the one jumps upon, the other also does so, and so on, showing that imitation functions so vividly in a situation where there is no scope for any social relation. Imitation in conflicts is, however, instinctive in the sense that it proceeds without reflection and that it is just reaction similar to some appropriate action.

It is indeed true that men in their normal life imitate one another. But there imitation does not function at haphazard. There are, on the contrary, certain principles to guide the process of imitation. Firstly, there is the desire in a man to possess what others possess, to enjoy what others enjoy, and this desire adds a zest to life and makes one of the conditions of progress, economic and other. It is because of this desire that men imitate each other in diet, dress, housing, etc. and create a common diet, a common dress, a common language and the rest, in short, a common way of living among different social beings or their different groups. At a developed stage of social life, even one society imitates another in respect of a law, a custom, a policy or constitution. In the matter of women's emancipation, for instance, the Eastern people, generally speaking, imitate the Westerners. The new nations imitate the democratic constitution of the major Western countries. Some peaceful nations follow India in her neutralism. And so on.

Secondly, the inferior people by and large imitate the people superior in education, culture, position and power. And the psychology that normally works in the minds of the imitators is that they could improve their state and status only by acquiring things like those which their superiors possess and enjoy. In this regard imitation is a great socializing force. But imitation itself presupposes social life, and, for that matter, social nature. Healthy imitation can be among men when they are already members of a social whole. Were they unrelated and indifferent to each other, there was no question of one imitating another. Therefore, imitation by itself cannot explain social nature.

(d) *The mutual aid theory of social nature.* Some sociologists maintain that mutual aid and division of labour are the essential marks of social nature. Wherever there is society there are, they argue, mutual aid and division of labour.[23] In their opinion, then, the social nature of man is explained by these two facts. It is doubtless true to say that in society there are groups each of which is given its peculiar function. Thus the cultivators till the land and produce food, the weavers weave cloths, the artisans make various other things needed in daily life, the intellectuals develop art and science, the army defends the country against aggression, and so forth. And, needless to say, the co-operative activities of these groups sustain society as a whole. Still, we cannot say that society as such is based on mutual aid and division of labour. The difficulty is that we cannot convert the proposition, "Wherever there is society there is mutual aid and also division of labour", and say "Wherever there is mutual aid and also division of labour there is society." We cannot, because there are cases of mutual aid and division of labour where there is not the least of society. Consider a living organism, human or other. A living organism, as we know, consists of millions of cells, and this thing as a whole is constituted by them in their totality and is sustained by their co-operative functions. Again, the different parts or organs of a living body have their respective places and functions. Each with its own work is the principle of their arrangement in the body to which they belong. Thus the heart, lungs, liver, brain, kidneys, eyes, ears, and the rest have each their distinctive positions and functions in the body. But by no stretch of imagination can we think that there is a society, in the strict sense, of the

23 Kropotkin, *Mutual Aid*, Heinemann, London, 1919.

cells or organs. Mutual aid and division of labour we discern among the ants and bees. But these are only instinctively determined and have no social implications. Ants and bees have existed for centuries but have not yet developed in them any sort of life beyond their instinctive mode of existence. Mutual aid and division of labour we find both within and without society.

Sometimes, as Giddings points out, and as we find ourselves, social life is without a trace of mutual aid and division of labour. It is a fact that at the earilest stage of society there was no division of labour and that division of labour came about by way of a progressive organization of society. So also about mutual aid. It became articulate gradually through the deepening of the social sense. In developed societies conflicts often occur between individual and individual, between group and group—conflicts of interests and purposes, wherein there is no mutual aid whatsoever. Though mutual aid and division of labour mark developed social life in general, they, far from explaining society, posits it, and therefore cannot account for social nature.

IV. *Social nature is natural or intrinsic in man : Aristole's view.* Unlike Plato who bases society or social nature on intelligence—perception of utility, Aristotle (384-322 B.C.) maintains that society was a growth, and was not deliberately made. According to him, social nature was determined by natural impulses which created the family which was the social unit or society at its minimum.[24] But when he says "that man is by nature a political animal"[25] he means to say that society is not possible without the State and that the growth of the State is spontaneous. And Aristotle's theory involves the risk of interpreting the social in terms of the political organization. Such an interpretation of social life would indeed becloud the problem of social nature as such. Some great thinkers, however, seem to support Aristotle's theory of social nature.

24 Leichtenberger, *Development of Social Theory*, George Allen and Unwin, London. 1924, pp. 46-80; Aristotle, *Politics*, 1252b, 10, 15, 20.

25 *Op. cit.*, 1252. b, 30; 1253a.

St. Thomas Aquinas (thirteenth century) held that society arose spontaneously and that social nature itself is an instinct which impels men to form into an association which later leads to a many-sided development. He nevertheless maintained that society and the State must be consciously organized so as to work out the pattern of life adumbrated in the teaching of Jesus Christ. However, the theory that social nature is an instinct does not explain social nature. It simply means that social nature is social nature.

Jean Bodin, like Aristotle, maintains that society had a natural origin from the impulses which brought the family into existence. From the families, he said, arose the civil society.

Now, if the family is the source of society, society as such is to be traced to a pair or pairs of individuals who formed the original families. But it is difficult to substantiate this position, for the organization of society is far too complex to be explained by this theory. We have already seen that social nature cannot be traced to the parental instinct and the concomitant tender emotion. If it is contended that families forming into an association was really the beginning of society, we have to look beyond the natural basis of the family for the origin of society, because the question: what brought the families together? remains to be answered.

Montesquieu rejected the contract theory and supported the theory of natural origin of society, According to him, Men originally lived in the state of Nature. But this state, in his view, was not a state of war of all against all. They lived more or less at peace with one another, and society evolved out of their natural lives.[26] Obviously, Montesquieu, like Locke, could not quite distinguish between the state of Nature and the state of society, for the state of Nature with its relative peace and "natural rights of men" was some sort of social organization. Montesquieu, therefore, takes society and social nature for granted, and does not explain it.

V. *The social nature of man is based on the nature of man as*

26 Bogardus, *A History of Social Thought*. p. 188.

self or spirit. It is, of course, another thing to say that social life is natural to man. It is natural to man in the sense that it is bound up with the nature of man as a self-conscious rational being. The point is that social nature, being basic to man, could not be derived from anything external to human nature. Broadly, then, social nature is the innate tendency in an individual man to seek and enjoy the company of other men. And it is because of the fact that every individual man is at bottom a self—a spiritual entity. Here, of course, we may insist on the principle of "like attracts like." But this is not quite the consciousness of kind. The consciousness of kind is varied if it is not quite vague. In the case of the gregarious animals, the content of this consciousness seem to vary from species to speeies. But the kind in question is not bodily shape, for the individual animals do not perceive their bodies as objects in any way, though they perceive the bodily shapes of other animals. But the kind in the case of men is, however, bodily shape *cum* the inner counterpart conveyed through bodily signs. Unlike an animal, an individual human being sees the image of his body in water or in some other things, and is aware of his personal identity. In the light of this personal experience he can now understand his experience of other men. But all this is a developed process and could be found only in a developed man. But the question that we are considering relates to the beginning of society.

How could men begin to be social beings? This is the question. We find that the minimum that was needed for the purpose was self-consciousness on the part of men, which involved the consciousness of other selves. One could be conscious of himself as a self as he was conscious of other selves. There was, in short, self-consciousness on the part of men at the beginning of social life. It was not consciousness of kind, but consciousness of self. If primitive men associated with each other and thus laid the foundation of social life, they were certainly guided by their mutual awareness, mutual feeling and their sympathetic behaviour towards each other. We cannot say that social nature was determined by intelligence, or by instinct. Social nature was, in fact, the expression of the spiritual nature of man under the urge to concretize itself. And it concretizes itself through the medium of an external organization which is nothing but an association of individual minds. Co-operation, particularly a common way of life, however inchoate it might be, developed under the sense of the self as the essence of man, was the beginning of social life; social nature was consequently the outcome of the nature of man as spirit, which is a self-conscious entity and is the seat of all values that human beings have been seeking to realize by their creative activities. "The self is free, according to Hegel, because in all its actions it deals with what is ideal and its own; its connexions with the world are those of feeling, thought and will — mental powers in which the unity and self-identity of the self is realized."[27] Self-consciousness is at first abstract in the sense that the self is itself, and is expressible in the analytic proposition "I am I". It becomes concrete by embodiment in some adequate way. Self-consciousness becomes concrete by apprehending that it is in relation to both external things and other self-conscious beings.

27 Reyburn, *The Ethical Theory of Hegel*, **Clarendon Press, Oxford,** 1921, p. 87.

CHAPTER VI

The Family

Is the family an association? A family at the minimum consists of a man and a woman united as husband and wife. On a large scale it includes their children if they have any.

According to some sociologists and social philosophers, a family is an association. They say, "………in modern society, as in all complex civilizations, the family becomes definitely an association, so far as its adult members are concerned."[1] We have already seen that an association is a group of men within society formed in order to fulfil some purpose or purposes. So an association is deliberately formed and is guided by some rules framed for it. But an association is more or less without a social sanction. A family is not like a Limited Company, University Teachers' Association, or a Football League. In the case of a family two individuals—a man and a woman—of course, enter into a sort of alliance. There is, however, much difference between a family and an association, as we have defined it above.

In the first instance, the partners in a family do not proceed by framing rules to abide by. They simply take the oath of ethical life and ethical responsibility to each other. This they do only by way of solemnizing the sex-relation on which the family is based. Secondly, the members of an association do not or cannot live in it, whereas the members of a family live in it. Thirdly, a family grows, though there is no denying that it starts with a pair, and a family grows in the sense that new members come into it by birth out of the pair. So, if the family be conceived as an association, the new members are not a party to whatever was the purpose behind the association, nor to the rules, if any, framed for the working of the association. It cannot possibly be said that the children become members of the family in

1 **MacIver and Page, *Society*, 1957, p. 13.**

question when they become adults, i.e., when they become conscious of the purpose of the family, and agree to it. But we must note that the purpose for which their parents were united with each other is no purpose of the children even when they become adults. And if there be no purpose common to the parents and their children, they cannot be conceived as forming an association. There is a dilemma here : if the family be an association, the new comers, i.e., the offspring, are no members of it; again, if the family is no association, there is no question of the new comers being members of it. But the point is that children are members of the family to which they belong. We can resolve the difficulty only when we see that the family is no association in the ordinary sense of the term, but that the family is a social unit or organization which consists of a pair, or of a pair and their children.

It may be pointed out that a pair without offspring, in any case, constitutes a family. That such a pair does so nobody can deny. But it ought to be clear to anybody that this is only the minimum of the family. Generally, as children come in, the family of two expands into one of many. Be that as it may, the fact remains that the family is based on marriage. And whether the family is an association or not depends upon our view of the origin of the family. The view established before does not, at any rate, make the family an association. Even if we look upon marriage as a contract, made by way of registration in a law court, between two individuals of opposite sexes, the family does not become an association. The conception of marriage as a contract emphasizes only the legal aspect of it as well as of the family. An Association, to be sure, is not based on a contract. Therein some individuals form an organization to fulfil some purpose or purposes. And there is no social sanction behind it. Such an organization may be formed and may be dissolved, and with this society has nothing to do. An association, in short, does not arise to satisfy any social need. The Calcutta University Students' Union, for instance, has been formed to promote the well-being of students of the University. This is no need of society as such. We may be told that mutual enjoyment is the purpose behind the alliance in marriage. But we have to recognize the fact that the fulfilment of this purpose does not depend upon the caprice of the parties to the marriage, but upon social approval. Even contract marriage in the legalistic sense is subject to social sanction. So it is clear that the family is not an association. It is simply an organization through which the sex-relation as well as procreation is regulated in society.

The earliest form of the family. Sociologists and anthropologists try to ascertain the earliest form of the family. But there is a wide divergence between them. According to some, at the earliest stage of human existence there was no family organization.[2] There was then nothing to regulate sex-life and consequently there was promiscuity or communism in sex-relations. Men possessed women in common.

Some seek to reach to the earliest stage of social life, and they choose three ways of reconstructing the social life of primitive men, namely, (1) a study of the biological and geological facts, (2) an analysis of the archaeological materials, and (3) a general parallelism between some features of the primitive society and some features of the lowest societies of the present-day savages.[3]

Biology is, broadly, the study of animal species; It traces the complex species to some original simple forms of animal life. Naturally, biology considers the question of the origin of men out of some species of animals. So biology, we are told, throws much light upon the earliest stage of social life. But the difficulty is that the biological theory regarding the origin of men—that they were descended from some anthropoid apes—is more or less a hypothesis. We do not yet know anything definite about the origin of the human kind.

Geology, again, studies the formation cf the layers of the earth, and in a way goes beyond biology. Geology in fact, studies the earth we inhabit and our progenitors inhabit-

2 Lewis H. Morgan, *Ancient Society*, Indian Edition, 1958, pp. 393-94.

3 Cf. F. H. Giddings, *The Principles of Sociology*, pp. 209-210.

ed in the past. Some layers of the earth indeed contain some relics of the past which indeed count as evidence for some primitive conditions. But in geology as in biology whatever theory we erect regarding the earliest stage of human life would only be a hypothesis and would fail to furnish us with any definite conclusion.

As regards archaeological materials, we should like to say that they point to a comparatively advanced stage of social life, at which primitive people learnt the art of making tools and instruments out of some material. Even if we know much by this means about the things they used, the kind of houses they lived in, the utensils they used, the cloths they wove and so forth, we can that way know little or nothing about the form or forms of family life that prevailed at that time.

Some anthropologists make much of parallelism between the existing savage societies and the primitive society. They point out that the civilized and savage societies have much in common. They share some beliefs, customs and superstitions. Belief in ghosts, for instance, is common to the savage and civilized men. This shows, they say, that civilization developed out of savagery and that the savage societies for some reason or other lagged behind and were in the end left in a state of stagnation. So, it is argued, the conditions of savage life of the present time approximate to those of primitive life. A thorough study of the savage societies of today would, we are told, help us to reconstruct the primitive society. There is no doubt an element of truth in this view. But we should not exaggerate it. When we seek to utilize our knowledge of the savage world in our effort to reconstruct the beginning of society we have to bear in mind the basic difference between the two sides. Modern savage people have in fact, been driven into jungles and "hilly barren tracts" by civilized men. The former are therefore at a disadvantage and live in cramping circumstances, while primitive men lived in free, open environments, had an abundant food-supply and were healthy, strong and stout. So there must be limitations to parallelism between the two peoples. It is indeed futile to try to gain an image of the primitive society by a study of the existing savage societies. Strictly speaking, we cannot say anything definite about the beginning of human society; we can only frame hypotheses, and one hypothesis is as good as another.

Morgan, for his part, posits promiscuity at the beginning of human existence, and maintains that family organization gradually evolved out of the initial chaos. Morgan's scheme of the evolution of the family is as follows.

I. *The Consanguine Family.*

The consanguine family was the first form of the family. It was based on the marriage of brothers and sisters in a group. We are told that there is definite evidence to support the theory of the consanguine marriage. In ancient Egypt and Persia, they say, the kings and princes married within their families because they attached a special virtue to royal blood, or because they wanted to prevent royal property passing into the hands of outsiders by way of wedding gifts to their sisters. Furthermore, the consanguine family is said to be prevalent in Siam, Burma, Ceylon, the Howaiian Islands, and Peru.

II. *The Punaluan Family.*

This form of the family was the second form to evolve. The word "punaluan" derives from the Howaiian relationship of punalua, meaning group marriage, i.e., "marriage of several brothers to each other's wives in a group, and of several sisters to each other's husbands."

III. *The Syndyasmian Family.*

The word "Syndyasmos" means joining two individuals together, and strictly the union of a male with a female in marriage. The Syndyasmian was the third form in the evolution of the family, and was based on a pair of individuals.

IV. *The Patriarchal Family.*

The fourth form of the family was based on the

marriage of one man to many women, the man wielding absolute power over the whole family.

V. *The Monogamian Family.*

This form of the family was the highest form and was the last form to evolve. As the very name indicates, this form of the family was determined by the marriage of one man to one woman.[4]

Morgan adds that Levirate—the marriage of a man and the childless widow of his brother—which prevails in some societies, seems to be a relic of the punaluan form of the family.

Morgan's position that in the remote past there was no family life, or that sex-relations were promiscuous has been rejected by some sociologists. According to Westermarck and others, there was some sort of family life at the beginning of society. Indeed much can be said on both sides. Still, whether family life in some form or other was there is a pertinent question. Though we cannot answer this question in the affirmative or in the negative, we can at any rate say that family life without marriage was possible at the earliest stage of society. In this matter the analogy of some animals would help us. We find that birds and beasts of some species live together with their young, though most of them do so for a short period. A hen with her brood resembles, though remotely, a human mother with her children; so also a cat with her kittens, and a bitch with her puppies. There are some animals that most resemble men. They are orang-utans, gorillas, and chimpanzees, who live in pairs with their young. But such temporary or relatively permanent grouping of the parent or parents and their young in the cases of some animals is undoubtedly determined more by instinct than by anything else. This seems to be a plan of Nature to preserve the species in question. However, an animal group of this kind cannot, properly speaking, be

4 Lewis H. Morgan, *Ancient Society*, Bharati Library, Calcutta, 1958, p. 28.

called a family. Likewise, the groupings of human parents and their children at the pre-social stage, if any, cannot be called families, and the reason is that a family is a social unit based on sexual union approved by society. Though marriage involves sex-relation, it by itself is no marriage. A man and a woman may have sex-relation with each other, though they are not married to each other. Such relationship is an illegitimate one and is considered anti-social. So, if in the pre-historical days parents lived with their children temporarily or permanently, they did so, like many kinds of animals, simply under the parental instinct, without the institution of marriage which is possible only within society. It is very difficult, in any case, to determine the earliest stage of human existence. This much, however, we can say that at the earliest stage there was some sort of family life in a very loose sense of the term, in the sense of a bare group of parents and their children.

As regards Morgan's scheme of the evolution of the family, we may consider some points. In the first instance, we should like to point out that incest, sexual connection between blood-relations, is viewed with horror, and that it was prohibited even in ancient society.[5] As we have noted before, Plato refers to this prohibition as an unwritten law. Incest is disallowed and disapproved in present-day savage societies in general. The so-called consanguine marriage Morgan refers to was no marriage in the strict sense; it was, if at all, a sort of sex-relation much near to the sex-relation in the lower animals. As to royal families wherein a brother married a sister, we should like to say that that was an affair of the royal families in question and was apart from the common run of men. This form of the family was allowed, if ever, under special circumstances. If there are societies in which brother-sister marriage prevails, they must be degenerate and do not represent any normal stage of social development. For some reason or other there must have been in them laxity in social relationship. Furthermore, Morgan might have confounded the *classificatory system* of

5 *Rig-Veda*, x, 10.

some savage societies with consanguine marriage. The classificatory system is just the application of some terms not to single individual persons but to the classes of relatives which may often be very large, e.g., brother, mother and cousin. In this system, some words are applied to people who have the same rank with the persons to whom the words are meant to be applied. Thus the word "father" is applied to all those male persons the father calls brother, and the word "mother" to all those women the mother calls sister. Boys and girls of the same age and rank call each other brother and sister. And so on. So very many words like these were used in a wide sense. From the point of view of the classificatory system therefore individuals—males and females—who were distant relatives or were not relatives at all call themselves brother and sister. There was obviously no bar to marriage between a male and a female among these individuals, because the classificatory system was wholly a matter of language. Morgan's theory might be based on wrong observation and an incomplete analysis of it. Therefore, we must be slow to accept Morgan's theory that the consanguine family was the first form of the family.[6]

Secondly, Morgan's theory of group marriage—the punaluan—was based on inadequate observation and a misinterpretation of some social practices of some savage tribes. As reports made by Christian missionaries about them contradict each other, sociologists now do not accept the conception of group marriage.

Thirdly, the line of evolution of the family as suggested by Morgan is not a correct one, for the patriarchal form of the family appeared only in civilization, and monogamy is found even in savagery.* Hence Morgan's whole scheme is

6 W. H. R. Rivers, *Kinship and Social Organisation*, Constable & Co. Ltd., London, 1914, pp. 2-3;

Encyclopaedia of Religion and Ethics, Ed. by James Hastings, Vol. VIII, Charles Scribner's Sons, New York, 1916, p. 425.

*Westermarck, *History of Human Marriage*, Vol. I. Macmillan & Co. Ltd., London, 1921, pp. 117-125.

wrong. The fact is that as we cannot ascertain the earliest form of the family or the earliest stage of society with its details, so also we cannot trace the evolution of the family organization. . There are no sufficient data to go upon, and it is no use making some wild hypotheses about the beginning and evolution of the family. We may only consider with profit the forms of the family that prevailed in civilized societies.

The Patriarchal Family. At a particular stage of civilization in ancient times the prevailing form of the family was patriarchal. In Engels's words, "With the patriarchal family we enter the field of written history...." We know this by a study of the Laws of the ancient peoples—the Greeks, Romans, Jews, Hindus, and Chinese.[7] But we cannot say that the patriarchal form was the earliest form of the family, for it represents an advanced stage of social life where customs had passed into laws.

The typical patriarchal family was the Roman family in which the power of the father—the *patria potestas*—was "absolutely supreme in his household." The father was the head of the family and exercised absolute authority over the family, which consisted of the father, mother, their children, all descendants in the male line, and slaves. When a daughter was married she joined her husband's family and submitted herself to the authority ruling there. In the families descent was traced through the father. The patriarchal families were *patrilineal*. As Mrs. Bosanquet tells us, in the Roman patriarchal family in its extreme form a woman's children were not related to her brother's children. There are two kinds of family relationship called *Agnatic* and *Cognatic* relationship. The idea ef Cognatic relationship is a modern one and is quite familiar to us. It is the relationship traced through "common descent from the same pair of married persons. Nowadays the descendants of a pair

7 Helen Bosanquet, *The Family*, Macmillan & Co, Ltd., London, 1906, p, 9;

History and Culture of the Vedic People, Vol. I, Ed. R, C. Majumdar, George Allen & Unwin Ltd., London, 1957, p. 384; Henry Sumner Maine, *Ancient Law*, John Murray, London, 1870, p. 123.

have this of kind relationship among themselves. But agnatic relationship prevailed in patriarchal societies, especially in ancient Roman families. This relationship was traced through the males only, and the authority of the father was its basis.[8] The status of the woman in the families was very low indeed. There was the institution of "perpetual Tutelage" of women. When the father of a female died she became subject to her nearest male relation or to some other male person her father chose for the purpose. When the husband of a woman died she came under the authority of her son who now became head of the family. The women in all circumstances were not free. They were considered inferior to their menfolk. The head of the family gave away his daughter in marriage and gave a wife to his son ; he had even the power of life and death over the other members of the family. Under the Roman Empire, howevrr, the absolute power of the father of the family came to be curtailed, and he exercised his power only within limits. Later, Roman Law further reduced the power of the head.

The Basis of the Paramount Power of the Father.

The paramount power of the father in the patriarchal family was a problem to the sociologists and social philosophers, and stimulated research about it. And there are some different views about the source of the power of the father.

According to one view, the father wielded absolute power over his family because of his superior physical strength. But this view seems to be absurd. Granted that the other members of the family were severally weaker than the head of the family, they could collectively overpower him whenever he proved to be a despot. Further, it is not thinkable that at a stage of civilization family life was organized and ruled by sheer brute force. The father was after all a human being and had his natural tender emotion towards his children, and his duties and responsibilities for his dependants. The point, however, is that in the case of punishing a member of the family

8 Maine, *Ancient Law*, p. 149.

for a misdeed the head of the family was the sole authority and his decision in the matter was final. As the head was responsible for all affairs of the family, his supreme power derived from his supreme responsibilities, and was approved by the law of the land. But that is another matter. It nevertheless appears that there was nothing in the social system to check him when he went, or wanted to go, too far in exercise of his power. The fact that the father of the patriarchal family wielded power even in his old age when he became physically weak points to a deep source of his power.

They say that there were three reasons why the patriarch had absolute power over all other members of his family.[9] First, the father was the progenitor and had power and rights over his family just as a proprietor had his rights over his property. Second, the father as the oldest member of the family possessed wisdom and wide experience by which he was best fitted for conducting the affairs of his family. Naturally, all the other members of the family were dependent upon him. Third, each family had its peculiar tradition which was handed down from generation to generation. The head of the family maintained and enhanced the tradition. This gave the head a privileged position in the family. His position became specially significant in the family in which ancestor-worship was the main creed. He knew the peculiar cult and performed the peculiar rites All this, we are told, gave him a supreme place in his family.

The first reason stated above has no force, for the head of the family was not necessarily a father. The oldest male member without children might be head of the family or *paterfamilias*. So we cannot say that the power of the head was supreme because he was the progenitor. The other two reasons are quite plausible. It is understandable that members of a family submitted themselves to the power and care of the head particularly because he with his wisdom and experience was best fitted for discharging his responsibilities regarding his family. Still, we feel that his power was far wider than was justified by his duties and responsibilities.

9 Helen Bosanquet, *The Family*, pp. 13-15.

Among the ancient Jews, Greeks and Chinese as among the ancient Romans the patriarchal family was in its extreme form. One fact that becomes clear from the above analysis of the patriarchate or patriarchal form of the family is this, that in patriarchal families women were subjected to men. In ancient Hindu families the emphasis was laid upon ancestor-worship. A list of the past generations of the family, in the male line was kept by the head of the family, and appropriate rites were performed by him. But the head of a Hindu family, unlike the head of a Roman family, had no absolute power or authority over the members of his family. In a Hindu family the right to worship the ancestors was vested in the male members in a hierarchical order in the line of succession to the headship. And the right to the ancestral property was commensurate with the right to ancestor-worship. But therein women had no property right except in the families which were governed by Mitākṣar, the law-giver who had given women also some share in the family property. In Hindu society most of women were economically dependent upon the male members of their families. We can say that in ancient times there was, generally speaking, a threefold dependence of women upon men. In her girlhood she was dependent upon her father, in her youth upon her husband, and in her old age upon her son. Recently or in the recent past, however, an overall change came upon the condition of womankind. Nowadays almost everywhere the rights of women have been recognized.

The Matriarchal Form of the Family. Some sociologists nevertheless plead for matriarchy as against patrirarchy. We have considered above in some detail the patriarchal form of the family. Let us now discuss the matriarchal form of it.

The matriarchal was the form of the family in which the mother occupied the position of absolute authority, and in which descent was traced through her, that is, relationships were metronymic. So the matriarchal family was matrilineal. We are told that in the matriarchal family the mother or wife was in power. In any event, in it a female was head of the family, whereas in the patriarchal family a male, generally the father, was head.

Westermarck emphasized the contribution of the male to the growth of the family. According to him, it was the male who by his power and impulse for exclusive possession of a woman brought order to sex-relation out of the somewhat formless conditions of primitive life. Westermarck suggests that the patriarchal form of the family was most ancient.[10]

Bachofen, the Swiss sociologist, in his book "Mütter recht" (Mother Right), however, lays stress upon the matriarchal type of the family and holds that the matriarchal was the earliest form of the family.[11] And R. Briffault in his *The Mothers* broadly supports Bachofen's view. According to Bachofen, it was the woman who brought order out of sexual chaos in primitive society. Some even go to the length of saying that at the earliest stage of human existence woman was in supreme power both inside and outside the family, and that there was a time, when women ruled society. There were, according to them, days of gynaecocracy.[12] Whatever evidence is there for this theory is furnished by some tribal societies. We are told that among the Hurons and Iroquois of North America, and the Eskimoes of Greenland women exercised authority. But as to the extent of their power accounts differ, and it is pointed out that the family organization in these tribes is not of the matriarchal type.

There are nevertheless some tribes which are really matriarchal. Among the Khasis of the Khasia Hills in Assam women not only supervise all family affairs, but also fnnction as heads of their families. The daughter inherits the ancestral property, and when she marries her husband leaves his family and joins hers and lives there under her authority. Descent is naturaly traced through the mother.

Minicoy is a small island about 230 miles off the Malabar Coast in the Arabian Sea. There the people are all Muslims. Early marriage is prevalent among them, and the girls are free to marry. The women are influential to the extent that all property of their families belongs to

10 Westermarck, *History of Human Marriage.*

11 Helen Bosanquet, *The Family*, p. 35.

12 *Vide* Wilhelm Wündt, *Elements of Folk Psychology*, George Allen & Unwin Ltd., London, 1916, p. 36.

them. The males have only the right of residence in the homes, and the right of maintenance. There is no system of *Purdah*. When a male person marries he goes over to his wife's family and takes over her name.[13]

In Manipur in Assam women are free in their movements and activities, and exercise much power and authority over their families, though we cannot say that the *Manipuri family* is of the matriarchal type. In the time of the battle of Kurukṣetra, about fourteen centuries before Christ, narrated in the *Mahābhārata*, which is an Indian Epic, there was a women's State in the eastern region of India. Historians locate this State in modern Manipur. There are obviously enough data to support the view that at some stage of social development in India women held positions of authority and were in fact heads of their families.

We cannot, however, definitely say that the matriarchal form was the earliest form of the family. As some thinkers suggest, it might be that both the matriarchal and the patriarchal forms prevailed at the same time either in the same society or in different societies. And both, involving as they did a complex organization, presupposed a stage of developed social life.

MacIver and Page, for their part, point out that there is a form of the family which appears to be a somewhat modified form of the matriarchal family.[14] Among some people, the Malays, for example, woman is in authority and her husband is a subordinate in the home. But therein a male relative of the wife exercises authority on her behalf, although the children trace their descent through the mother. In this form of the family matrilineal descent is often associated with "matrilocal residence", meaning that children are born and reared in the home of a male relative of the mother. There might be other different forms of the matriarchal form of the family. But they are not our immediate concern. We are only to consider, and we have considered, the contrast between the patriarchal and matriarchal forms of the family.

13 *Cf. The Statesman*, August 16, 1956.

14 MacIver and Page, *Society*, p. 248.

We have analyzed some details and come to the conclusion that they do not throw light upon the problem of the earliest form of the family, though it is true that both point to a distant past.

The patriarchal and modern family. Though the patriarchal family in the strict sense is now a thing of the past, yet some elements of it still persist in the modern family. Generally speaking, the father is the head of the modern family, and upon him falls the whole burden of the family—he has to support and maintain it. As we have seen before, ancestor-worship was the main plank on which the patriarchal family was based. It is debatable, however, whether ancestor-worship was ever a stage of religion any more than totemism was. The fact, nevertheless, remains that ancestors were remembered with reverence and were adored by their progeny in every age and every country. Even today every family in every society more or less observe Remembrance Day in memory of the ancestors when prayers are made to God for their well-being. This practice we should call *worship for ancestors*, not ancestor-worship, as sociologists in general call it. In some present-day societies the head of the family performs rites for ancestors on an appointed day. So the father as head still holds a position of authority in the family, which corresponds to his responsibilities. But the power of the modern father is limited. In a way his responsibilities are greater than his power. He has to feed the members of the family, to rear the children, and give them a sound education, and so forth. But he cannot do whatever he likes about his family. There is law to restrain him. His wife and children, even his servants, have the right of maintenance by him, and in case he neglects his obligations, they can seek redress from the State.

In the patriarchal form of the family, the head had a monopoly of wisdom and experience. But nowadays education is widespread, and knowledge, being disseminated through books, is open to all. The spread of education has broken the monopoly of knowledge and wisdom the heads of the patriarchal families had. But the father as the progenitor has some basic right on his children. He would serve the family according to his means and would often chastise his children when they would go wrong. In one respect, however, the father in some societies is absolute authority. The ancestral as well as his personal property is at his disposal where there is yet private property[15]. He may still give away some of his children as a gift to some of his relations or to someone else. But he cannot in any way inflict grievous injuries on, or kill, any member of his family. If he ever does so, he would be dealt with as a criminal.

The Basis of the Family. According to Mackenzie, the child is the basis of the family. The nurture of the child with a view to making it a true citizen of the State is he says, the chief concern of the family. So it is the well-being of the offspring that, in his opinion, holds the family together[16]. And it is on matter, we are told, that a child is born of the union of husband and wife, for he is logically prior to the union in the sense that the idea of the child functions behind the marriage-tie between them. There is no doubt point in this contention if it is that marriage is determined by a desire for offspring.

This view seems to be plausible but is difficult to establish. We may advance some arguments against it.

First, there might be cases in which the people concerned marry for the purpose of having children but they do

15 As we have seen before, in some tribal societies, the family is, even today, matriarchal, and the father has no authority there. Again, under the Dāyabhāga (one Section of Hindu Law), according to which, the sons (the daughters are left out of consideration in the matter of property right in the presence of a son) do not acquire any interest in ancestral property while the father is alive, a Hindu father could dispose of the property in any way he liked. Under the Mitākṣara Hindu Law, however, the sons of a person are entitled by their very birth to their respective shares in the family property. So in the families governed by this law the father is not absolute authority over the property (Mulla, 1959, pp. 4·7-473). However, the new Act—*The Hindu Succession Act*, 1956—has abolished the Dāyabhāga and the Mitākṣara law, and given the males and females each an absolute right over the family property. This is only a right of succession But, while living, the father is free to dispose of his property as he likes.

16 *Outlines of Social Philosophy*, George Allen and Unwin Ltd., London, 1956, pp. 77-81.

not have any child. Still, the families they form do not break up.

Second, there is indeed one secret purpose of Nature, which is the preservation of the species, especially the perpetuation of the human race by new births, which she fulfils by means of union of a male and a female of the same class or kind. But how prove that the secret purpose of Nature becomes a conscious purpose in man ? Even if we grant that there is a secret purpose of Nature behind the process of procreation, we cannot deny that this purpose is all unconscious in the lower animals and that this purpose is effected there through the mediation of the sex-instinct. In insects, birds and beasts, as we know, the process of reproduction is determined by the blind sexual connection between a male and a female of the same kind. Man, though rational, is an animal because some instincts, including the sex-instinct, constitute the sensuous basis of his being. It cannot be denied that the instincts and impulses are sought to be ordered by reason in him. But instincts qua instincts play their part in human life and are not quite rationalized. Therefore, it is reasonable to say that a man and a woman are attracted towards each other, when they are so attracted, and are finally united with each other through the sex-instinct. This sexual union as sanctioned by society is what we call marriage. If some married couples came to have desires a for offspring, that was obviously an after-thought, which was determined by certain circumstances of life.

In reference to the Vedic age, they say, "The fulfilment of the desire for offspring, and male offspring in particular, was the chief aim of marriage."[17] Then we have to say that the Vedic people were coldly rational and that they proceeded in a matter like marriage in a cool and calculating way. Were they so, any woman was sufficient for a man, and any man for a woman to fulfil the purpose; there could evidently be no need for any sexual selection. And, what is worse, the Vedic women might be, in that case, con-

17 *The History and Culture of the Indian People*, Vol. I, Ed. R. C. Majumdar, George Allen and Unwin Ltd., London, 1957, p. 390.

sidered only child-producing machines. If, on the contrary, marriage in Vedic times was based on sexual preference, there was behind it some natural impulse, not an ulterior motive like desire for offspring.

Third, if desire for offspring were the motive force behind marriage, few people would go in for it. Only those who had enough for the purpose of rearing and supporting children should marry. Consider the state of poor people, especially that of destitutes. They marry though they have not the means to support their families. They have no houses to live in, no clothes to wear except rags and have little to eat. If they still marry and do so for offspring, they are abnormal to a degree. Otherwise, we can by no stretch of imagination conceive that they marry to fulfil their desire for offspring.

Fourth, the eagerness with which people have taken to birth control shows that after marriage children come in as a natural consequence of it, over which they have ordinarily no control. Children are born to a pair even if they do not desire them. All this implies that the child is not the basis of the family. Were the child the basis of the family and child-production the sole purpose of marriage, why should Government seek to foil this purpose by prescribing and encouraging birth control in the families we wonder. But birth control is birth control, and strictly, is control of the sex-relation between husband and wife. But it means control over the physical or physiological process of the sex-act so as to prevent child-birth. But this control does not mean control of the sex-desire, but only control of one natural consequence of marriage—the flow of babies into the families. There is therefore something in the marriage-relationship which accounts for the birth of a child and which is really the foundation of the family.

Some may point out that there is in this argument a misunderstanding of the purpose of the Government. They may say that Government in their attempt to prevent over-population in the country only propose birth control as a means of limiting the families, that they are never for whole-sale birth control. So birth control as proposed and sponsored by Government does not, they may argue, make against the position that the child is the basis of the family. But we have to take note of the fact that many married people are taking advantage of birth control just to enjoy sex-life without encumbrance. These people only utilize the Government's policy and plan for their personal enjoyment, showing thereby that the child is only an offshoot of the family, and not its basis.

Fifth, many people posit some worthy motive for marriage in order to cover up their sex-desire of which they are apparently shy. This happens in a bride or bridegroom or in both who are advanced in years. Everything has its time : youth is the time for marriage. Naturally, in an aged couple the sex-desire seems to be out of place and masquerades as desire for offspring.

Sixth, one cannot possibly misinterpret the view of this or that social philosopher. In this context one may quote Plato as saying, "The bride and the bridegroom should consider that they are to produce for the State the best and fairest specimens of children which they can."[18] We must here mark the word "should" and need not discuss the view of the sex-relation Plato expresses in the *Republic* where he pleads for communism in women as against the family.[19] If we look into the sentence quoted above, we shall find that Plato does not mean that two individuals enter into the marriage-relationship with the obvert purpose of having offspring. He only means that a married couple have one duty to the State; that they have to contribute to its man-power by producing "the best and fairest specimens of children which they can." The idea is that they should utilize the marriage-relation for the good of the State. But if they in fact produce children with a view to strengthening the State, it does not follow that their purpose behind marriage was to produce children for the State. In Plato's communism a man and a

18 Frederick Copleston, *A History of Philosophy*, Vol. I, Burns and Oates Ltd., London, 1961, p. 236; Plato, *Laws*, Jowett, IV, 709 E, VI, 775, D, E.

19 *Republic*, V, 459-461.

woman in their sexual union were to produce children who were to be reared by the State. In that case, there was no question of a family, let alone the child forming the basis of the family. Suppose that a man has earned a vast fortune by hard labour and that he is asked by the Government to contribute a considerable sum towards the industrialization of the country. Suppose now that he contributes a sum for the purpose. But it does not mean that he earned money only to contribute towards the well-being of his country. It may be that he simply utilizes some of his earnings for the good of his country.

Seventh, it is no use arguing that the State itself posits the desire for offspring as the motive behind marriage. But there is scarcely an equation between the State's desire and a citizen's desire in so far as the marriage-relation is concerned. During the last World War, Hitler in Germany and Mussolini in Italy devised some means of increasing the population of their countries. They encouraged and rewarded parents for more and more children. Here, we see, the Political Authority wanted an enormous increase in the population in view of warfare. But this desire on the part of the Authority concerned could not be the desire of the married people at large of the country in question. If they responded to the appeal of the Authority, and produced more and more children, they did so only out of greed. If it be argued that the people might have identified themselves with their leader, with his ideas and desires, and that they married, when they married, with the sole purpose of producing children, it may be pointed out that the people there were simply mechanized. The mechanization of men means that they have ceased to be normal men and have been reduced to things. In that situation, marriage as a matter of free choice and free consent loses all meaning.

Eighth, if the child is the basis of the family, how can there be divorce between husband and wife with a child or some children ? But divorce is fact and is sanctioned by Law. A child torn between two claimants on the scene of divorce is the most tragic thing in the world. A child is, again, often left to its own fate. The fact of divorce and its tragic consequence is the unanswerable criticism of the view that the child is the basis of the family.

The Economic Condition as the Basis of the Family—Helen Bosanquet in her *The Family* refers to the theory that the family is "only a temporary product of a particular stage of economic development, and that it would disappear with the disappearance of private property. The father is the economic centre of the family in the sense that all other members are dependent upon him for sustenance. The point is that in olden days women for their sustenance were dependent upon men. So a woman generally chose a man who could or would look after her. It was in this way, say Marx and Engels, that they formed a union, which as sanctioned by society was called a family. The economic condition was thus the basis of the family. This idea is conveyed when Marx says that institutions, moral conceptions, law, customs, etc., were directly determined by the means of production.[20]

Engels in his *The Origin of the Family, Private Property and the State*, plans to present "the results of Morgan's researches" regarding the family, and seems to accept his theory in broad outline.[21] He, however, supplements it with his own conceptions. He seems to hold the view that the family was originally based on sex when he says, "The old society based on sex groups bursts asunder in the collision of the newly-developed social classes; in its place a new society appears, constituted in a state, the lower units of which are no longer sex groups but territorial groups, a society in which the family system is entirely dominated by the property system in which the class antagonisms and class struggles, which make up the content of all hitherto *written* history, now freely develops."[22] After having considered the evolution of the family at the three stages of human existence, savagery, barbarism, and civilization, Engels fixes on monogamy. He

20 *Cf.* Emile Burns, *What is Marxism?* Peoples Publishing House Ltd., Bombay, 1952, p. 8.

21 *The Origin of the Family, Private Property and the State*, Foreign Languages Publishing House, Moscow, 1952, p. 7.

22 *Op cit.*, p. 10.

points out that monogamy as a form of the family arose out of the accumulation of wealth in the hands of a man and out of his desire to bequeath his property to his children.[23] At a particular stage of social development people became monogamous because of their anxiety for their private property. Monogamy, therefore, had some economic causes. This view obviously lays emphasis upon the economic as the cause of the monogamic form of the family. But the conclusion does not follow from the premises. Granted that wealth accumulates in the hands of a man and that he has the desire to bequeath it to his children, we cannot say that wealth is the cause of this form of the family. Rather the form of his family, i.e., monogamy determines how he deals with or disposes of his property. If the man bequeaths or wants to bequeath his wealth to his children, it is because of his love of them. A social institution or organization is not a simple thing, but a complex one in the sense that diverse elements combine to constitute it. The economic condition is one of the most important conditions of some social phenomena, and the economic value is just utility. But there are deeper values than this; for them we have to look into human nature as well as into human evolution. Details apart, we can say that the marriage-relation, being a human relation, is based on human nature. The economic condition is only relevant to the stability or otherwise of the family.

As to the view that the members of the family hang together because most of them are dependent upon the father, we should like to say that it cannot stand scrutiny. Were the basis of the family economic, the economic independence would have dispersed the family. On the contrary, the members generally lived together even though they earned their living independently. We, again, find that a male and a female enter into the marriage relation though each of them is economically independent, giving the lie to the economic theory of the family.

Furthermore, the view of Marx and Engels in regard to the interpretation of history contradicts the economic expla-

23 *Op. cit.*, p. 123.

nation of the basis of the family. They both require three things for the interpretation of history : (i) the primal needs—eating, drinking, clothing and housing; (ii) the satisfaction of those needs producing other needs; (iii) the family—the earliest form of co-operation and division of labour between man and woman in reproducing their kind.[24]

We are, therefore, justified in concluding that the family is based on marriage, which in its turn is based on the sex-instinct in the human kind as modified by self-consciousness. As human beings are rational, they guide the functioning of the instinct by their intelligence. The instinct as regulated by reason takes the form of conjugal love, which is a peculiarly human emotion. At first it is all inward, although it is expressed in the behaviour and attitude of husband and wife towards each other. Later, of course, it is externalized in the child, which is the joint product of the husband and the wife, and in loving it they love each other more intensely than ever. The child indeed becomes the visible bond of connection between them. When this emotional basis of the family is destroyed the parties may continue to live together but in spirit they become separated. In that case, the child ceases to be the centre of their interest and becomes only an episode of their physical union. And their spiritual separation one day leads to a physical break between them.

The Status of Woman in Ancient Society—In some ancient societies women freely moved about and enjoyed somewhat equal rights with men, although they always remained under protection of their guardians. In Vedic times, for example, women were not confined in the hearth and home; they had freedom in the selection of their husbands.[25] In ancient Egypt,women enjoyed many privileges and moved about with

24 *Vide* H.P. Adams, *Karl Marx in his earlier writings*, George Allen and Unwin Ltd., London, 1940, p. 148.

25 *The History and Culture of the Indian People*, Vol. I, Ed. R. C. Majumdar, George Allen and Unwin Ltd., London, 1957, pp. 288-391.

their husbands.[26] As we have seen before, in the matriarchal family woman was supreme authority and even descent was traced through her. In the patriarchal family, however, man wielded power; the father was generally the head of the family of this type. All the other members, including the women, were in every way dependent upon him.

The Modern Family—Though the orthodox patriarchal family disappeared in the course of time, yet the tradition of man protecting the family has continued into modern times. There were, again, complex political conditions which compelled women to remain indoors, and they willy-nilly accepted the situation. They did so with understanding, not under pressure from men. Some nevertheless interpret this state of affairs as persecution or torture of women. But this was not so. For example, there was no *purdah* in India in the pre-invasion days. Later, however, to avoid the vulgar gaze of the invaders and to escape molestation at their hands Hindu women preferred the seclusion of their homes. "It is a commonplace of history how Rajput women performed the *Johar-brata*—self-immolation in the sacred fire to avoid the invaders of the land. They preferred death to losing their purity".[27] Whatever the reasons, the restrictions under which women lived in the past appear rather hard and obviously kept them out of the spheres which they were fitted by nature to enter. The idea was that man and woman had their division of labour based on the difference in sex between them. It is indeed true that a man cannot bear a child. Child-bearing is the appropriate function of a woman. But a woman cannot produce a child by herself. She needs the co-operation of a man. However, some people committed a fallacy when they thought that this basic difference between man and woman should differentiate all their duties and responsibilities, forgetting that natural gifts and aptitudes are equally distributed among men and women, as Plato pointed out. In intellectual powers, for example, women are visibly equal to men—some even excel men. Even in physical

26 E.S. Bogardus, *A History of Social Thought*, p. 36.

27 A C. Das, *A Commentary on the Life and Teaching of Sri Ramakrishna*, General Printers, Calcutta, 1958, p. 66.

strength some women are found to be superior to men, at least equal to them. For example, some women, including a Bengali woman—Arati Shaha—swam the English Channel. There was therefore no reason whatever why women should be shut up in homes with their natural faculties undeveloped. Woman in her various capacities is the partner of man in life. So she should not go along with man in a lopsided manner. She should develop along with him. Some may nevertheless tell us that the views of some thinkers of the past are entitled to respect. According to Aristotle, a woman is a failure of Nature to produce a man; according to Napoleon a woman was only a child-producing machine, and St. Augustine identified woman with sin. But the fact remains that these are only some men's conceptions based on prejudice.

Women were not to remain in this state for long, however. A movement was on foot in the recent past both in the West and in the East for emancipation of women. Mary Wollstonecraft's *A Vindication of the Rights of Woman*[28] was the Magna Carta for women. She repudiated the idea that women were merely things to be enjoyed by men, pleaded for broad female education to make them fit for all sorts of work in society and in the State. As she puts it, "It is vain to expect virtue from women till they are in some degree independent of men; nay, it is vain to expect that strength of natural affection which would make them good wives and mothers."[29] And again, "business of various kinds they might likewise pursue, if they were educated in a more orderly manner, which might save many from common and legal prostitution.[30]

Raja Ram Mohan Ray (1774-1833), the great Indian reformer, expressed his indignation at the corruptions rampant in eighteenth century India, saying, "A Brahmin generally marries a large number of women for the sake of

28 MacIver and Page, *Society*, p. 251.

29 *A Vindication of the Rights of Woman*, Walter Scott, London, 1891, (First published in 1792), p. 199.

30 *Op. cit.*, p. 209.

money. He then leaves most of them with their parents, only visiting them occasionally to collect money from them. How degraded ! The Brahmins talk glibly of God and often quote from the scriptures but in practice they worship mammon. On the other hand, those women who live with their husbands enjoy a life of dedication. They do their utmost to make their in-laws happy. They do all domestic duties, including cooking and serving meals in their families. And if they are poor; they even draw water, prepare cow-dung for the fire, and so forth. So ungrateful are the men to their womenfolk that when the latter are widowed they consider it a great religious act to burn them on pyres."[31]

Much has happened since. The fight for the rights and privileges of women continued in the East as well as in the West. And now women have come into their own. Their legitimate rights have been recognized almost in all countries. They now take advantage of the general diffusion of education and most of them are now fitted for diverse functions in society on an equal footing with men. Women are now teachers, doctors, scientists, philosophers, pilots, engineers, magistrates, judges, Governors, even Prime Ministers. Women have by now a vote at elections and can be elected to Parliament and other legislative bodies. Social reform and advancement has brought immense good to society in general and to womankind in particular. Women have, in short, come out of the cramping corners of their homes and are contributing to, and sharing in, the cultural achievements, i.e., achievements in art, literature, philosophy and science. Knowledge they attain and impart lights up every nook and corner of their lives, and gives their families new perspective and a new outlook. But women, generally speaking, in the first flush of their victory in the fight for their rights made slight of the deep values of life and this paved the way to social degradation. Female emancipation, as it is called, has had its repercussion upon the family itself. Let us then consider the conditions of the modern family.

31 *A Commentary on the Life and Teaching of Sri Ramakrishna*, p. 68.

(*a*) *Higher Education and the Sense of Independence.*

At the present time higher education is open to all. So girls who want to complete their education, generally, do not or cannot marry until they attain mature age. A long course of education undoubtedly serves to develop their personality and in fact fosters in them a sense of independence, and their mind is swayed by the dualism of man and woman; they extol the rights of woman as against the rights of man. This has a far-reaching consequence.

When they come to marry they think of their rights and their status of equality with men. This attitude beyond doubt renders marriage into a contract. But this attitude contradicts the very principle of marriage, which is in the strict sense the union of two individuals of opposite sexes into a single person. Therein the parties surrender themselves to each other and thus form an identity in difference. In that case, the husband finds himself in his wife and the wife herself in the husband. But if they enter into the marriage-relation with a sense of their rights against each other, the union they form would be a flimsy one, and would break up at the slightest shock. Divorce is the inevitable consequence of such contract marriage.

(*b*) *The Family and Free Love.* In the educated circles romantic marriage or marriage by courtship has come to stay. An educated girl or an educated boy nowadays chooses his or her partner of life independently of the consent of the parents, except in cases where the consent is absolutely necessary. Formerly, in most countries of Europe the marriage between a boy and a girl was arranged by parents on both sides. In some, again, the marriage of a girl was contingent upon the consent of her father. But the old order was long ago yielding place to the new, and there has now been a change in the marriage-situation in the West. The emphasis is now laid upon individual choice and mutual love between the parties to the marriage-relation. America is the most advanced country in this respect. There this form of marriage prevails in an acute form because of the sense of self-importance in educated men and women. In the Eastern countries, in India especially, the traditional form of marriage prevails, roughly speaking. But it cannot be denied that in educated Indian families there is already a tendency towards free love without consideration of caste and creed. And there have already been many sporadic cases of the Western form of marriage.

If love is or should be the basis of marriage, marriage by free love seems to be the ideal form of marriage. But the difficulty is that there is a very high rate of divorce among the people who practise free-love marriage. This gives us pause. And we have to say that such marriage is based on passion which is not true love. Passion is nothing but the urge for the satisfaction of the sex-desire. When it is satisfied for a time the satisfaction leaves a vacuum, while real love is a constant emotion based on a deep-laid relation between a male and a female. It is such that the very presence of one satisfies the other. In this relation sex becomes secondary. Romantic marriage seems to have about it an exuberance of feeling. But in such a case divorce can never occur unless the exuberance has evaporated altogether.

There are some obvious reasons why romantic marriage generally proves futile. During the period of courtship both the man and the woman concerned show themselves at their best to each other. Naturally, they cover up their faults, defects and deficiencies. When they get married and the exuberance of their feelings abates they come to see each other in their true colours, that they are more unlike than they are like in temperament, taste, ideas and ideals. This discovery, as they make it, is found to loosen the marriage-tie between them. We cannot say, however, that marriage by courtship or free love always leads to disaster. In many cases, free love, which is real love, becomes the basis of a stable family-life.

(*c*) *The Family and late Marriage.* Formerly, more or less in all countries people were married in early youth—just at puberty when the sexual urge is at its intensest and is expressed as the desire for friendship or companionship. So a girl and a boy, if united by wedlock at their tender age in the rosy way, they say, they would develop between them deep mutual affection. Their affection now entails the constant company of each other and as such makes up for whatever deficiencies they might have had. Even when an ugly disease overtakes either of them the other sacrifices all to serve and save the partner of life.

Nevertheless, we cannot support early marriage. We disapprove of it for sundry reasons. In the first instance. early marriage stands in the way of the self-development of girls and boys. Adolescence and youth cover the period when they grow both physically and mentally. During this time they take up courses of study and receive training in arts, crafts, and science, which are designed to make them full citizens of the State. Boys and girls therefore should not become fathers and mothers at their formative period.

Secondly, we do not approve early marriage for eugenical reasons, Eugenics is the science which studies the method or methods of improving the race and analyzes the conditions of procreation and their effects on the progeny. If the conditions be premature, their consequences must be harmful to the offspring. The word "eugenics" derives from the Greek word *eugenia*, which means "well born". Eugenics is therefore defined as the science of the agencies and conditions "under social control which may improve or impair the racial qualities of future generations, physically and mentally,"[32] Procreation has three sides : physical or physiological, psychological and economic. The parties to the marriage-relation must be physically mature in order that they produce healthy children. Ill-formed and weak children are the products of a physically immature pair. A judicious sexual selection presupposes mental growth and the power of judgment. Boys and girls with their undeveloped minds do not quite know what things produce what effects. They cannot comprehend the responsibilities they take upon themselves. This ignorance on their part may in the long run bring disappointment to them, or even ruin their lives. One fact a prospective husband should consider. It is whether he would be in a position to support the family he would raise. And a prospective wife should consider whether she would be able to adjust herself

32 *Encyclopaedia Britannica*, Vol. 8, 1959, p. 806.

to the economic conditions of her would-be husband. But boys and girls are, to say the least, unable to judge about one vital matter of their lives. It is for this reason that the sex-relation is regulated by society from some different points of view.

According to the Hindu Marriage Act, 1955, the bridegroom must have completed the age of 18 years and the bride the age of 15 years.[33] According to Plato, men must marry at 30 and women at 20.[34]

It may be urged, however, that in some societies the marriage of a boy with a girl is arranged by their parents, and that the responsibility for it rests on the latter. But parents wise enough to see the future of their sons and daughters are very rare. Even if it is true to say that early marriage is mere betrothal and that the consummation of marriage takes place when the boy and the girl become adults, there is no justification for yoking them in marriage when they have no idea what it is like.

It is difficult to controvert the position that marriage should take place at mature age. Such marriage is sound eugenically, psychologically and economically and is in keeping with the modern conditions of life.

(*d*) *Religion without hold on the Modern Family.* Formerly, people had an intense religious consciousness and considered the marriage-relation itself as part of the religious life. They regarded marriage as divinely ordained. So husband and wife could not separate without committing sin. But religion is now at a discount, and for many marriage has no religious significance. Marriage, generally speaking, is now regarded as a human affair with a human end in view, and the solemnization of marriage as a mere formality. As a result, the marriage-relation in modern society tends to be a very shaky foundation of the family.

33 D.A. Mulla, *Principle of Hindu Law*, N. M. Tripathi, Private Limited, 1959, p. 799.

34 F. Copleston, *A History of Philosophy*, Vol. I, Burns and Oates Limited, London, 1961, p. 236; Plato, *Laws*, IV, 721; *Republic*, V, 460.

(e) *Eagerness for enjoyment of a variety.*[35] There is a tendency in man and also in woman to enjoy a variety of sexual relation. It was this tendency which was more responsible than the economic condition for the perversion of family life in the past. In former times, religion had a check upon this tendency. It seems to be boosted by the loosening of the hold of religion upon most social individuals at the present time. Suppose that a man and a woman make love and become husband and wife. Deep love between them indeed puts a brake upon the aforesaid unwholesome tendency. But if their love ebbs, either of them is, or they both are, in quest of fresh love. When there is no higher value to adjust the ebb and flow in the conjugal relation, disorder in the family, or even disruption of the family, is the result. The urge for fresh love, i.e., varied sexual enjoyment is certainly the main motive behind adultery and the frequency of divorce in modern society.

Nowadays, the legality of birth control has opened up an opportunity to the seekers of variety-enjoyment. We can well imagine sexual chaos prevailing in society under the sanction of Law itself unless the sense of value comes to the rescue of the people. But moral and spiritual values are now slighted. All this cuts at the stable foundation of the family. The family in modern society seems to be only a place of rest in the adventure of sexual enjoyment. One tends to set the marriage-relation at naught whenever one finds it convenient to do so. This trend in present-day societies must be arrested by all means.

(f) *Industrialization and its effects upon the Family.* Modern industrial development has changed the economic structure of society. In most countries, the machine has taken the place of man, the producer. In the highly industrialized countries the necessaries of life are now being produced on a mass scale in factories. But there are labourers to work the factories. They are drawn from the families, and in some countries all able-bodied men and women are compelled by Law to work in the factories, or to assist in working the

35 MacIver and Page, *Society*, p. 273.

machinery of Government. Therein the emphasis is laid upon the State with the result that part of the duties and responsibilities of the families has been taken over by the State. Thus there have developed public nurseries and crèches where mother-workers deposit their babies and children before they join their work in the factories. They indeed take back their young ones when they return home. So in these countries motherhood is not a full-time job. The mothers there do not and cannot devote their whole attention and care to their children, for which, however, there is a better and more efficient substitute, care by the State. Nevertheless, the estrangement of children from their parents, though temporary, is sure to have an unwholesome psychological effect upon the former, even upon the latter. That would at any rate make family life more or less mechanical and would lessen the importance of the family as a social unit. The family would then remain, if it in the end remains, only as the means of preventing sexual chaos. This would indeed degrade the family.

(*g*) *Provision for Divorce in Modern Society*. Ancient Law made provision for divorce, and in ancient times sterility was the main reason for it. But polygamy that sanctioned many wives eliminated or tended to eliminate this reason. The Hindu lawmakers or legislators allowed divorce under some conditions, such as incurable disease, lunacy, cruelty, etc.[36] But divorce was not quite practised in Hindu society until recently. Under the Marriage Acts in the East and West divorce is permissible for some specific reasons : malignant leprosy, cruelty, desertion, adultery, and so forth. There is also provision for judicial separation between husband and wife on account of cruelty, leprosy, venereal disease, lunacy and adultery on either side. But there should be no confusion between divorce and judicial separation. There is a clear distinction between them. A decree for divorce dissolves marriage, while a decree for judicial separation only suspends the operation of the marriage-relationship. In the case of

36 *The Laws of Manu*, S.B.E. XXV. *Cf*. R. Levy, *The Social Structure of Islam*, Cambridge University Press, 1957, pp. 121-123.

judicial separation, after a space of time the husband and the wife may resume cohabitation.

The Divorce Act makes provision for divorce but does not by itself cause divorce. The Act only removes the obstacles to it and affords an opportunity to those who are badly in need of it. Nevertheless, divorce, though sanctioned by Law, may not be practised by the people concerned. Many people in every society, we believe, loathe divorce in spite of the legitimate reasons for it. The remarriage of Hindu widows was legalized by the Hindu Widows' Remarriage Act, 1856. But it remained only an Act. Ninety-nine per cent of Hindu widows did not and do not remarry, though they had or have the age and ability to do so. The idea of remarriage outrages their moral sense and their sense of chastity.

The whole thing depends upon the social individuals and their sense of value. If we let go moral and spiritual value, our life loses its moorings and is tossed up and down on the heaving sea of passions. The increase in the cases of divorce in some quarters around us points to the instability of the modern family, and we are reminded that some forces are already at work to sap the sound basis of the family.

CHAPTER VII

MARRIAGE

Is marriage all sex? According to the popular conception of it, marriage is all sex; it is just the sexual relation between a male and a female. But mere sexual connection is not marriage. According to some sociologists, at the pre-social stage of human existence the sex-relation was promiscuous. That is to say, men and women often mated together to satisfy their sexual desire. But there was nothing like marriage. Even today the illegitimate sex-relation without the marriage-relation is mere sexual connection. If marriage meant merely this, it could be extended even to the animal world. But as a matter of fact marriage is relevant only to men.

Marriage is rooted in the family. According to Westermarck, "Marriage is rooted in the family rather than the family in marriage."[1] He is right if he means that historically family in the large sense of the term, existed before marriage. He perhaps relies on the analogy of the way of life of some species of animals. As we know, monkeys and some other animals live in groups with their offspring. Westermarck may mean that at the earliest stage of human existence males and females formed into families with their childern, and that marriage came about when the sex-relations formed by way of families were recognized and sanctioned by society. But here the analogy of the animal world is not helpful to us. There is no way to disprove the view that at the earliest stage of the human world sex-relations were promiscuous, and that order came into sex-life when marriage was established as an institution. If people had already settled down into families, sex-life was ordered to a great extent, and there was hardly any need for an

1 Bertrand Russell, *Marriage and Morals*, George Allen and Unwin Ltd., London, 1961, p. 27; Westermarck, *History of Human Marriage* Vol. I. Macmillan and Co. Ltd., London, 1921, p. 72.

institution like marriage. Westermarck seems to make much of the family when he says that marriage is rooted in the family.

Marriage as the means of getting an assistant in domestic work. Some make light of sex in the marriage-relation. They maintain that a man and a woman seek each other as a companion and that a man takes a woman to wife particularly because she would do all domestic work for him. They mean to say that marriage is not so much a matter of sex as one of division of labour between a man and a woman. In New Guinea, we are told, a Kai does not quite marry for sexual enjoyment, which he manages outside his home and without responsibility for it. He marries only to have some one to do the cooking and some other work for him.[2] For the data on which to base this view we need not go to Australia or elsewhere. Even in our own society we find much to suggest such a view. We often hear some people say that they need wives to help them in their work. This is particularly true of the lower strata in every society where women are still considered to be inferior and means to men. But this is not the complete analysis of the fact.

If a Kai, as stated above, marries a woman to cook his food, to work in the field with and for him, and not for sexual enjoyment, why does he take a woman for these purposes? A suitable man would have done well for him. On the other hand, why does a woman marry a Kai at all? If there be no question of compulsion, a woman marries a man because of her sex-desire, not for the sole purpose of serving him. If a Kai seeks sexual satisfaction outside the marriage-relation, how about his wife? The sexual behaviour of a Kai, if correctly reported, only shows that the sex-relation is not yet perfectly regulated in his society. The fact is that people, generally speaking, are very shy of sex. And they seek it by substitution.

2 *Encyclopaedia of the Social Sciences*, Ed. by Edwin R.A. Seligman and Alvin Johnson, Vol. X, The Macmillan Company, 1953, New York, p. 148.

That is to say, they put the need for an assistant in their domestic and other work as the obvert plea for marrying a woman, while really they take her under the urge of the sex impulse. If a man and a woman are united with each other by marriage they are to co-operate with each other in the discharge of the responsibility their relation entails. This responsibility is obviously the consequence, not the cause, of the marriage-relationship. The above view therefore puts the cart before the horse. Marriage indeed involves the sex-relation between a male and a female. But it is sanctioned by society and is more than sex. So it is necessary to consider marriage from some different points of view.

Different aspects of marriage. We can analyze marriage from the physical, psychological, ethical and spiritual points of view[3].

Physically, marriage is the union of a male and a female, which is determined by the sex-instinct as guided by reason. There seems to be a secret purpose of Nature behind the functioning of the instinct, which is nothing but the perpetuation of the human species. If fresh individuals do not come in, the species would soon run out of existence. But individuals do not drop from the clouds; they come and can come only through the sexual union of a man and a woman. It seems that Nature herself makes provision for this. There is obviously mutual attraction between the sexes. This is visible even in the animal world. Among many kinds of animals, as we see, the male attracts the female. Observe the peacocks, cocks, pigeons, etc. They with their plumage and colours attract their females. In some animals the sexual urge is only periodic, however. Cows, dogs and some other animals have their breeding seasons. In the case of human beings, women, generally speaking, attract men for sexual relation, though it cannot be denied that there is more or less mutual attraction between them. In the animal world the

3 H. A. Reyburn, *The Ethical Theory of Hegel*, Clarendon Press, Oxford, 1921, pp. 206-210.

males somehow recognize the females of their kind, and the sexual act presupposes this recognition. In the human world, however, sexual selection is far more precise. So a man normally does not get into sex-relation with any woman, nor does a woman get into such a relation with any man. This shows that in the sex-relation there is something more than the physical urge. If a man and a woman consider physical contact to be all about the sex-relation, they certainly behave like lower animals.

Psychologically, marriage involves an emotion between husband and wife. In contrast with the lower animals, two human individuals united on sexual basis are marked by an appropriate tender emotion towards each other. It is the sex-instinct that excites this emotion because of the fact that in human beings the instinct is guided by reason. As Havelock Ellis puts it,

> "The attractive characteristics of a loved woman or man, from the point of view of sexual selection, are a complex but harmonious whole leading up to a desire for the complete possession of the person who displays them."[4]

Marriage perhaps begins with a passion for physical enjoyment. But it in the long run evolves into mutual affection and in the end deepens into conjugal love which makes for the stability of the relation within marriage. B. Russell says,

> "Love is something far more than desire for sexual intercourse; it is the principal means of escape from the loneliness which afflicts most men and women throughout the greater part of their lives."[5]

"She is a phantom of delight" represents only the exuberant feeling of the first stage of the marriage-relationship. But "sex intercourse apart from love has little value."

4 Havelock Ellis, *Studies in the Psychology of Sex*, F. A. Davis Company, Philadelphia, 1923, p. 1; MacDougall, *An Introduction to Social Psychology*, p. 388.

5 *Marriage and Morals*, p. 64.

Ethically, marriage involves "a free surrender of the private self" of the one party to the other[6] and implies a kind of common life between them, in which their respective narrow and selfish interests are curbed and they sacrifice their petty preferences in order to adjust themselves to each other. They thus find an opportunity to transform their natural selves by means of a common end they both value. Such control indeed makes for moral development, especially because they together bear the burden of duties and responsibilities which the unity they form entails.

Spiritually, husband and wife form one concrete unity. As Jesus said,

"Wherefore they are no more twain, but one flesh"[7]

Love is not mere liking, but is the passion for companionship that informs one's whole being with the feeling of delight. True love means identification of the lovers. Husband and wife therefore see the identity of the one in the other. They together form a higher person, and recognize that one's spirit is present in the other[8]. In the Upaniṣads it is said that one supreme Self manifests itself in the things and beings of the world. So one's love for another is ultimately love for the supreme self, and, for that reason, husband and wife in loving each other love and seek the supreme self which is in them. This is high metaphysics; we need not go so far. We only take the word "spiritual" to mean just commerce between spirit and spirit, between one self and another. And this sort of commerce is possible only on the basis of a deep-laid relation like that between husband and wife. "Love (between husband and wife) requires a blending of each other ranging from physical intercourse up to intellectual and spiritual comprehension."[9]

6 Hegel, *Philosophy of Right*, tr. by T. M. Knox, Oxford, 1942, p. 115.

7 *Matthew*, XIX, 6.

8 Hegel, *Op. cit.*, p. 112.

9 Keyserling, *The Book of Marriage*, Janathan Cape, London, 1927, p. 17.

Plato speaks of three kinds of love: a love of the body, a love of the soul, and a mixed sort made up of both.[10] Conjugal love is of the third kind. The growth of the family brings into bold relief this aspect of the marriage-relationship. When children are born of a pair a new transformation comes upon the latter. They are now saturated with deep tender emotion towards their offspring, which has not the remotest resemblance to the sexual passion with which their union began. This emotion makes the spiritual aspect of their being concrete.

In the Old Testament marriage is a sacrament. Therein marriage is considered sacred as it has received approval from God. And God approves of it for biological and social needs.[11] In the 8th century B.C. prophet Hosea denounced the double standard of morals for man and woman and enjoined his hearers to avoid divorce as far as possible.[12]

Marriage as an institution. Marriage arose in the past as a social necessity, as the means of regulating the sex-relationship. If such relationships were promiscuous, there could be no ordered life, and without ordered life there would be no development in the individuals. Being rational, men must be responsible for their actions. Though sex is an instinct, it does not function in men in the same way as it does in the lower animals. Men seek the satisfaction of the instinct in an organized way which is guided by reason or intelligence. The regulation of the sexual relationship between man and woman is indeed a social need which is fulfilled by marriage--the sexual union between two individuals of opposite sexes sanctioned by society. Marriage, as we know, is solemnized in every society, and the solemnization testifies to the fact that marriage is regarded as an institution. Marriage is an institution in the sense that it is a relation between two individuals which fulfils a social necessity.

Some may point out that civil marriage is a legal

10 *The Dialogues of Plato*, Jowett, Vol. V, 837.

11 *Book of Genesis*, Chap. II.

12 Bogardus, *A History of Social Thought*, pp. 60-61.

affair and takes place by registration in office without any rites. It seems that there is a point in this contention. But the parties to this kind of marriage take an oath of fidelity to each other and seek recognition of it by society by holding a reception or feast in celebration of their wedding. All this is enough solemnization.

Some, again, tell us that in some society people enter into the marriage-relationship without solemnization as there is nothing like it there. Elizabeth Elliot reports that the Auca Indians, a primitive tribe living in the Amazon Jungle near the eastern border of Ecuador, enter into the marriage-relation without any rites or rituals.[13] But the point is that when a man and a woman of this territory get married to each other they become husband and wife and are recognized as such by their society. Social recognition is the main purpose of solemnization of marriage. Marriage, in any case, is not merely an affair between two individuals, but is to be sanctioned by society. This recognition of marriage as a social need renders it an institution in the sense that it functions as the means of development of the parties to the marriage relation.

Forms of marriage—Modern researches in the field of sociology have brought to light the fact that family life as such was based on marriage. However, marriage as an institution became the basis of the family only at a definite stage of social development. But social philosophers and sociologists are not agreed how marriage evolved out of indefinite sex-relations which supposedly prevailed at the beginning of human existence. Of the evolution of marriage they give different accounts. Some hold that for the sake of offspring—sons and daughters—primitive men sought to make family life stable, and that to this end they provided for social recognition of the sex-relation through the solemnization of the sexual union between a male and a female. And socially recognized sexual union came to be called marriage. Others, on the contrary, maintain that marriage was the result of the endeavour on the part of the strong man in the

13 *Reader's Digest*, January, 1963, pp. 151-165.

tribe or community to regulate sex-relations. He formulated, we are told, a law or laws regarding sexual union, which were binding on all members of the tribe. There is still a third view, according to which, primitive men became tired of sexual chaos and hungered for peace and order in the community. They thus created the convention of marriage, which indeed served a pressing need of society.

The three views mentioned above are mere hypotheses, and one is as good or bad as another. The truth, however, is that we cannot quite determine the nature of primitive society, and that we cannot say anything definite about it. But nevertheless marriage as a social institution evolved out of whatever irregular sex-relations existed at first. And we can only distinguish between some forms of marriage.

According to some, the original form of marriage was monogamic. The word "monogamy" means either the practice of marrying only once or that of marrying one person at a time. Without considering the double sense of "monogamy", we can say that as different forms of marriage prevail among the savage people of the present time, it is thinkable that there were some different forms of marriage in ancient times. Though we cannot quite determine these forms, we can well consider the forms of marriage that prevailed on this side of primitive society, particularly those of the present time, that are found in both savagery and civilization. We distinguish them as follows.

1. *Temporary Marriage.* This is a form of marriage which is a little more than promiscuity. In it a male and a female are united and live together till a child is born to them, or it grows up to be independent of the parents. It might be that marriage started like this. Temporary marriage was indeed the minimum of marriage. This form of marriage is found among some Australian tribes.

Temporary marriage has another form which is called marriage at convenience. This is a form of marriage which allows the man to live with his wife at his convenience and gives him the right to take a new wife, and the woman the right to take a new husband. And sometimes a man takes several wives and a woman several husbands at the same time. This peculiar form was perhaps crystallized into polygamy and bigamy.

2. *Trial Marriage.* In some present-day societies, particularly among some savage tribes, a form of temporary marriage is coming into vogue, though it is not yet recognized by society. It is called trial marriage. In it a man and a woman come together with a view to marrying each other. This form of union is only temporary, only a trial for marriage and no marriage in the strict sense of the term. This form is obviously based on individual caprice and fails to impress the people who have a strong social sense.

We are told that in ancient Egypt a woman had often been taken on probation for a year or so before she permanently became a wife.[14] This peculiar form indeed anticipated the modern conception of trial marriage.

3. *Companionate Marriage.* Judge Lindsay speaks of a form of marriage which he calls companionate marriage. But he does not quite propose any new form of marriage. He only means that companionate marriage is already there in society. It is a form of marriage which is to be distinguished from procreative marriage. Every young couple today, he says, begins with companionate marriage and ends with the procreative. Companionate marriage is not, however, trial marriage in the ordinary sense of the word. Every marriage in the beginning nevertheless is trial marriage in the sense that nobody can "predict the outcome of any union." Trial marriage in the usual sense, on the other hand, means a tentative or provisional sort of union. The conception of trial marriage, however, implies that people want a permanent relationship through marriage. Lindsay says, "Companionate marriage is legal marriage; and every childless marriage wherein, by mutual agreement, the parties can obtain a divorce if they want it, is a Companionate."[15] The point is that when the parties in the marriage-relation prevent pre-

14 Holland, *Elements of Jurisprudence.* Thirteenth Edition, p. 178.

15 *The Companionate Marriage.* Brentano's Ltd., London, 1928, pp. 140-141.

gnancy by artificial means for exclusive enjoyment of their union, the marriage is to be considered companionate marriage, and that the conception would be complete if divorce by mutual agreement in their case be sanctioned by law.

4. *Polygamy and Bigamy.* Polygamy is a form of marriage in which a man has many wives, while bigamy is a form in which a man has only two wives. These two forms prevailed at different stages of social evolution. They are found even in some present-day societies. In ancient Egypt polygamy was practised by the wealthy people.[16] Polygamy is sanctioned by Muslim society, for example, and in Hindu society, bigamy and polygamy were widely practised until a law was enacted prohibiting these forms of marriage.

We, however, find that a man takes a second wife when his first wife dies, a third when the second dies, and so on, up to a limit. So he does not have two wives at the same time; he has one wife at a time, although he contracts many marriages or more than one marriage. Here there is the conception of many marriages as against that of many wives. The word "polygamy" is indeed taken to mean many wives at the same time. But the fact of two or many marriages needs a new word. Bigamy is clearly the effect of two marriages and polygamy the effect of many marriages. A plurality of marriages could, of course, be obviated by mass marriage. But we do not know whether mass marriage was ever practised anywhere.

Some take the word "polygyny" to mean many wives and "polygamy" many marriages. But as one has or can have many wives by many marriages, the two words are synonymous with each other. By either of these words we fail to cover the fact that when a man's wife dies he takes another woman to wife. Polygamy or polygyny is generally contrasted with polyandry.

5. *Polyandry.* Polyandry is a form of marriage in which a woman has more than one husband. It is an awkward form of marriage, which outrages the moral sense of women themselves. It appeared at a certain stage of history. But

16 E.S. Bogaddus, *A History of Social Thought*, p. 36.

assuredly, it was not much in favour with society and soon passed out of vogue. We are, however, told that this form of marriage is still found in some parts of Tibet and Ceylon. A conspicuous case of polyandry is mentioned in the *Mahābhārata*. Some time during 1950-1400 B.C. the five Pāṇḍva brothers—Yudhisthira, Bhima, Arjuna, Nakula, and Sahadeva—together married Draupadi, daughter of King Drupad.[17] There was, however, some order in the brothers' relation to their common wife. During the period between her two consecutive monthly courses she lived exclusively with one of her husbands and avoided sexual connection with the others; so that if she conceived during this period, the father of the child was clearly known. In any case, many compatriots of the Pāṇḍavas looked askance at this form of marriage, and some regarded it as a relic of a practice long past. Some sociologists point out, however, that the Todas of the Nilgiri Hills practise polyandry even today.[18]

6. *Monogamy.* Monogamy is a form of marriage in which a man and a woman form a family for life. It is a life-long union between a man and a woman. According to some, society started with monogamy. But there is hardly any evidence for this view. Strictly, monogamy as a form of marriage presupposes a good deal of social development, a deep sense of social and moral value. For this reason, as Bernard Shaw points out, few people are physiologically and psychologically fit for monogamy. Monogamy nevertheless evolved in civilization and was an institution among the Greeks and other groups of the Aryan people. By this form of marriage pure and peaceful home-life was indeed promoted and the development of the character of the children as well as the security of their future ensured. Monogamy as the stable basis of the family came about at a stage when there was a division of labour between man and woman. Woman had then her appropriate work in procreation as well as in

17 *The History and Culture of the Indian people*, Vol. I, Ed. R.C. Majumdar, 1957, p. 300.

18 John Lubbock, *The Origin of Civilization*, Longmans, London, 1875, p. 87.

the household. Women performed domestic duties and menfolk did outdoor work—work in the field, for instance. So each needed and supplemented the other, and their mutual help made their relationship stable; they became life-long companions with each other. And above all they in their marriage-relation had love for each other, which was indeed enhanced and deepened by the incoming of their offspring.

7. *Beena Marriage.* In savage life a man generally chooses a woman of his own group. Sometimes, however, a man leaves his horde and joins another group wherein he takes a woman to wife. But there he cannot exercise any authority over his wife and children. He there submits to the laws and customs of the horde of his adoption. This form of marriage prevailed among some people in Ceylon and was called Beena marriage.

According to some, two forms of marriage prevailed in Ceylon, namely, *Deega* marriage and *Beena* marriage. In the former the woman went over to the house of her husband, while in the latter the man crossed over to the family of his wife.[19]

8. *Marriage by Capture.* The hordes of savages are not only different from, but are more or less hostile to, each other. Among them the capture of women is a common event, and very often two groups come to clash with each other over the stealing of a woman of one group by the other. In such a case, the woman is at the mercy of her captor and is compelled to marry him. She is regarded as property and is generally ill-treated by her owner.

Marriage by capture is not confined to the savage communities, however. It often happens even in civilization. Sporadic cases of forcible marriage occur all over the world.

If we reflect a little, we shall find that marriage by capture is a misnomer, for in it a woman is united with a man against her will. Marriage, as we have seen, is based on mutual attraction between a man and a woman and their mutual consent. Marriage by capture is indeed extreme tor-

19 John Lubbock, p. 73.

ture to which a woman is put for no fault of hers. Hence so-called marriage by capture is temporary as it rests upon the lust of the man concerned, and divorce is the necessary consequence. In savagery the children born of a forcible marriage are regarded as the property of the horde of the captor. This custom prevails especially among the Tasmanians[20].

In social evolution, nevertheless, Beena marriage and marriage by capture played an important role. The members of a primitive group married within the group. But in Beena marriage a man left his group and joined the group of his wife. He did so or had to do so presumably because he broke one custom of his group by marrying outside it. In marriage by capture, again, a woman of a horde was forcibly taken away by a hostile horde. These two forms of marriage therefore brought two or more hordes into blood relationship, which had previously no relation whatever with each other. Perhaps this way of relationship in the end led to the formation of a clan out of some hordes.

9. *Group Marriage.* Group marriage is said to be prevalent in a tribe in South Australia, which is divided into two classes.[21] We are told that every man of each class is the rightful husband of every woman of the other class, and conversely every woman of each class is the rightful wife of every man of the other class. This theory was based on the data furnished by the English missionary, Lorimer Fison, concerning the tribe under consideration here.

If there is a foundation to this theory, the sex-relations in the tribe in question are promiscuous and there could be no family life among these people. Rivers discards the phrase "group marriage" and posits instead a state of "organised sexual communism in which sexual relations are recognized as orthodox between the men of one social group and the women of another."[22] He goes on to say that sexual communism represents a stage of social development.

20 *Cf.* Giddings's view.

21 Helen Bosanquet, *The Family*, pp. 28-29.

22 Rivers, *Kin hip aud Social Organisation*, Constable and Co. Ltd., London, 1914, p. 86.

But other writers oppose the theory of group marriage by their research about the Australian tribe under discussion. Curr, who studied the tribe, maintains that in it there is no community of wives, that a man possesses one wife or more than one wife, and that the husband is the sole authority over his wife or wives. The two accounts—one furnished by Lorimer Fison and the other by Curr—contradict each other. And it is difficult to decide whether Fison or Curr is right in his contention. It is suggested, nevertheless, that Fison might have observed that the members of either of the classes did not marry among themselves, but married outside their group. If, in any event, there is anything like group marriage in the said Australian tribe, we have to agree with Rivers that group marriage is just sexual communism; or we have to say that so-called group marriage only represents exogamy. Let us consider here briefly endogamy and exogamy.

Endogamy and Exogamy: In primitive times men and women generally married within their tribe, but the marriage-relation excluded blood relations such as father, daughter, mother, son, brother and sister. This practice of marrying within one's group is known as endogamy, and a people who followed this practice were or are regarded as endogamous.

Some tribes nevertheless abandoned endogamy and practised exogamy, which was the practice of marrying outside one's tribe. But a tribe might consist of a number of groups of which some were endogamous and the rest exogamous. Some speak of hypergamy as existing in some civilized society. Hypergamy is the practice of taking a wife from a lower class or caste, and this practice prevailed in some section of society in Kerala, one of the States of India.[23] So we may redefine exogamy as the practice of marrying outside one's group. But the question is : If primitive people were originally endogamous, how could some of them become exogamous ? It is pointed out that there were at least two things to explain the origin of exogamy, marriage by capture and totemism.

23 *India's villages*, Ed. M. N. Srinivas, Asia Publishing House, Bombay, 1963. p. 44.

Marriage by Capture : Hordes or tribes which were hostile to each other often came into conflict with each other, and the victors quite often carried away some women of the vanquished and forcibly married them. According to some, such marriage by capture later led to the mode of marriage known as exogamy.

John Ferguson McLennan (1827-1881) coined the word "exogamy", and developed the theory that primitive people who were originally endogamous became exogamous because of female infanticide among them. For some reason or other they disliked daughters, we are told, and so they practised killing female infants at birth. In consequence there was among them a scarcity of women. That was why the people of one group seized women of another and forcibly married them. In this way endogamy ended and exogamy began.[24] But modern researches in sociology and anthropology show that in primitive society infanticide or marriage by capture was never a widespread practice. They were exaggerated by McLennan. His theory of the origin of exogamy is therefore untenable. Most sociologists are now agreed that marriage by capture only occurred in the tribes which often came to clash with each other, and that marriage by capture was never a normal mode of marrying in primitive society.

Totemism. According to some, it is totemism that throws light upon the origin and development of exogamy. Fetishism and totemism represent two stages of development in primitive society. Fetishism was a form of primitive religion, or the most primive religion, in which primitive men worshipped natural things. At sight of a thing, let us imagine, they were seized with wonder and regarded it with reverence. Thus a stone with a peculiar shape became with some primitives the object of worship. An ear of maize became a fetish with the Negro, for instance. Fetishism, in short, developed as the expression of the original sense of the

24 *Encyclopaedia of the Social Sciences*, Ed. by R. A. Seligman and Alvin Johnson, Vol. X. The Macmillan Company, New York, pp. 29-30; also McLennan, *Studies in Ancient History* and *Primitive Marriage.*

mysterious primitive men had around natural things. But Fetishism, we believe, had nothing to do with exogamy. We mention fetishism here so as to understand the meaning and implication of totemism in contrast with the former.

Totemism definitely developed out of the sense of weakness and limitation of power on the part of primitive people. They had recourse to "some outside agency"[25] to make up their deficiency. Totemism was nothing but an organized practice of this kind. While fetishism is confined to individual things, totemism concerns species or classes. A totem is generally a species of animals, rarely a class of things, which is regarded by a group or clan as the seat of the mysterious and as the protector of the clan as well. Every member of the totem species or class is treated with softness and reverence, and no harm is done to it by anyone of the clan. Bear, cow, buffalo; eagle, parrot, tiger, lion, etc. are taken as totems. Plant totems also are found and are widespread among the Red Indians of North America. Totemism also prevails in Australia, Africa, Melpanesia, polynesia, and India. B.W.E. Armstrong enumerates some features of it[26], which are as follows:

(1) Totemism represents association of groups of persons with groups of animals or objects. (2) Totemism implies that a tribe is divided into several totemic groups, and (3) one kind of totemic group is commoner than another, namely, the exogamous group, i.e., the group the members of which marry outside the group. Totemism in this its aspect is bound up, we are told, with exogamy.[27] But some totemic groups in Africa are endogamous.

In this connection we may refer to the conception of *gotra* in Hindu society. *Gotra* is not identical with caste or class, as different groups of people of the same caste have different *gotras*. And the *gotra* of a family indicates the sage

25 Lubbock, *Origin of Civilization*, p. 326; W. Schmidt, *Origin and Growth of Religion*. Macmillan and Co. Ltd., London, p. 104.

26 Article on Totemism in *Encyclopaedia Britannica* 14th edition.

27 J.G. Frazer, *Totemism and Exogamy*, Macmillan Co. Ltd. London, 1910, Vol. II, p. 133.

to whom it is affiliated. The idea is that a family traces its origin to asage of the past, and if some families have the same *gotra*, they are descended from the same sage, and they are of like blood. So though Hindus, specially the upper-class Hindus, marry within their castes or classes, they do not marry within the families that have the same *gotra* as they have for eugeinc reasons. It ought to be clear that *gotra* is not a totem. The former is based on the conception of descent from a high personage of the past, while the latter implies a mysterious power in a species or class which protects a clan or a group of men who accept it as such.

10. *Forms of Hindu Marriage.* The Hindu Law-makers mention eight forms of marriage, which came into vogue in the course of social development. They are: Brāhma, Daiva, Ārṣa, Prājāpatya, Āsura, Gāndharva, Rākṣasa, and Paiśāca.[28] Let us consider the forms and begin from the end of the list.

(1) *The Paiśāca*: Some of the eight forms of marriage were prevalent among the Vedic people and some of these are sanctioned by society even today, while the rest disappeared a long time ago. Let us begin our analysis by considering the Paiśāca form of marriage. It is a form of marriage which does not involve the free consent of the woman concerned. She is deceived or drugged and in her state in which she loses control of herself she is ravished by the man. This is only a sex-act by which the man satisfies his momentary sex-desire. As the woman is wronged by the man, society compels him to marry her. This is the lowest form of marriage since lust is the motive force behind it. Cases of marriage by deception no doubt occurred in the past, and are not rare even at the present stage of social life. The Paiśāca form of marriage was sanctioned at

28 *Manu Saṁhitā*, Chapter III, S.B.E., Vol. XXV, pp. 79-80;
Grihya-Sūtra, S.B.E. Vol. XXIX, pp. 281-283;
Dharma-Sūtra, S.B.E., Vol. II, p. 194;
The History and Culture of the Indian People, Ed. by R.C. Majumdar, pp. 510-511;
Radhakrishnan, *Religion and Society*, pp. 165-167.

one stage of social development only to bring relief to the woman who was wronged by a man.

(2) *The Rākṣasa*: The Rākṣasa form of marriage prevailed during the period when women were counted among the booty of war. This form is really identical with marriage by capture. As we have seen before, when two hordes clashed with each other, the victor often carried away a woman or some women of the vanquished and married them against their will. This is also not a valid form of marriage because it is not based on the mutual consent of the man and the woman. Therefore, the Rākṣasa form, like the Paiśāca, was discarded by society. The former is nevertheless often revived under modern conditions of political chaos in some country or countries. This is unfortunate.

(3) *The Āsura*: In the Āsura form of marriage the husband buys the bride. This is "marriage by purchase", and is as old as the *Rig-Veda* but is surprisingly practised even today in some societies. If we ponder over this form, we find a very interesting fact about it; it is the question of supply and demand in the marriage market. If in a community girls are much fewer than boys, there would evidently be a competition among suitors in having girls to wives, and a girl would naturally be given to the highest bidder. Money is a great force in society. So some men offered the parents of a girl a large sum to induce them to make a decision in their favour. Marriage by coemptio among the Romans was marriage by purchase.[29]

The conditions under which the Āsura form of marriage prevailed, if ever, are there even today in some Indian societies as possibly elsewhere. There is one social phenomenon well worth investigation, namely, that in the upper-class families in Bengal especially, the number of girls is far greater than that of boys. On the contrary, in the families of the low-class people, in which both men and women make a living by physical labour—cultivators, weavers, smiths, and so on—girls are by far fewer than boys. So in such families the girls are assets in the sense that their marriage brings

29 Lubbock, *Origin of Civilization*, p. 2.

their parents a large sum of money. This is practically the Āsura form of marriage.

There are some obvious defects of this form of marriage. Firstly, the parents of the bride are the sole authority to make a decision about her marriage, and with them money is the main consideration. They do not consider so much the suitability of the bridegroom for their daughter, or her future happiness. They are in the matter led only by greed of gain. The parents sink below the human level. Secondly, as a price is put upon the bride, she is reduced to a marketable commodity. This militates against the dignity of a human individual and the sanctity of the human personality. Thirdly, the bride falls a victim to a double social evil—her parents' love of gain and the sex-desire of the bridegroom. You call this marriage!

There is a converted form of the Āsura marriage, however. In this form the bride purchases the bridegroom. In the upper-class families of Bengal, perhaps also of other States, the girls are a liability. Their marriage is a problem, and in their cases there is a competition among the families in having bridegrooms. The parents of a girl had or has to spend a considerable sum over a suitable bridegroom. This form is really a converted form of the Āsura. In the original form the parents of a bride make a good bargain out of the marriage of their daughter, whereas in the converted form the parents of a bridegroom make a lucrative business by their son's marriage. Both, however, share the same defects, and show the moral and social degradation of the people concerned. Indeed the conversion of the Āsura form of marriage was the root of the dowry system at marriage. In independent India there has been an enactment against this practice, and dowry is now a crime.

In Sumatra there are three kinds of marriage: (1) the *Jugur*, (2) the *Ambel-anak*, and (3) the *Semando*. In the *Semando* husband and wife stand on terms of equality. In the Jugur the man purchased the woman, while in the *Ambel-anak* the woman purchased the man.[30]

30 *Op. cit.*, pp. 71-72.

Sociologically, the Āsura form of marriage is very significant. It gives the lie to the Marxian theory that the cause of the family was all economic in that the family and the forms of it were determined by wealth and production of wealth. Here is at least one form of marriage which was determined by some special extra-pecuniary circumstances. As we have just seen, the original Āsura form of marriage was determined by the paucity of girls as against the large number of boys, and the converted form by the paucity of suitable bridegrooms as against the large number of girls. And the economic matter—payment of money to the parents of a bride or to the parents of a bridegroom is only an effect of these circumstances. This would surely give Marxists pause.

4. *The Gāndharva or Romantic form of Marriage.* This form of marriage is based on mutual consent and free love. There is no solemnization of this form except an exchange of personal oaths of fidelity, and no rites are performed to indicate that it is sanctioned by society. It seems as if this sort of marriage is an affair of two lovers—a man and a woman. An exchange of garlands or rings between the lovers is the least solemnization, if there is any at all, of this form of marriage. In Vātsyāyana's *Kāma-Sūtra* the Gāndharva is regarded as the ideal form of marriage, for in it the idea of two individuals—a male and a female—forming a unity, which is the ideal for marriage to achieve, is realized. In this form of marriage there is an immediate and spontaneous merging of the parties into each other. This form is well illustrated by the marriage of Dusyanta and Sakuntala in the Sanskrit drama, the *Sakuntala,* by poet Kalidasa. King Dusyanta, while hunting in a forest, came on the chance of meeting Sakuntala, a girl of saint Kanva's Āsrama (hermitage). They fell in love at first sight and were married to each other by mutual consent and free love. The king then went back home, leaving Sakuntala behind at her place. But when later she went to her husband's palace to join him as his legitimate wife he at first could not recognize her. The poet suggests that the Gāndharva, being based on the momentary sex-impulse, is not likely to be a stable relationship.

This form was therefore disapproved by society, and modern Hindu society does not recognize it at all.

We may feel inclined to call the Gāndharva form of marriage marriage by courtship or romantic marriage. But, really, there is difference between the Gāndharva and marriage by courtship. In the former the decision is determined by impulse and is made in a moment, whereas in the latter wooing the woman spreads or may spread over a length of time. Secondly, there are no solemnizing rites, in the strict sense, around the Gāndharva, but marriage by courtship is as a rule solemnized by usual rites. There is much affinity, however, between the two types in that in both the union between husband and wife is determined by their personal liking of each other. *On the decision to marry* no outside influence works, not even the influence of the parents of both parties, not to speak of the question of social rank, caste or creed. In this sense both the Gāndharva and marriage by courtship is romantic marriage. In the story narrated above Dusyanta's love for Sakuntala was so ardent that it overrode the obstacle that he was a king and Sakuntala was a mere forest girl.

Sociologists and social philosophers make their different assessments of romantic marriage, or marriage by courtship or mutual love. MacIver and Page so nicely define romantic love: "By romantic love we understand an engrossing emotional attachment between a man and a woman, exclusive and individualized, transcending at need all sorts of obstacles, involving some kind of idealization, and enveloping the sex relationship in an aura of tender emotion for the personality of the loved one."[31]

According to Hegel, "Love is not mere liking or inclination, however strong the passion may be. Love is the feature of a stable form of life."[32] Some are of the opinion that the instability of the family, or the increasing rate of divorce in

31 *Society*, 1957, p. 252.

32 Reyburn, *Hegel's Ethical Theory*, p. 205: Hegel, *Philosophy of Right* tr. by T.M. Knox, Oxford, 1942, p. 118; W. T. Stace, *Philosophy of* Hegel, p. 409.

the Western world is due to romantic marriage or marriage by courtship. We think Hegel is right when he says that the stability of the family life is the test of true love between husband and wife. It is a fact that passion often masquerades as love. And the question is: passion or love? So whatever be the form of marriage, love between the parties to the marriage-relation is the main consideration. If it is lacking, the foundation of the family becomes shaky. There is, again, ebb and flow in conjugal love on account of the complex circumstances of modern life. We cannot therefore hold one particular form of marriage, say, romantic marriage responsible for the frequency of divorce in the families. The increasing rate of divorce is a complex phenomenon which has a complex cause. And we have to analyze it patiently. The fact, however, remains that personal choice is the most important factor in the marriage relationship. If marriage by courtship is really based on mutual liking, mutual understanding of husband and wife, we cannot say that this form of marriage is based simply on passion. If there are very many cases of divorce against marriages by courtship, the reasons perhaps lie in the modern conditions of life plus the perverted sense of value. If Law permits divorce, it may occur irrespective of forms of marriage.

5. *The Ārṣa Form of Marriage.* In this form of marriage the father of the bride accepts a cow and a bull from the bridegroom. This is obviously a modified version of the Āsura form and was considered a low form of marriage.

6. *The Daiva Form of Marriage.* This form of marriage prevailed in Vedic times. Those were the days of sacrifices to gods and goddesses. The sacrificer often offered his daughter to the priest performing the sacrifice. This form is called the Daiva since the marriage is arranged by negotiation in the course of the performance of a sacrifice to a god or goddess. People looked down upon this form of marriage for the simple reason that the arrangement of an earthly relation like marriage should not be mixed up with religious rites. Naturally, the Daiva form of marriage disappeared with Vedic sacrifices.

7. *The Prājāpatya.* In this form of marriage the bride

bedecked with ornaments, fine linen and flowers is offered to the bridegroom with due rites. They are enjoined by the priest and parents of the bride to remain united throughout their life discharging moral and religious duties.

8. *The Brāhma Form*, This one form is very popular among all classes of Hindus. In it the couple pray to God that their love and friendship be everlasting.

The form of marriage that generally prevails in Hindu society is or seems to be a combination of the Prājāpatya and Brāhma forms, though the form tends to vary.

It was the duty of the Vedic Indians to marry. The idea was that a man or a woman was not complete unless he or she was married. By marrying they performed their duties to the family and to society.

9. *The Svayaṁvara or Marriage by personal choice of the Bride.* There was, however, a ninth form of marriage in ancient India, namely, the Svayaṁvara, in which the bride chose her husband directly from among the suitors assembled in her father's house. In this form the suitors' choice was taken for granted; the assembly implied that they were willing to take the girl proposed to wife. But the ultimate decision lay with the bride. The man upon whom her choice fell became her husband. She was taken round the assembly and the suitors were introduced to her by turns. Details regarding their family, wealth, etc. were narrated before her. The bride considered the narratives as well as the personal charm of the suitors and then made her choice. And she demonstrated her decision by garlanding the man she chose.

The Svayaṁvara was a specific form of marriage and was confined to royal families, to kings, princes and princesses.

In one form of the Svayaṁvara the bride's choice was staked on the performance of a feat by the suitor. This form was prevalent among Kshatriyas (the fighting class). Thus, as we have it in the *Rāmāyaṇa* in hoary antiquity, Ramachandra,[33] son of King Dasaratha, married Sita, daughter of

33 During 2350-1950 B.C.—*Vide The History and Culture* of the Indian People, Vol. I, 1957, Book IV, Chap. XIV, p. 288.

King Janaka, by breaking a massive iron bow. As is narrated in the *Mahābhārata*, Arjuna[34] performed the feat of shooting a fish-image through the eye constantly revolving within a wheel fixed up high in the sky, while looking at the reflection of the image in the water below, and obtained Draupadi, daughter of King Drupad. The feat in question provided a test of the physical strength of the suitor. Those were the days when women, princesses specially, admired the physical strength of the bridegroom more than his personal charm, Kings and princes had to protect their women against aggression by their enemies.

The Svayaṁvara continued for a fairly long time and has in fact continued into modern times. But partly because of a change in the old political set-up and partly because of Western influence upon the general conditions of life in the East this form of marriage has disappeared.

The ideal Form of Marriage: From the above analysis it ought to be clear that though marriage is ultimately based on love between tbe parties thereto—a man and a woman—marriage should not be left entirely to them. We have already considered the merits and defects of romantic marriage or marriage by courtship. We have seen that therein the choice is made under the sex impulse of the moment, and that the deficiencies on both sides, if any, were unconsidered in the exuberance of their feelings for each other. When, however, they are discovered disillusionment occurs on both sides and makes for divorce in most cases. To avoid the evil consequences of romantic marriage, some therefore plead for arranged marriage. Notwithstanding the different forms of marriage that prevailed at different stages of social development, the common run of men and women practise arranged marriage. This form of marriage is settled by negotiations between the parents or guardians of the bride and the bridegroom who meet each other for the first time at the marriage ceremony. Previously, arranged marriage prevailed in Asian and European countries, especially in Germany, and is now found mostly in Eastern countries, especially in India.

34 During 1950-1400 B.C.—*Vide Op. cit.*, pp. 294-300.

Hegel was deadly against romantic marriage.[35] According to him, the sex instinct reflects itself in the mind as emotion, but love is not a mere impulse. Love, in his opinion, is a relatively permanent disposition or attitude. Hegel, again, holds that the two individuals in the marriage-relation form into one concrete person in the sense that the man finds his identity in the woman, and *vice versa*. They should therefore meet together as separate individuals, and out of them as differences an ethical unity is to evolve—ethical in the sense that each finds self-development in the unity they form. This is the main reason why marriage between near blood relations, i.e., consanguine marriage, is banned. As they are already intimately related with each other, they have not the independence and difference required for the purpose of marriage, of forming an ethical unity between husband and wife. Hegel goes to the length of saying that there should be no friendship or intimacy between the parties before marriage, the idea being that marriage between a male and a female should be arranged by the parents or guardians on both sides. But, in our view, arranged marriage of this kind and romantic marriage are extremes. It is not understandable why the parties to the marriage-relation should blindly submit to the choice made by a third party in a matter that vitally concerns their lives.

It may be argued that the parents always have the well-being of their children at heart and that the former can be depended on in the affair of their children's marriage. This contention is theoretically all right. But in practice it is often found that in the case of marriage of their children the parents look to their own interest rather than to the interest of the children. If the parents themselves behave in this manner, we can imagine what the guardians, who are not the parents, would be like. The old patriarchal idea that the father as the procreator is the proprietor of his children still persists, although it has been curbed by modern Law. The father nonetheless exercises some rights over his childern. And in virtue of these rights he often makes or tries to make

35 *Vide Philosophy of Right*, p. 115.

a profit out of his children's marriage. This obviously leads to degradation in the marriage-situation. Granted, however, that the parents, more than anybody else, are anxious for the future of their children and consider pros and cons when they get their children married, one thing they cannot quite ascertain. It is whether, all relevant facts considered, the bride and the bridegroom agree to the proposed relationship. As marriage is to take place at mature age, the parties should be allowed to meet each other and make their final choice, of course, with the help of their parents or guardians. This is the most rational way of arranging marriage between a young man and a young woman. The marriage-relation is a human relation and must be rationally determined. But it does not mean that marriage would be without emotion. There should be no confusion between the determination of this relation itself and what ensues out of it. Marriage, being the relation between two individuals of opposite sexes, the parties, agreeable to the relation, become from the very beginning of their conjugal life saturated with tender feelings towards each other, which in the course of a short time deepen into love which indeed unifies them into one person.

Chapter VIII

VARṆĀŚRAMA DHARMA

OR

DUTIES OF THE DIFFERENT STAGES OF LIFE OF THE FOUR CASTES OF HINDU SOCIETY

"Varṇāśrama is a compound word and consists of "varṇa" and "āśrama". "Varṇa" means colour or class, and "āśrama" a stage of life. And the word "Dharma" means duty or right conduct.[1] The phrase "Varṇāśrama Dharma", then, means the duties of the different stages of life of the four classes of people. Historians tell us that originally the people of India had only two colours, fair and dark. The Aryans who had come to India from somewhere in Central Asia were fair-complexioned, while the aborigines of the country were rather dark. The former could only settle down in the new territory after having subdued the latter who were called the Dāsas or Dasyus. Therefore, if one colour signified one distinct class of people, there were originally two classes in India, the Aryans and the natives of the country, now called the Dāsas. But "varṇāśrama" in its earlier use meant the different stages of life of the four classes of people—Brāhmaṇa, Rājanya (Kshatriya), Vaiśya, and Śūdra, who together constituted society. In its later use, however, the word meant four castes having these four names. Here, then, two problems arise : how could "varṇa" be used as the collective name for the four classes, and how did the classes harden, if ever, into the castes ?

Four Colours for four classes. Some maintain that the four classes now had their distinctive colours, and that the variation in the colours of the three upper classes who were all Aryans was caused by their intermixture with the non-

1 P.V. Kane, *History of Dharmaśāstra*, Vol. II, Oriental Research Institute, Poona, pp. 3-25.

Aryans, then admitted into the Aryan fold. There is no doubt that in ancient times there was an intermixture through intermarriage of Aryans and non-Aryans in India. But whether or not this intermixture gave rise to some distinctive group-colours, or, exactly what colours it caused, is a matter of mere conjecture. The above view is moreover contradicted by the historical fact that the four classes came about by way of the functional organization of society. It was by no means the fact that each of these classes was formed on the basis of an identical colour a number of people possessed. It is indeed true that the word "varṇa" was later used to cover the classes. And there was no difficulty about it. "Varṇa" now meant the two colours as it had meant before. The word, however, had now an expanded meaning in that it meant the four classes under the two colours, as well as their distinctive functions. If the four classes were ever called four *Varṇas*, they were so called, and they were indeed so, in the secondary sense, in the sense that they were four classes originally covered by the two colours, fair and dark. In any case, "varṇa" in the phrase "Varṇāśrama Dharma" means the four classes or castes—Brāhmaṇa, Kshatriya, Vaiśya, and Śūdra.

The Fourfold organization of the Vedic Society. Now as regards the fourfold organization of the Hindu society, we should like to say that there was a stage of the Vedic people when there was no functional division among them. Even the Rig-Veda points to this stage. At that time individuals, especially the heads of the families which are said to have been patriarchal in type, did all sorts of work, including production of food, family worship, and defence of the homeland. But, as time went on, the circumstances in which they lived became increasingly complex, and it became far too difficult for one man to perform multifarious duties. Thus there arose the need to organize society on division of labour. Those who had the aptitude for learning, wisdom and worship were grouped into one class and were called the Brāhmaṇas. Those who were fitted by their physical strength for defence of the land were entrusted with this work and were called the Kshatriyas. A third class of people had their allotted task, that of producing food and wealth and were called the Vaiśyas, the fourth class was formed by the Śūdras, aborigines absorbed in the Aryan society, who were just labourers and whose sole duty it was to serve the three other classes. This was, in short, the fourfold organization of the ancient Hindu society. It was seemingly a simple affair. But in the course of time the organization became highly complex.

Training and discipline for the classes. Eventually, the idea arose in the minds of the people that a group or class could not perform its proper function at haphazard, that it would perform its duties properly only by training and discipline. Therefore, the life of the people of the different classes was planned with an eye to their respective functions. And it was planned according to the duties they were to perform at the different stages of life. There are, as we know, three stages of a man's life—boyhood, youth and old age.[2] Needless to say, every man normally passes through these stages. Each of the four classes we have mentioned above had its social function, and it could perform it properly if the individuals of the group each lived ordered life by doing their normal duties to themselves and to their families. Law-makers and legislators gradually came up and thought out details about the different stages of life of the four classes and the respective duties assigned to them. It is not definitely known whether there were some distinct periods of the codification of rules regarding *Varṇāśrama,* such as those of the Śrauta-Sūtra, the Grihya-Sūtra and the Dharma-Sūtra plus the Dharma-Śāstra or the Smriti. We can, in any case, distinguish between the period of the Sūtra and that of the Śāstra.[3]

The Śrauta-Sūtra prescribes and explains the details of some sacrifices for householders. But these were not binding upon them or anybody else. The Śrauta-Sūtra apparently has no significance for Varṇāśrama Dharma. The Grihya-

2 *Kaumāraṁ Yauvanaṁ jarā, Bhagavadgītā, II, 13.*

3 *The History and Culture of the Indian people,* Vol. I, Ed. R.C. Majumdar, Allen Unwin Ltd., London, 1957, pp. 506-507.

Sūtra,[4] as the name indicates, prescribes and expounds the duties that are binding upon the householder. But while discussing the duties of the householder, it was led to discuss the duties of others also. The Dharma-Śūtra and Dharma-Śāstra, however, consider the duties of the four castes, as they call them, their social rank and status in relation to each other. There is indeed difference between the Dharma-Sūtra and the Dharma-Śāstra. But the difference is only a verbal one, in the sense that while the Dharma-Sūtra consists of aphorisms, the Dharma-Śāstra is written in verse.

Origin of the four Castes. We are told that the Dharma-Sūtra either presupposed the formation of the four classes into castes, or "witnessed the hardening" of the classes into castes. Formerly, as we have seen before, each of the four classes was determined by its peculiar social function, and the function itself by the requisite quality or qualities. Thus one who was pure in heart and intellectually alert could become a Brāhmaṇa; one who was physically strong enough to share in the defence as well as administration of the country became a Kshatriya ; and so on. The classes, to be sure, were fluid with the exception of the Śūdras, forming a class as they did by themselves because they lacked qualities for any significant social function. New individuals came into the three upper classes in virtue of the requisite qualities they possessed. But now the classes became petrified. The process of their formation by proper quality stopped since the emphasis was now laid upon birth. That is to say, the class, an individual belonged to, came to be determined by birth, not, as before, by quality. The son of a Brāhmaṇa was a Brāhmaṇa, though he was ignorant and immoral, the son of a Kshatriya was a Kshatriya, though he was a weakling. Historians point out that the hardening of the classes into castes took place when the Aryans moved from the Indus Valley towards the eastern rigion and settled down in the middle of the country in relative peace and security to spin out a web of complex social relationships.[5]

4 *S.B.E.*, Vol. XXIX, pp. 5-16.

5 *The History anl Culture of the Indian people*, Vol. I, pp. 386-387.

In the ninth Book of the Rig-Veda, some different crafts and occupations are mentioned. But it seems that they were not castes yet. In the tenth Book of the Rig-Veda, however, there is an explicit mention of the four castes. In the *Puruṣa-Sūkta,* the account of the origin of the castes runs as follows :

"From the mouth of the supreme Being proceeded the Brāhmaṇa, from his arms the Rājanya,[6] from his thighs the Vaiśya, and from his feet the Śūdra."[7]

This hymn has been much discussed by historians and Vedic scholars. According to some, one part of this hymn, that part which deals with the origin of the castes, is an interpolation, and they give reasons for their view. But all this relates to acute scholarship with which we are not here concerned. It might be that there was no caste-system during the time the hymn was composed. But during the latter half of the Vedic period there was definitely the fourfold organization of society, and in the later period the four classes were, perhaps, just on the way to being hardened into castes. That it was so is indicated by the attempt to put the classes in a hierarchy and to give sanctity to them by tracing their origin to the Supreme Being, the Lord of the universe. But the four classes formed into a hierarchy from the nature of the case. Intelligence, wisdom and spiritual virtue, which were the intrinsic qualities of the Brāhmaṇa, were higher than the physical strength and courage of the warrior. Physical strength without guidance by intelligence is blind. The strength and courage of the warrior was, again, higher than the qualities of the producer who beyond doubt required protection by the warrior against enemies. And it goes without saying that the labourer (the Śūdra) represented the bottom rung of the ladder as he lived only by serving or only to serve the other classes. But it will not do to neglect the organic relation between the upper classes, that one was incomplete or ineffective

6 "Rājanya" means Kshatriya—the warrior, but the word "Kshatriya does not occur in the Rig-Veda

7 Rig-Veda, X, 90.

without the others. One class was indeed higher than another as we have explained them. But it was not on that account superior to another. The transition from class to caste could be effected only by shifting the emphasis from quality to the accident of birth, that is, by making birth the standard of social rank.

In this connexion much is also made of a text of the *Bhagavadgītā* wherein Sri Kriṣṇa says :

> "The four classes were created by me
> according to quality and work."[8]

Commenting on this text, Dr. S. Radhakrishnan says, "The emphasis is on guṇa (aptitude) and karma (work) and not jāti (birth). The varṇa or the order to which we belong is independent of sex, birth or breeding."[9] Truly, this text refers to class and not to caste. Human beings are born inequal, and their inborn aptitude and temperament determine the inequality among them. Their qualities could not be created in them by any artificial means. They just have them from Nature, as we may say, and can develop them only by training. Far from giving sanction to the four castes, the *Bhagavadgītā* emphasizes the principle of the functional organization of society, i.e., the organization of society according to quality and work, in which an individual or a group of individuals is entrusted with a function which they are best fitted by their qualities and aptitudes to perform.

Plato in the *Republic* outlined his scheme of an ideal society or State organized on the principle of division of labour, or the principle of "one man one trade", not on that of "one man many trades."[10] Plato mentioned three cardinal virtues as excellences of character, namely, wisdom, courage, and temperance. Wisdom resides in reason, courage is "the right and perfect condition of spirit," and temperance results from the ordered functioning of the appetites.[11] And

8 *Bhagavadgītā*, IV, 13.

9 *The Bhagavadgītā*, George Allen and Unwin Ltd., London, 1948, pp. 160-161.

10 *Republic*, II, 37 , Ed. A.D. Lindsay, J.M. Dent and Sons Ltd., London, 1923, op. 55.

11 A. E. Taylor, *Plato*, Constable Company Ltd., London, 1922. p. 102.

there is a fourth virtue. But it is not a single one like any of the three mentioned above ; it is just harmony of the three virtues. Plato now conceived the State or society on the analogy of the individual soul or the individual man. According to him, "the State is only the individual writ large."[12] In a community there are three classes which correspond to the three parts of the individual.[13]

They are the guardians (rulers), the auxiliaries (soldiers), and the artisans or craftsmen (producers and traders). And in virtue of theses classes the city is wise, courageous temperate and just. Wisdom belongs to the rulers, courage to the soldiers, temperance to the producers, and justice in the city consists in harmony among the three classes.

> "But we have surely not forgotten", says Plato, "that the city was just by reason of the three classes within it each doing their own work."[14]

From this sketch of Plato's conception of a community, brief as it is, it is pretty clear that his threefold scheme, on the whole, corresponds to the fourfold order of the ancient Hindu society. But there is difference between the two sides, and the difference lies in the fact that whereas Plato was left with his conception of an ideal city without having an opportunity to put it into practice, the early Vedic society was really a fourfold organization in which the four classes discharged each their proper functions and thus maintained order in society. So we may have the liberty of saying that Plato's idea of an ideal society was in truth achieved and lived by the Vedic people in ancient India many centuries before the birth of Plato. His theory, nonetheless, has supreme value in that it shows that the fourfold Hindu organization had a rational foundation. It may be pointed out, however, that the transition from class to caste in Hindu society was a deviation from the path of reason. We think we can safely say that towards the end of the Rig-Vedic period the transformation of class into

12 *Op cit.*, p. 103.
13 *Republic*, IV, 441.
14 *Ibid.*

caste was complete, that the status and rank of an individual was determined solely by birth. Families were now fixed up as Brāhmaṇa, Kshatriya, Vaiśya and Śūdra families, and individuals born into them were respectively called the Brāhmaṇas, Kshatriyas, Vaiśyas and Śūdras. These castes, as they were now called, were put in a hierarchy with the Brāhmaṇa at the top and the Śūdra at the base, and every caste was considered inferior to the one or ones which were above it, so that the Śūdras were inferior to all three other castes, the Vaiśyas to the Kshatriyas and Brāhmaṇas, and the Kshatriyas to the Brāhmaṇas. The emphasis was obviously laid on the difference rather than on the organic relation between them with the result that the fourfold order ceased to be dynamic. At all events, there were some circumstances which made for the change we have just indicated.

In the first instance, the rites and rituals became more and more complex and required specialization in them as well as a tradition of the proper performing of them, which was to be handed down from generation to generation. Likewise, defence *plus* law and order became an intricate art—no less so was agriculture and industry—with the gradual expansion of the Aryan society. Even the Śūdras specialized in service by training in their families. So the emphasis was shifted from the individual to the family. And they thought that that way society could be organized in a more effective way than ever before. But the trouble was that the son of a Brāhmaṇa was not necessarily endowed with the qualities of a Brāhmaṇa, the son of a Kshatriya was not necessarily endowed with the qualities of a Kshatriya, and so on. On the other hand, many individuals who belonged to a non-Brāhmaṇa caste had the qualities of a Brāhmaṇa, and many of the Brāhmaṇas were indeed inferior to many Kshatriyas and Vaiśyas, and so forth. All this is beyond doubt a severe criticism of caste. But one justification at any rate seems to be there. It may be pointed out that quality or no quality, an individual had his caste according to the occupation of the family. It was no matter whether he followed the occupation perfectly well or not. Thus caste came to stay, and in later times there indeed arose a multiplicity of castes and sub-castes according to arts and crafts, such as weaver, carpenter, blacksmith, cultivator, fisherman, oilman, and so forth.

Relationship between the castes. Now fixing on the four major castes, we find that though generally they were exclusive of each other, there were degrees of exclusiveness between one caste and another. This would become clear to us if we consider the duties (dharma) of the different stages of life of the individuals of the four castes as prescribed and explained by the Hindu Law-makers—the authors of the Grihya-Sūtra, the Dharma-Sūtra, and the Dharma Śāstra. Let us consider their teachings in some detail.

These Sūtras and Śāstras relate to the social process in the post-Vedic period in which there was a gradual hardening of the castes. But the Śrauta-Sūtra was rather liberal in its attitude towards the castes. Therein some sacrifices, the Vājapeya, for instance, were prescribed for the priest, king, and Vaiśya alike, showing that the castes did not become very rigid yet. But the differentiation of the status, occupations, duties, etc., of the four castes is found in the Grihya-Sūtra. The Brahmaṇas constituted the priesthood, and it was their duty to study and teach the Veda and to perform sacrifices, rites, and rituals for themselves as well as for others. They were most honoured in society, and they deserved well of all because of their learning, wisdom, ethical purity and spirituality. In status the Rājanyas—Kshatriyas—were next to the Brahmaṇas, and noble was their work—to maintain order in society against internal strife and external aggression. The Vaiśyas, the producers of wealth, of course, had to do some gross sort of work such as tilling the land to raise crops, cattle-rearing, and trade. Judging the nature of their work, we find the Vaiśyas nearer to the Śūdras than to the two upper castes. They, nevertheless, did things which were extremely useful to society. The Śūdras were indeed apart from these three castes. But they were not outcastes. They in fact formed part of the Aryan society itself, though they were given the lowest status and a lowly sort of work, i.e., service, because they had no capacity, we are told, for any higher work. They were denied all rites and rituals except the marriage-rites and the one they performed before they were admitted into the Aryan fold—the rite called Vrātya Stoma which purified the Dāsas. The position of the Śūdras in Hindu society was somewhat analogous to that of the slaves in Greek and Roman societies. They did all sorts of manual work, including cooking, perhaps.

In the Dharma-Sūtra, however, the differentiation of the castes became acuter. Now differential treatment was accorded to the different castes even in the same social and legal affairs. Nevertheless, during this time intermarriage between the three upper castes, and also between these castes and the Śūdras gave rise to some sub-castes. But it seems that the Dharma-Sūtra discouraged, even prohibited, interdining with the Śūdras, let alone intermarriage with them. As it is said, "If a Śūdra touches him (while eating), then he shall leave off eating.....Food offered by people of any caste, who follow the laws prescribed for them, except that of Śūdras, may be eaten."[15]

Stages of life and their duties. In the Law-books, then, four castes are expressly mentioned. "There are four castes, Brāhmaṇas, Kshatriyas, Vaiśyas, and Śudras. And each caste is superior by birth to the one following."[16] For the three upper classes there were four orders or stages of life, namely, "that of the student, of the householder, of the hermit in the woods,"[17] and of the ascetic. The individuals of the three upper classes were called the twice-born in the sense that they were born twice. Each of them was indeed born of his parents; it was his physical birth as he derived his body from his father and mother. But when he was initiated to the Vedic study—sacred knowledge a spiritual awakening occurred in him. This was regarded as his second birth—his spiritual birth. "He from whom he gathers the knowledge of his religious duties is the teacher, who causes him to be born a second time by imparting to him sacred knowledge."[18] As

15 *Āpastamba* in S.B.E., Vol. II, p. 67.

16 *Dharma-Sūtra*, S.B.E. Vol. II, pp. 1-2.

17 *Gautama*, Op. cit. p. 190.

18 *Op. cit*, p. 276.

Manu puts it, "In the second birth, the Sāvitrī—the rite of initiation is the mother and the teacher the father."[19] The twice-born, i.e., the three classes, excluding the Śūdras, passed through four stages of life, performing the respective duties attached to the stages. The Grihya, and Dharma Sūtras, and the Dharma-Śāstra detail the duties of these stages. We can only deal with them in broad outlines.

As we have said above, student life was the first stage of life. It began with the rite of *Upanayana* or initiation, and this rite consisted in presenting the child to the teacher for the purpose of teaching, who in his turn introduced him to the sacred study. The initiation of the Brāhmaṇa took place in the eighth year from conception, of the Kshatriya in the eleventh and of the Vaiśya in the twelfth year.[20] On this occasion the child performed some elaborate rites and is invested with the sacred thread which he wore over his shoulder and was given the *Gāyatrī*, a Vedic formula.

After initiation the student lived with the teacher and performed his daily duties. He revered his teacher, touching his feet and serving him, studied the Veda, learnt sacrifice to the fire and "to tend the fire." He took a seat lower than that of the teacher, did not eat any pungent, salt meal, or meat, must not sleep in the day-time, must not indulge in any luxuries. He must avoid gossiping, wear an upper and a lower garment, tie a knot of hair on the crown of the head, cropping the rest of the hair. He should practise restraint, control of sensuous desires, and say twilight prayer. "During the earlier twilight he should stand repeating the Sāvitrī till the sun is distinctly visible, during the later twilight he should sit till the stars are clearly seen."[21] He was also to beg in the morning and in the evening.[22] When grown up he was to observe continence. And so on.

According to Manu, the females were not to go through the elaborate process of initiation and to take up residence

19 *Manu-Smṛti*, tr. by Ganganath Jha, Vol. I, Part II, University of Calcutta, 1921, p. 459.

20 *Op. cit.*, p. 276.

21 *Op. cit.*, p. 364.

22 S.B.E., Vol. II, p. 11.

with the teacher. For them marriage took the place of initiation; serving husband and doing domestic work were their duties.

Student life covered 36 years or half that time or a quarter. When the student had finished his study of the Veda the ceremony of the *Samāvartana*(returning home or Convocation) was held at which the teacher enjoined him to continue his study while doing other duties and ever to be honest and virtuous. As it is said, "The teacher shall dismiss the pupil after he has performed the ceremony of the *Samāvartana* and has finished his studentship with these words :

"Apply thyself henceforth to other duties."[23]

The student now took a girl of the same caste to wife and was at the second stage of his life, the life of a householder. The duties prescribed for this new life were as follows :

(1) "He shall have two meals, one in the morning and one in the evening.

(2) He shall not have intercourse with his wife in the day-time.

(3) He shall lie with his wife during copulation and be separate from her at other times.

(4) Both husband and wife shall bathe everyday.

(5) He shall never abandon sacred learning.

(6) With the sacred fire kindled at the wedding he shall perform the domestic ceremonies, and the five sacrifices, and with that fire he shall cook his food.

(7) He shall give cooked food to beggars, but not for illegal or immoral purposes.

(8) He shall feed his guests, the infants, the sick, the pregnant women, the females under his protection, the aged and the poor who take shelter in his house. And so on.

When the householder became advanced in age, when his skin wrinkled up, his hairs became all grey, and when his sons had sons, he retired into the forest. This was the third stage of life—the life of a hermit. He now built a hut out-

23 *Dharma-Sūtra*, S.B.E., Vol. II, p. 32.

side the village and lived there "with his wife, his children and the sacred fire, or he lived there alone", meditating on Brahman, and sustained himself by gleaning corn from the field and also by fruits and roots. He often went to a village for food. But he was not to hoard against the future; he was to procure food daily.

Further on there was the fourth and final stage of life, the life of an ascetic. A hermit became an ascetic when he left his hut for good and wandered from place to place, meditating on Brahman and sustaining himself by begging.

As we see, and as they say, the order of the householder was the centre of the four-stage organization of the Hindu society. The householders were producers or procurers of food and other necessaries of life, and in fact supported students, hermits and ascetics. So the healthy working of the *varṇāśrama dharma* depended upon the efficiency of the householder. So the emphasis was laid upon the household. All three—the student, the hermit, and the ascetic—emerged out of the household. So we have it :

> "A twice-born man who seeks liberation without studying the Vedas, without having begotten sons and without having offered sacrifices, sinks downwards."[24]

The four stages of life of the twice-born were determined by the fourfold end of their life: Dharma, Artha, Kāma, and Moksha—virtue, wealth or possession, enjoyment, and liberation. These ends were conceived and arranged in order of worth thus : wealth, enjoyment, virtue, and liberation. Wealth or property by itself had no value; it had value only as a means to enjoyment, for things to enjoy were procured by means of wealth. But unbridled enjoyment degraded man. So enjoyment must be regulated by virtue or moral life. That is to say, enjoyment one sought should be commensurate with moral goodness. And enjoyment and all that was regulated by the pursuit of virtue for the ultimate purpose of liberation. Therefore, liberation or spiritual realization was the highest ideal and the three other ends in relation to each other were the means to the realization of this ideal, which was clearly a

24 *The Laws of Manu*, S.B.E., Vol XXV, p. 205.

concrete one in the sense that its realization, far from negating life, occurred through the mediation of the four grades of life. Usually a man passed through these four stages, and some common virtues were prescribed for all four stages. They were : "purity, truthfulness, absence of spite, abstinence from cruelty, etc."[25]

Some Law-makers, however, permitted sannyāsa or renunciation immediately after student-life or the life of a householder.[26]

However, it ought to be clear to anybody that the pursuit of this ideal was a monopoly of the three upper classes, and was denied to women, and also to the Śūdras whose summum bonum of life consisted in eating, drinking and serving the former classes. Moreover, the Śūdras were in many ways exploited, even subjected to harsh treatment by the higher castes. If a Śūdra ever reviled or assaulted a twice-born, he was deprived of the limbs with which he offended. This sort of punishment amounted to the modern sort called lynching.

As the caste of a man was determined by birth, the four castes became increasingly rigid. So to deal with intermixture of castes the Law-makers framed some specific rules. The Dharma-Sūtra refers to the existence of mixed castes, and sanctions two types of intercaste marriage, namely, the *Anuloma* and the *Pratiloma*. In the *Anuloma* form of marriage, a male of a higher caste took to wife a female of a lower caste, and the rule was that the children born of this union belonged to the caste of the father. In the *Pratiloma*, on the other hand, a male of a lower caste married a female of a higher caste. But the female lost her caste. This form of marriage was not much in favour with the higher castes. In any case, a Śūdra coming into the picture was not tolerated. If a twice-born man ever in his folly married a woman of the Śūdra caste, he degraded himself and his children. If a Brāhmaṇa, for example, had a Śūdra wife, he would "sink

25 Kane, p. 93.

26 P.H. Prabhu, *Hindu Social Organization*, Popular Book Depot, Bombay, p. 91; Manu, vi, 38.

into hell". "The offspring of a Śūdra male and a Brāhmaṇa female became an outcast," the Law-givers say. And so forth.

Forms of marriage. The Āśvalāyana Grihya-Sūtra and the Dharma Sūtra mention eight forms of marriage.[27] These forms of marriage are stated in these Sūtras according to the degrees of validity they possess. Thus we have: (1) The Brāhma, (2) the Prājāpatya, (3) the Ārṣa, (4) the Daiva, (5) the Gāndharva, (6) the Āsura, (7) the Rākṣasa, and (8) the Paiśāca. In the Brāhma form of marriage, the father gives away his daughter dressed in two garments and decked with ornaments to a person who possesses learning and character, with a prayer for their happiness.

In the Prājāpatya form, the bridegroom receives the bride decked with best linen, ornaments and flowers, and the couple are enjoined with the formula, "Fulfil ye the law conjointly", to perform the duties of their new life.

In the Ārṣa form of marriage, the bridegroom presents a cow and a bull to the father or guardian of the bride, while in the Daiva the bride is decked with flowers and ornaments and is given away to the officiating priest at a sacrifice.

The Gāndharva form is apart, however. It is based on the mutual consent of a male and a female, and the union is inspired by spontaneous love for each other.

In the Āsura form of marriage, the bride is virtually purchased by the bridegroom. He satisfies those who have authority over the girl with money before they have given their consent to the proposed marriage.

In the Rākṣasa marriage the bride is forcibly taken away by the bridegroom or his party. It is in fact marriage by capture. In the Paiśāca marriage, on the other hand, a girl is ravished by a man against her will or without her knowledge, i.e., when she is not in her senses.

The Law-givers are more or less agreed that the daughter is to be given in marriage before she attains the age of puberty, but are not agreed about the eight forms of marriage detailed above. According to some, the first four, according to others, the first six, are valid. In ancient times, however,

27 *Gautama,* S.B.E., Vol. II, pp. 194-197, *Āśvalāyana-Gṛhya-Sūtra,* S.B.E., Vol. XXIX.

all eight forms prevailed, and social sanction was given to the Rākṣasa and Paiśāca forms in order to give relief to the women victimized by wicked men. These forms, nevertheless, changed in the course of time; some definitely went out of vogue and the others assumed new forms. In spite of the vicissitudes of society, the form of Hindu marriage which prevails at the present time seems to be a combination of the Brāhma and Prājāpatya forms, which has indeed local variations in different parts of the country, and involves elements of some lower forms up to the Āsura. The current Hindu marriage ceremony consists of some details which are as follows:

(1) The bride is adorned, and both the bride and the bridegroom are purified by some rites.

(2) They are given wedding gifts by the parents or guardians and relatives of the bride.

(3) The bridegroom ceremonially arrives at the home of the bride's parents or guardians and is received with rites.

(4) The father or guardian and relatives of the bridegroom, who accompany him to the bride's place, are feasted along with the invitees to the ceremony.

(5) Then the marriage-rites proper begin. The bride and bridegroom are brought to a place in the house specially chosen and sanctified for the purpose. And in the presence of a select gathering there, in token of mutual acceptance the bride goes, or is taken, round the bridegroom seated in a chair, and she goes seven times round, describing seven circles, so to speak, implying that she entwines him with her life for good.

(6) The seven-circuit item is followed by the main rite which consists in the formal giving away of the bride to the bridegroom. Clothes, utensils, and other daily necessaries are given to the bride and bridegroom. Oblations are offered to the sacred fire with prayers for peace and happiness of the new couple. The bride and bridegroom together sit before the sacred fire and chant Vedic *mantras*

(hymns) with the assistance of the priest, the purport of which is that they—the bride and bridegroom—solemnly form a union and start out in life for mutual enjoyment as well as moral and spiritual development.

(7) Now comes the *Saptapadi* which marks the culmination of the marriage ceremony. The *Saptapadi* means walking seven steps and is indeed a symbolic function. The bride and bridegroom go arm in arm from the sacrificial fire and walk seven steps, indicating that they together are pledged to life-long companionship.

The performance of the marriage ceremony produces or is calculated to produce in the new couple the sense that marriage is a sacrament and not a contract, and that they have to take their new life seriously.

Castes and sub-castes. As time went on, castes multiplied and there was a large number of sub-castes along with the major four castes. There were as many castes as there were occupations: and a gulf was created between the higher and the lower castes. Even interdining among some of them was prohibited, not to speak of intermarriage. And, what is more surprising, the lower castes themselves became exclusive of each other.

Moreover, the conception of *gotra* made for division within a single caste. *Gotra* broadly means descent from a great saint or sage of the past. The families of each caste now had their respective *gotras*, meaning that they were descended from the great persons whose names constituted their *gotras*. So families with the same *gotra*, though they belonged to the same caste, avoided, and even today avoid, the marriage-relationship between them for reasons of like blood. Some may explain *gotra* in terms of totemism. But the difficulty is that human totems were very rare. Further, totemism stands for a particular kind of belief in a savage tribe about the relation between itself and a species of plants or animals. But the conception of *gotra* was developed in civilization. So we cannot trace the conception of *gotra* to totemism. While the people of a savage tribe or clan believd that a particular species of plants or animals had the power to protect the tribe, the Hindu families believed, and even to this day believe, in their *gotras* in the sense that they were descended from some great sages of the past.

But *gotra* is a social fiction. It is not believable that all the Hindu families were descended from ancient sages, for there was no stage of Indian history when the population consisted only of some sages and their families. Further, the sages, whatever might be their number, certainly were fewer than the people at large of their time: they were known for their wisdom and spirituality, not for their being prolific. The fact, however, is that *gotra* means only the glorification of the past and an urge in the believers concerned to link themselves to the creators of their spiritual culture and civilization. There is, to be sure, no historical truth at the basis of this conception. The Hindu Marriage Act, 1955, therefore, makes marriage within the same *gotra* valid. Dr. Gour's Act, Act XXX of 1923, had already permitted intercaste marriage. But there still remains a line between the legal and the social. Legal sanction is not necessarily reinforced by social sanction. In spite of provision made by Law for intercaste marriage and marriage within the same *gotra*, the Hindu orthodoxy holds on to the old practice. There have indeed been revolts against casteism over the centuries. Sri Kriṣṇa in the *Bhagavadgītā* emphasized four classes against four castes, and also the life of a householder doing his duties in a detached way. He depreciated outer renunciation which became a sort of formalism, and laid stress on inner development which could be achieved, he pointed out, through the performance of one's proper duties as worship of God. As he puts it, "The renunciation of works and their unselfish performance both lead to the soul's salvation. But of the two the unselfish performancc of works is better than their renunciation."[28] The Buddha, Sri Chaitanya, Swami Viveka-

28 *Bhagavadgītā*, V. 2, Radhakrishnan, p. 175.

nanda, and Mahatma Gandhi and other great religious leaders denounced caste. They each indeed had a following. But the body-politic remained adamant with their age-old beliefs and practices. Nay, Hindu society has become worse than ever before because of its multiple castes and sub-castes. It is, in short, a mess. The caste of a man or woman is fixed by birth regardless of his or her qualities and the occupations they follow. And these anomalies the Hindus tolerate primarily because their minds are swayed by the Law of Karma as well as by the belief in pre-existence and future life. The low-caste people reconcile themselves to the social inequalities and social injustice they suffer, thinking that their position and status in this life is determined by their past Karmas. But there has recently been a change in the situation. By the teaching of Mahatma Gandhi, particularly through the political regeneration of the country, a new awakening has come upon the people. Above all, the recent enactments by Parliament against untouchability and disabilities of individuals for reasons of sex, caste, and creed have thrown open equal opportunities to all people. Nonetheless, the mess in Indian society continues. The gradations or stratifications are still there in society, though castes and sub-castes interchange their functions. The higher-caste people very often follow the occupations of the lower or low castes. A Brahmaṇa, for example, becomes a cook, porter, sometimes deals in hides, takes to grocery, dyeing and cleaning, and so forth, and a low-caste man takes to learning and becomes a teacher at a school, college or at a university. Sometimes, again, a man follows more than one profession. He, for example, does agriculture, horticulture, building-construction, and so on. Brāhmaṇas along with the lower-caste people participate in the administration of the country, which was formerly the sole function of the Kshatriyas. All right-thinking men in the country are ever aware of this criss-cross of ideas and functions, and this awareness, we believe, is going to become wide-spread through the spread of general education. The Government cannot change the ideas and beliefs of a people overnight, who inherit them from the past. They can change them only by persuasion. But age-old beliefs die hard. A process of vast change is, however, afoot. We must have patience and do all we can to help and guide the process towards a classless or casteless society in which there would only be gradations of individuals by the degrees of culture they attain and in which only qualities and abilities would count.

Chapter IX

INDIVIDUAL AND SOCIETY

The problem of the relation between individuals and society. We have already seen that society is a group of human beings living together for all purposes in mutual help and co-operation. Now the question arises : What exactly is the relation between individuals and society? The relation is differently conceived by different sociologists. And these conceptions are somewhat parallel to some different conceptions of whole. Thus we have the conception of a heap, that of a mechanical whole, of an organism, and also that of an organization.

(1) *The individualistic or atomistic conception of society.* As we know, a large number of things put together or arranged in a pyramidal way constitutes a heap. Thus there is a heap of grains, or a heap of bricks, or a heap of sands, sugar, and so forth. If we analyze such a whole, we shall find that it does not contain anything besides the units that are there. In a heap of bricks, for instance, there is only a large number of bricks. They simply exist together in a loose sort of arrangement. When, however, the bricks get scattered, the whole they formed disappears.

Some sociologists conceive society in terms of a heap. They maintain that when a number of individuals exist together for the purposes of life they constitute society. That is to say, society is nothing but individuals living together, who were with their nature in tact when they did not form into society. The idea is that individuals by themselves were or are real and that society is an accident. When they would separate from each other, society would come to an end. Such a view is implied by the Contract Theory of Society. It posits individuals with intelligence, power of judgment, and the sense of utility before the origin of society. But this is only imagination. The history of man shows that the bodily and mental development has been possible only through the evolution of society or social life. So we cannot say that society came about only by way of external relations between some individual human beings. If individuals themselves developed both physically and mentally through the development of society, the latter is obviously a structure which is objective and independent of any definite individuals. It ought to be clear to anybody that individuals come and go but society remains and grows when it grows. Therefore, we reject the atomistic or individualistic theory about the relation between individuals and society.

(2) *The mechanistic theory*. We all know that a machine is an artificial thing. It does not grow, but is made by men. These are the days of science and technology, and up to now different kinds of machines—railway engines, engines of many other kinds, electric pumps, cranes, sewing machines, and so forth—have been manufactured to serve the purposes of men. Consider the nature and structure of a machine. Clearly, it is a whole which consists of some parts. There is, however, much difference between a machine or a mechanical whole and the kind of whole we have analyzed above, i.e., a heap. The units of a heap are loosely connected in the sense that they are only spatially related to each other. And the points of space they occupy are near enough to each other. In a machine, however, there is much more than this. In it the parts are fitted to each other in view of the purpose they together serve. Thus in the engine of a motor car each part has its definite position and definite function. The parts in their mutual relations constitute the car and in their proper functioning make it move. In a mechanical whole, like this, nevertheless, the parts are external to each other. That is to say, although they are elements in the whole, when they are taken out of the whole they remain independent pieces of matter, and as pieces they remain the same as they were in the whole.

Now some conceive society just as a mechanical whole produced by geographical conditions in relation to a large number of human beings. It is said that physical conditions *plus* human individuals constitute society. In it the elements are external to, and, in their nature, independent of, each other, though they come together and form the social whole which, however, breaks up when some of the elements fall out. But there is a difficulty about this conception of society.

A machine has, of course, a purpose to serve. But this purpose is external to the machine. For instance, an engine is designed to move something or to produce movement in something. But this movement is no purpose of the machine itself. A railway engine moves a train, and in moving it serves a purpose, only the purpose of the people who want to travel from place to place without walking. A railway engine indeed produces movement in itself. It moves and in moving carries a train. But it is no purpose of the engine itself to move along. It has a purpose, nevertheless, though external to it. What, then, is the purpose of the mechanical whole called society ? And what is it that brings individuals and physical conditions together? The point is that society grows and is never made; it, unlike a machine does not serve any purpose external to itself. It may be contended that society is not an end in itself, that it is only a means to an end. We have to admit that society has an end. But this end does not fall outside it, but is immanent in it. Physical conditions that are said to be among the elements of society are all inert and cannot have an end or purpose for themselves. Purpose is relevant only to self-conscious beings. A human being is self-conscious and rational and considers himself as an end in himself. He seeks to realize himself as an end by appropriating things from outside, or by modifying them so as to serve his purposes. So if we take human individuals to be some of the elements that make up the social whole, it is difficult to conceive it as a mechanical whole—a whole which is solely determined by mechanical laws. So we cannot accept the position that society is a mechanical whole.

(3) *The organismic conception of society.*[1] According to some sociologists, society is an organic whole and individuals can exist only in society. They are like the limbs of a living

1 *Vide* P. Sorokin, *Contemporary Sociological Theories*, Harper And Brothers, New York, 1928, pp. 196-198.

body, which, when separated from it, perish. An organism is quite different from a mechanical whole or machine. The limbs of an organism are indeed the parts of which it consists. But the relations between them and the whole to which they belong are very intimate, intimate to the extent that if they are separated from the whole they decompose and disappear in the long run. If we take out a finger, or a hand, or an eye, or any other limb from a body, it withers away altogether. There are some other characteristics of an organism. It, as we see, grows and is never made. A plant or an animal organism grows out of a seed by some stages. An oak, for instance, develops out of an acorn. Likewise, men, horses, cows, monkeys, and the rest grow out of their respective seeds. An organism, again, sustains itself by absorbing food from outside and assimilating it into itself. A plant, for instance, draws sap from the soil with its roots, and gathers carbon from air with its leaves by the help of sunlight. An animal organism sustains itself by taking in vegetables, flesh, fish, and water, and by digesting and transforming them into blood and tissues of the organism. An organism is also self-healing. If minor damage is done to any part of an organism, it heals up the damage itself. We may be told that the different systems of medicine contradict this conception, that the healing comes from outside and not from within of an organism itself. Nobody can deny that a bodily ailment is more often than not cured by medicine. But the science of medicine says that medicine is only an aid to Nature. It, in short, presupposes the healing power or process in the organisms themselves. If such power were not there, medicine could not function in an organism. Lastly, an organism as such passes through the stages of birth, growth, and decay or death. These are the cycles of its existence.

As has been stated above, some conceive society quite as an organism. In their opinion, individuals were or are never found outside of society; they are the constituents of society and develop along with the development of the social whole. Individuals are to society what limbs are to an organism. That the relation between individuals and society is organic is sought to be proved by showing that a human infant kept out of and away from society does not grow to be a human being. There are some test cases on record.[2] A wolf boy is here a case in point. Some books have already been written on wolf boys. To cite one case which happened in India some years ago. A wolf boy was found in a jungle of U.P. He was fourteen or fifteen years old but walked on hands and feet. He had no language except the language of inarticulate signs and sounds. He had obviously been stolen away from home by a wolf and reared by it there in the jungle. But he grew up to be an animal and no human being. This clearly shows that human infants could not become human beings if they were kept outside of social surroundings, and that the relation of human individuals to society is organic in the sense that the development of their nature as men depend upon society. If human infants be segregated from society, they would certainly grow up to be denizens of the animal world.

This organic or organismic conception of society is as old as the study of society. It is found in Plato, Aristotle and some other ancient philosophers. In the nineteenth century we meet with the very conception in Auguste Comte who founded sociology as a science to investigate society and social phenomena. Herbert Spencer who did much towards developing this science adopted the organic conception of society. But he told us that we should not press the conception too far. Sensory experience, he pointed out, accrues to a human organism through the senses and sense-organs. But in it the seat of sensation, or a common senseorium, as it is called, is there in the brain. Through the functioning of this common organ the sensations coming through the different senses are synthesized into the perception of a thing. Now, if society is an organism, it must have experience other than those of the individuals and that through a common sensorium in the individuals. But, in Spencer's opinion, society is not presented to us as one organism and far less has a common sensorium. Herbert Spencer therefore accepts the organic conception of society with a grain of salt. "*To speak of society as if it* were a physical organism", says

2 *Vide* MacIver and Page, *Society*, p. 45.

Hobhouse, "is a piece of mysticism, if indeed it is not quite meaningless".[3] He, however, maintains that the relations between individuals are organic in the sense that they are interdependent, that they sustain each other and that "through their mutual support comes a common development." There are nevertheless some staunch advocates of the conception that society is an organic whole. They are: A. Shaffle (a German sociologist), J. Novicov (a Russian), A. Fouillée (a French thinker), and some others.

In any case, some criticisms are urged against this conception of society. They are as follows :—

(1) Firstly, if we insist on the organic conception of society, we mean that there is a relation of necessity between organic relation and society or social life, that wherever there is organic relation, there is social life. But there is a difficulty about this view. An animal organism, as we know, consists of millions of cells. These in their mutual relationships constitute the organism and each of them exists and lives only as an element in the whole. They do not constitute a society, however, or have any social relations among them.

(2) Secondly, if society is an organism, sociology is a part or branch of biology. Biology, it is needless to say, is the science of animal organisms; it investigates their nature and structure and also how out of some simple forms of organism the complex forms evolved or evolve. But, definitely, there is difference between biology and sociology. As we have seen before, biology studies changes or effects produced upon organisms by environmental conditions In it changes in the organism are regarded as effect and the external objects as cause. In sociology, on the other hand, this relation is reversed. Society consists of human individuals, and each individual is a body plus a mind. Individuals are self-conscious thinking beings, and they in their attempt to realize or fulfil their desires mould or modify their environment and produce a structure like society. Obviously, the individuals are the cause and a change in the environment

3 *Social Evolution and Political Theory*, The World Press Private Ltd., Calcutta, 1962, p. 87.

the effect. Sociology is different from biology in both its standpoint and approach to its subject matter. In the circumstances sociology cannot be regarded as a branch of biology, and society cannot be taken to be an organic whole.

(3) Thirdly, the fact that grown-up persons can leave their own society with their individual nature in tact shows that individuals are not organically related to society. In individual or collective emigration, persons leave their native land and society to settle down in another country and another society. On a tour, or on business people leave their country and society, and live in another temporarily. They go from and come back to their own without detriment to their individual nature and personality. All this serves to show that society is no organism and that individuals are no inalienable parts of the social whole.

(4) Fourthly, the reform and reconstruction of society by individuals proves that society, far from being an organic whole, is more or less created by individuals. We generally say that society grows. But they say that it grows through the labour of individuals. The growth of society is then said to correspond to the growth of individual minds. It is only in the light of the growing ideas of individual minds that society is moulded or reconstructed.

A double relation between individuals and society. The above criticisms of the organic conception of society have much force. But some of them are overdone. It is indeed true to say that a case of organic relation is not necessarily a case of social life. As stated above, the cells of a living body are organically related to it and to each other. They perish as soon as they are taken out of the whole to which they belong. However, those who advocate the theory that individuals are organically related to society do not mean to say that wherever there is organic relation there is society. There are obviously different kinds of organism, plant and animal organisms, the latter, again, being one-cell and multi-cell organisms. However much a plant may differ from an animal organism, they nevertheless represent the same kind of relationship between their parts. These cannot exist outside the organism in question. Now to these two kinds is added one special kind of organism or organic whole—special in the sense that individuals who are conscious beings are the constituent elements of this whole. The question that we now have to answer is whether the social whole is really an organism. The critics point out that it is not, particularly because grown-up individuals are rather independent of their society. They may go wherever they please without injury to their individual nature because of their separation from their society. But there is another side to the thing. This we can only grasp if we consider human infants in relation to society in so far as their development into human beings is concerned. We have seen before that a human infant reared outside of human society does not grow to be a human thing; it becomes and can become a human individual if and only if it is nurtured in the social *milieu*. So it is clear that individuals are organically related to society up to a definite stage of their development. They could not become what they are now without society. But when they have attained majority, i.e., average development, they become somewhat independent in the sense that they now afford to live, if they want to, outside their own society. This, however, does not mean that they remain or can remain unaffected by society. Society still continues to influence them. *Individuals are therefore in a double relation with society; they are organically related to and independent of society according to the stages of their development.*

The relation between society and social reformers. The relation between society and those great men who reform and reconstruct society is another matter which is worthy of special consideration. We have to recognize the fact that everybody cannot be a reformer however hard he may try to become one. Sometimes society stagnates because of obstacles from both anti-social and pseudo-social forces. A reformer is he who has the genius to grasp the needs of society and canalize its growth by reconstructing worn-out customs and institutions. This we say from the side of the reformer himself. Early in the nineteenth century Raja Ram Mohun Roy, for example, rose against the superstitious and evil customs of Hindu society. He did much for it. He is in fact the maker of modern Hindu society. But he did not drop from the clouds. He was born and brought up in that society. We wonder how a man could rise out of the society which he later reformed root and branch. Deeply viewed, however, the reformer only appears to be an expression of a necessity of society. Society; is a living whole, and it often makes progress through the mediation of an element which exists within itself. He was originally a human infant indeed, and was nurtured in society he, like other individuals, was a child of society. But as he grew up, he came to a stage where he found himself in a position to mould society, and he moulded it. The reformer appears to be linked to the depth of society. Therefore, he is not independent of society as other grown-up individuals are. He does not at will get away from it, but is connected with it by an inner necessity.

Is society, then, an organism ? Evidently, it does not follow that society is an organism even if we admit that individuals at a certain stage of life are inseparably related to society. By definition society consists of individuals or individual minds. Empirically, individuals are distinct from each other and are or have distinct minds. One's life and experiences are not identical with the life and experiences of another. Further, each individual is an end in himself and seeks to realize himself by appropriating things from outside. It is by no means the case that the organisms of different individuals coalesce into just one organism to be called society, with a central sensorium and a central sensory experience. An animal organism, as we have seen, consists of an indefinite number of cells. But the cells have no purpose of their own. There is only one purpose. That is the unity of the whole which they hold together. As every individual is an end in himself and considers society as the medium of realizing this end, the conception that society is an organism breaks down. But this view does not contradict the statement made above, namely, that *human individuals in their birth and growth are organically related to society*. Here "organically" means only "very intimately", or "inseparably." In a building bricks, mortar, and beams, for instance, are inseparably related to each other in the sense that if they separate, the building will come down. But nevertheless the building is not an organism. Life and sunlight are inseparably connected in the sense that in the absence of sunlight the earth would become so cold that there would be no living thing on it. Still life and light are no elements in an organism in the strict sense of the term.

(4) *The conception of society as an organization.* The above consideration brings us to a fourth conception of society, namely, that society is an organization of individuals. It is conceived to be so, because they establish among themselves, we are told, a system of relationships so that they can live and realize themselves in co-operation and mutual help. As we say, human infants are born into society. But what society? Society which is already there as constituted and maintained by developed self-conscious individuals. But there is one danger. The conception of society as an organization may create in our minds the impression that fully formed individuals were there, to begin with, and that society came up through the efforts of these individuals. We have seen that this is an error which the atomistic or social contract theory commits. In any case, society is not an organization like a business organization. A Life Insurance Company or a bank, for example, is organized purposely by a handful of individuals. But society was never organized in like manner. We, of course, cannot say exactly how society began. We can, however, say that as in the beginning human individuals were barely conscious beings, they came together more by an impulse than by anything else. Later, whatever common way of life they developed reacted upon their inner nature. Thus for ages the outer conditions and the inner nature of individuals acted and reacted upon each other and made for development in both till at last individuals as units of an organized society evolved. The fact, however, remains that individuals at all stages of society began as human infants. And as they could not grow into human beings, even undeveloped, without the aid of society or social life, an inchoate form of society is a postulate with us in our study of society. If we, then, conceive society as an organization of individuals, we have to recognize that as infants, individuals have to pass through an organic relation to society before they attain to the state of

autonomy in their relationships with each other.

We then conclude that the relation of individuals to society is a complex one, and that it is not possible to conceive it in a stereotyped way. The relation is a peculiar one, and we can best conceive it by conceiving society as an organization of individuals, which involves at bottom (in the birth and growth of infants) a relation between the two sides which is obviously an organic one.

CHAPTER X

EDUCATION AND EDUCATIONAL INSTITUTIONS

Education is a social fact. We have already seen that a social fact is different from a fact of Nature, in the sense that the former is created by men out of the latter. They modify by their co-operative activities their surroundings in their attempt to live according to their desires. Judged by this standard, education itself is a social product. It is designed to develop body and mind which we have from Nature. Education, therefore, consists of a course or courses of training that make for the health of both body and mind. Whatever might be the method or methods of education employed in primitive society, in ancient times some great thinkers developed their theories of education.

Plato's theory of education. Plato in the pre-Christian era developed his conception of the ideal State. He in the *Republic* says that this State would consist of the guardians or rulers, the auxiliaries and the producers, and that the State would be organized on division of labour. These classes of people are, then, graded according to their qualities. Those who belong to the first class possess the best possible qualities and are like gold. They are best fitted for guiding and ruling over their fellow-citizens. Those who belong to the second class are "upholders of the doctrines of the rulers" and have the responsibility for defence of the State against aggression as well as for internal peace and order. They are like silver. And those who compose the third class are the agriculturists, traders and artisans, who produce food, wealth and other useful things. They are like iron and copper. Each class has its tasks. Plato says that they would find it easy to fulfil their tasks if they are properly trained for their respective purposes. Hence Plato draws up an elaborate scheme of education for these classes.

Plato believes that only a very few people are born philosophers and are able to guide others. The other persons must therefore be put through a process of education framed by the philosophers. They are then to be picked out for jobs according as they develop appropriate qualities. In ancient Greece, education consisted of music and gymnastic. Plato accepts this scheme as a suitable one for general education. He is, however, of the opinion that early education must be imparted by tales that are imaginative and fanciful. They might indeed be false, and it may be that they narrate no facts. But this is no matter. They must nevertheless aim to produce noble character in the pupils by presenting to them what is good and wholesome, for whatever a child "receives and believes at that early age is apt to become permanent and indelible." The poets have a specific role to play in so far as this stage of education is concerned. The stories they would tell and write about men and gods should produce in the hearers honesty, courage, and other good qualities. Poetry, therefore, must conform to a set standard and must not run wild.

Gymnastic for the body and music for the soul.[1] The next stage consists of music and gymanstic. The contents of poetry are not very important. Its form, style, and rhythm are of prime importance for children. Poems make music when they are set to tunes, and music produces soft and gentle qualities in the hearers by stimulating in their souls the sense of beauty, harmony and rhythm. It thus prepares them to conform to the beauty and rhythm of reason. But too much music makes one too soft and gentle. So music must be supplemented by gymnastic. It relates to the body and proceeds on the principle, "Sound mind is in a sound body." The body is then to be healthy and well formed by proper exercises. As Plato points out, bodily disease and the desire for medicine indicate lack of education, or bad education, that the individual concerned is not properly educated. "He that is trained in music will follow the same path in his pursuit of gymnastic, and may, if he will, be independent of medicine except in extreme cases".[2] Gymnastic is, of course, immediately concerned with

1 *Republic*, 376.
2 *Op. cit.*, 410.

the body. But really, according to Plato, both music and gymnastic are meant for the soul. Mere gymnastic makes a man beast, rough and ignorant, and deprives him of rhythm and grace. So music and gymnastic must be combined to give men a steady character.

According to Plato, at the top of the State would be those who are by nature and training best fitted to guide the rest of the people. Them he calls the guardians or rulers and proposes for them a special scheme of education, which is apart from general education. In his opinion, those who would be at the helm of the State must be wise, just, and good. And they can be so only if they have known the truth of the universe. Philosophy as a human study is concerned with the ultimate truth or reality, and a philosopher is he who has seen the truth and only a philosopher would rule with wisdom and justice and seek the good of all without selfishness. "Unless", says Plato, "philosophers bear kingly rule in cities, or those who are now called kings and princes become genuine and adequate philosophers, and political power and philosophy be brought together, ... there will be no respite from evils, ...for cities, nor I fancy for humanity."[3] The guardians, then, have to become philosophers, not indeed star-gazers, but seers of truth. They must possess reality, and, being poised in wisdom, steer the ship of the State. The special education of the guardians therefore would consist in a course covered by mathematics and philosophy. Philosophy by definition is concerned with reality which is spiritual in its essence and is difficult to grasp. Mathematics is an aid to philosophy as it studies abstract entities like point, line, figure, etc. It, again, takes the help of symbols and diagrams. As Plato points out, one cannot rise to reality and grasp it by one sweep. One has to proceed gradually, stage by stage, from the sensuous to the non-sensuous abstract realm and thence through pure ideas to the highest which is "the brightest blaze of Being."

Plato in the *Laws* lays no emphasis on a coming kingdom of philosophers. He, of course, does not banish from the State the philosophers along with the poets. But definitely he

3 *Republic* (Ed. by Lindsay), 473.

ignored them. In this Dialogue religion takes the place of philosophy and helps to regulate the ethical life of the citizens. Now there is the law-giver or legislator to frame laws with a view to all virtues. The *Laws* does not contain any conception of an ideal State; it rather exhibits the State as organized in the light of human psychology, motives and feelings. The emphasis on the soul is, however, retained. The citizens are no longer under the Government of philosophers. The sexes are on an equal footing. Men and women are to eat from common tables, share in common pursuits; women are to serve even in war. They are to have a common education as they have it in the *Republic.* The scheme of education outlined in the *Laws* is much lower than that found in the *Republic.* In the former Plato deals with popular education which includes mathematics and preliminary sciences as they are very useful in practical life. The rulers are to de trained in all knowledge; there is no special scheme for them. Education has, as in the *Republic*, two branches, namely, gymnastic and music. The former is concerned with the body, whereas the latter with the soul. Gymnastic, again, has two parts—dancing and wrestling. One kind of dancing aims at rhythm and harmony and is much akin to music. The other kind is concerned with the training of the body and has health, beauty and agility as the objectives.

Aristotle's theory of education. Aristotle in his *Politics* develops his theory of education. In it he broadly adopts the principles Plato lays down in the *Laws.* According to Aristotle, politics is a supreme practical art.[4] It is the business of the statesman to legislate and to rule. The work of the statesman is really an art, a supreme art in the sense that it prescribes and provides conditions under which all other arts thrive. He has one practical end in view. That is the well-being of society as a whole, and he must have requisite qualities for the discharge of his responsibilities. These qualities he may acquire, or develop if they are natural in him, by training. A scheme of education is therefore relevant here. For ordered life in the State the individual citizens, including the statesman, must acquire certain qualities of mind and body by a

4 A. E. Taylor, *Aristotle*, Nelson and Sons Ltd., London, 1945, p. 125.

course of education, which is the same for both men and women.

Happy life is indeed the end of all men. But how could men be happy? Plato speaks of three features of happy life. It is an end in itself and is not a means to anything else. It must satisfy us completely and is a way of life a wise man lives. Aristotle broadly agrees with Plato. As Aristotle points out, everything and every being in the world has its proper work. The eye, for instance, sees and seeing is its proper work. So also the work of the ear is to hear. The main function of a living thing is to live; the life of "feeding and growing" is common to all living organisms; the life of sensation, impulse and feeling is the life of a conscious animal organism. On the other hand, the life of pure thinking is the life lived by God. The life of man is, however, different from these forms of life. It is a life which consists in controlling passions, instincts and impulses by reason. And happiness, strictly speaking, consists in living such a life. The rationalization of the lower nature is therefore the end man seeks or should seek. This is the good he endeavours to attain. Aristotle tells us that this end one can only attain by following a rule, a right rule. If one cannot find it out himself, he has it from the legislator or teacher. Living by a rule is a discipline which engenders the goodness of character. Goodness is inborn in some, while it is acquired by others. Goodness is to the soul what health is to the body. Health is just the balance of the functionings in the body, while goodness is the balance of reason and unreason in man. The legislator is the wise man; he knows the conditions of the well-being of the community, and frames a rule accordingly. The best life, according to Aristotle, is the life lived in co-operation and mutual help in the State. All education should therefore aim to make individual men good citizens. He nevertheless says that there is a life yet higher than political life, and the highest which is the kind of life God lives in thinking Himself in His unity. He means to say that the highest life is the life of contemplation and appreciation of art, literature and music, far above mundane life, to which we can rise by the help of a discipline which necessitates an elaborate scheme of education.

Aristotle works out some details of what he calls "liberal education". Education is so called because it, in his opinion, makes men free, free to think and free to act. There is illiberal education, nevertheless. It covers the mechanical crafts which are today called technical or vocational studies and which enable one to follow a profession to earn a living.

In Aristotle's opinion, for the first five years a child should be allowed to live a spontaneous life of play and kept away from servants or slaves lest their low tastes and evil qualities enter into them. As he tells us, a child should be put to school at the age of seven years. And there should be a graded course of education. Like Plato, Aristotle insists on music and gymnastic as parts of education. The rhythm and harmony of music develop the soft side of human nature by suggesting and stimulating different tender feelings. Plato, however, puts a ban on exciting music on account of its evil effects on those who enjoy it. He wants to abolish tragic art. Aristotle, on the other hand, commends the "most sensational forms of music for their purgative value." As we know, a purgative is a medicine which, when taken, cleanses the bowels. Sensational music or a tragedy with its sensational rendering of the calamities of the hero of a piece, likewise, purifies the mind of emotions like fear and pity that accumulate there. Aristotle is obviously much of a psycho-analyst. Gymnastic would be part of the education of the adults, for bodily exercises would not only make the body strong and free from disease, but also produce the steady qualities of grace and courage in the trainees. Like Plato, he suggests that adults in their later teens must have a course of military training for two or three years. Young people are to take a course in science and high intellectual culture when they have passed out of their teens.

Education in ancient Rome. In ancient Rome, education was given to children in the family, which was Patriarchal in type. In it the father was the supreme authority and it was he who gave instruction to his children in moral, civic and religious duties. It is not definitely known whether there were any schools in the Roman State of that time. Roman education, in any case, was practical and trained the youths to behave properly as citizens and moral agents. Later, however, Greek culture made its way into the Roman Empire and as a result some great centres of learning grew up in Alexandria and some other places where several subjects such as rhetoric, logic, metaphysics, etc. were studied.[5]

Education in the Middle Ages. Politically, the mediaeval period of history begins with the fall of the Roman Empire in 476 A.D. and ended in the fifteenth century. During this period, education in Europe took shape through the agency of the Christian Church. Rome in its shattered state had some emperors who came one after another. But, as they were weak in their authority and power, they were always suspicious of the people. There were already cultural institutes all over the Empire, where people assembled for intellectual pursuits. Justinian, the Roman Emperor, suspected that people were therein conspiring against the State, and issued a royal decree in 529 A.D., closing down all centres of culture. And since that date commenced the Dark Age which extended to the end of the eighth century. Culture was in eclipse during this time. Some culture was, however, preserved in the secret corners of the cathedrals where the clergy pursued some studies, including theology.

Towards the end of the eighth century, Charlemagne "who was crowned Emperor by the Pope in Rome", brought order out of the political chaos of Western Europe and established the Holy Roman Empire with the co-operation of the Western Church. He was a vigorous person with political sagacity. "He could not read or write, but he inaugurated a literary renaissance."[6] Under his patronage there was a general revival of culture. The clergy now came out into the open and established schools all over Europe and began to teach different subjects there. The curriculum comprised rhetoric, grammar, dialectic, theology and some sciences such as arithmetic, geometry, astronomy and music.[7]

5 *Encyclopaedia Britannica*, Vol. 7, p. 965.

6 B. Russell, *A History of Western Philosophy*, George Allen and Unwin, London, 1946, p. 413.

7 D.J.B. Hawkins, *A Sketch of Mediaeval Philosophy*, Sheed and Ward, London, p. 11.

Charlemagne invited some scholars from England and Ireland. By the end of the eleventh and in the course of the twelfth century, some universities arose out of the Cathedral Schools, including the University of Paris in France and the University of Oxford and the University of Cambridge in England. The earliest University of Europe is said to have been established in Bologna and the University of Paris was the greatest of the mediaeval universities.

In the universities, studies were pursued under four faculties, namely, arts (grammar, literature and logic), theology, law and medicine.[8] Therein the pattern of modern university education was set up.[9] The Degree course, research-studentship, and the post-graduate Degree of modern universities correspond respectively to the three stages of higher education marked in the mediaeval universities, namely, Baccalaureate (Baccalaureus), Licenciate, and Mastership (Magister). The emphasis was laid on the third course. No one was allowed to teach without mastery over the subject in question as well as speech. Most of our present-day teachers fall short of this high standard of efficiency. The Convocation of a university, nowadays held annually, is a mediaeval innovation.

Some important theories of education were developed in modern times. Here we consider only the theory of John Locke and that of Rousseau.

Locke's theory. Locke works out his theory of education in the *Thoughts concerning Education*, The *Conduct of the understanding* and The *Second Treatise of Government*. According to him, the training of the mind is the end of education. But it does not mean that the body is to be neglected. He in fact emphasizes physical education. For the health of the body he prescribes sufficient open air, exercise, sleep, a balanced diet and suitable clothing.[10]

The child is to be stimulated by example and is to form

8 *Encyclopaedia Britannica* Vol. 7, p. 967.

9 Will Durant, *The Story of Civilization*, Vol. IV, (The Age of Faith, Simon and Schüster, New York, 1950, pp. 1939-40.

10 Robert R. Rusk, *Doctrines of the great Educators*, Macmillan And Co., Ltd., London, 1937, p. 120.

good habits. Locke does not want that the child should become a prodigy. He simply wants him to conform to the common social standards or rules. He, therefore, lays emphasis on practice. Habits are to be formed by imitation. But the fittest time for children to attend to anything is when they are in good spirits and are well disposed to learn a thing. The whole responsibility for making provision for the education of the children falls on the parents. Locke says,

> "The power, then, that parents have over their children arises from that duty which is incumbent on them, to take care of their offspring during the imperfect state of childhood. To inform the mind and govern the actions of their yet ignorant nonage, till reason shall take its place and ease them of that trouble, is what the children want, and the parents are bound to.[11]
>
> "Nay, this power so little belongs to the father by any peculiar right of nature, but only as he is guardian of his children, that when he quits his care of them he loses his power over them, which goes along with their nourishment and education, to which it is inseparably annexed, and it belongs as much to the foster-father of an exposed child as the natural father of another; so little power does the bare act of begetting give a man over his issue, if all his care ends there, and this be all the title he hath to the name and authority of a father."[12]

The parents must engage a tutor for their sons, who should be taught rules following which in practical life they would form wholesome habits.

The curriculum, according to Locke, would include reading, play, writing, drawing, shorthand, and French. When he can speak and read French he would proceed to Latin. But while he learns these foreign languages he should not neglect to learn English. Besides these, Locke's curriculum includes geography, astronomy, chronology and also some

11 The *Second Treatise of Government*, Basil Blackwell, Oxford, 1956, p. 29.

12 *Op. cit.*, pp. 32-33.

parts of history, geometry, ethics, law and English.

Locke himself discusses the question: "To whom should grammar be taught?" He answers by saying that men learn a language for communication and social intercourse and that so far as this purpose is concerned the way of learning a language by conversation will suffice; for this purpose grammar is not necessary. However, there are others who should speak and write their language properly and correctly. According to Locke, they should study grammar among other helps to speaking it well. There is, again, a third group of men who try to master two or three learned languages. They indeed need to study the grammar of the language they want to learn. We believe that logic and rhetoric are the means of training the intellect. Locke, however, discards this view. In his opinion, the pupil derives no benefit from such studies. He nevertheless contends that memory is necessary to all conditions of life and that it should be developed through proper exercise. He says that mere book-learning is useless. One cannot possibly live on books. He tells us that the pupil must learn a trade, and the trades he recommends are gardening, husbandry, and "working in wood as a carpenter."

The education of a young English gentleman, as Locke calls an English boy, would not be complete without travel. Travel indeed expands the sphere of one's knowledge and broadens one's outlook. But, according to Locke, travel should be undertaken by the pupil when he has grown up. It appears that he has no programme of education for girls.

Rousseau's theory : According to Rousseau, there are two types of education that are apparently opposed to each other, namely, public and private education. The former is common to many, while the latter concerns and is confined to an individual.[13] For an explanation of public education Rousseau refers his readers to Plato's theory of education, which is worked out in the *Republic and the Laws*. He nevertheless explains it to some extent himself by saying that it is one of the tasks of the State to make provision for public education. He seeks to clarify his position by citing the systems of education that prevailed in

13 Rusk, p. 140.

some countries such as Sparta and ancient Persia.[14]

In the *Emilĕ* and other works, on the other hand, Rousseau gives an account of private education, which he calls the education of the home. In it the mother is presented as the centre of home life. He there brings to light the duties and responsibilities of the parents. According to him, there are three factors in education, which must be considered. They are: "the endowmnnt, the social environment, and the physical environment of the world." And an ideal system of education involves the interaction and harmony of these factors.

Rousseau divides the pupil's life into four periods: infancy; childhood—up to the age of twelve years; boyhood—from the age of twelve to that of fifteen years; adolescence—from the age of fifteen years onwards until the pupil attains manhood. "Education begins at birth," says Rousseau.[15] So he prescribes a course for the care of the infant. Like some other educationists, he lays stress on the role of habit in education, although about habits he often makes contradictory statements such as "Education itself is but habit". "The only habit the child should be allowed to contract is that of having no habits." The contradiction disappears, however, if we recognize the fact that in the first statement by "*habit*" Rousseau means the natural habits of the body, whereas in the second by "habit" he only means conforming to social customs and usages. He obviously condemns the latter because customs consist in control and compulsion. He attaches value, however, to the habit of man to follow the rule of reason.

Rousseau says that freedom is the greatest good. And a man is truly free when he is able to follow and does his desires. The rules of education indeed derive from this maxim. So he tells us that the child should be allowed to indulge in his plays, pleasures and delightful instincts. He deprecates the system of education that imposes restrictions upon the child and mars the joys of his life by the hope of a happy future which

14 *Op. cit.*, p. 141.
15 *Emilé*, Book I.

would never come. Such freedom in the child is possible only within certain limits. These are determined by the nature and necessity of things and his own weakness. In order to promote freedom in the child education must act positively and also negatively. The negative aspect of education is just bringing the child to realize that there is no conflict between freedom and necessity and that he can command Nature only by obeying her. In any case, Rousseau wants to form in the child the habit of right action, and, in his opinion, the child can form such habits only by following the laws of nature. He must find necessity in things and not in the arbitrary creation of men.

There are in fact two kinds of dependence, dependence upon things and dependence upon society. The former is non-moral, whereas the latter leads to virtue or vice. So the basic principle for early education up to the age of twelve years is: "keep the child dependent on things only." This is amoral or non-social education. This is teaching through games, songs and amusements. This period of the child's life is very important. and we have to take good care of it. During this period the child should be educated outside society. The child should not be punished. If he deviates from the nature of things, he would suffer as a natural consequence. But it does not mean that Rousseau is opposed to morality or moral life. According to him, morality is the ultimate aim of education. Still, the only moral maxim he wants to impart to the child is: "Never hurt anybody." The child should not be taught by fables, he says, for out of them he would choose only what is wrong.

Rousseau nevertheless wants to give the pupil some training for social life. It would consist in imitating actions which we like to form into habits. The pupil must not be given any verbal lesson; he would proceed only by experience. Rousseau relegates the study of languages to the lumber room of education. It is all useless. Geography is only teaching the map. At the early stage the pupil should not be put to the study of history, for it presupposes knowledge of the State and political action. The course of early education would comprise physical exercise and the proper application of the senses.

The second phase of education which covers the period of twelve to fifteen years must fulfil the pupil's present needs.

The principle of utility must be the guiding principle here. The pupil should not be taught science. He should only be led on to it. He should learn a trade, and the trade which is most useful, according to Rousseau, is that of the carpenter. "Teach by doing" and "Learn by doing" should rule the mind of the teacher and also the mind of the pupil. The child should learn to observe and must observe things for himself.

The third phase of education covers the period of adolescence. During this period, the pupil must begin to study himself in relation to his fellow social beings. This is the crucial stage in the development of the pupil's mind, the previous stages being only a preparation for it. It is here that the pupil develops his moral sense. "Let him know that man by nature is good, let him judge his neighbour by himself; but let him see "how men are depraved and perverted by society." At this stage subjects like history would be included in the curriculum. There are difficulties, however, about the study of history. According to Rousseau, history records the evil rather than the good. It does not present men as they live and grow in their peaceful lives in their families and among their friends.

Rousseau now considers the problem of religious education. By religious education he does not mean that the pupil is to be affiliated to a religious sect. By it he only means that sort of training which would help the pupil to form a conception of God by the right use of his reason. By this training people would have a common belief and thus be prevented from coming into conflict with each other in their private opinions. Intuitionism is the philosophy on which the religious creed is based, and really proceeds out of the inner light. He says, "The Being who moves the universe and orders all things is what we call God." He in fact emphasizes the teleological argument for the existence of God. There are signs of design in Nature, and there is need for a cause of this design. He adds that men have freedom of the will in spite of the fact that God is the Ordainer of the universe.

In addition to instruction in ethics and religion Rousseau would at this stage introduce the pupils to the study of aesthetics. But their physical training should not be minimized.

As regards sexual instruction, Rousseau points to the laws

of Nature and to the consequences to which the violation of the laws would lead. Marriage is to be regarded as a sacred bond, and the pupil should be taught to respect it and the duties and responsibilities that surround it. He should imbibe the idea that his health, happiness, courage, virtue—in short, all that is good for him—would depend upon his sexual purity or chastity. The sexual instinct dominates human life. So, according to Rousseau, this instinct must be transformed by directing the energy involved in it towards the ideal of true womanhood.

Rousseau recognizes the fact that there is difference between man and woman. So he speaks of a double standard of education. "A man seeks to serve, a woman seeks to please ; the one needs knowledge, the other taste." "Liberty is the watchword of the boy's education, restraint is that of the girl's." And so on. He seems to be of the opinion that the boy's religion is based on reason and that the girl's is based on authority. This antithesis between boys and girls, between men and women suggests that the education of woman should complement that of man. Rousseau, however, maintains that woman is only to be a source of delight to man and that the education of woman should be planned accordingly. But such a double standard of education was repudiated by Plato in ancient times and is discarded by most of the educationists of the present time.

Education of ancient India. At a certain stage of social development in ancient India, there was a fourfold organization of society, and there were four classes or castes with their respective duties. The four castes were : Brāhmaṇas, Kshatriyas, Vaiśyas, and Śūdras. For the three upper castes there were four orders or stages of life, namely, that of the student, of the householder, of the hermit, and of the ascetic in the woods. Student life was the first stage. The child at the proper age was presented to the teacher for education. After initiation into the sacred formula and being invested with the sacred thread, the pupil began his study. He lived with the teacher and served him in all possible ways and studied the Veda along with some subsidiary subjects, namely, *Śikshā* (pronunciation), *Chhanda* (metre or prosody),

Vyākaraṇa (grammar), *Nirukta* (etymology), *Jyotish* (astronomy), and *Kalpa* (sacrifice). He rose at dawn and retired at night at the prescribed time. He worked and rested in the day-time. Student life in ancient India was indeed a strenuous sort of life and a hard discipline. The course of education covered 36 years or half that time or a quarter thereof. When the student had finished his studiest he ceremony known as the Convocation was held at which the teacher enjoined him to continue his study and do the duties appropriate to the next stage of life. The student now took leave of the teacher and with his blessings entered upon the second stage of life.[16]

The scheme of education prescribed in ancient Hindu society was meant for the males belonging to the three upper classes and was exclusive of the Śūdras and women of all classes. The Śūdras were originally non-Aryans and were taken into the Aryan fold after proper purification. They thus formed the lowest class, and their main work was to serve the upper classes. For the purpose of serving other people there was no need for any education for the Śūdras. The aim of education in ancient India was indeed very high. It was to give training to the pupil both in body and in mind for the purpose of spiritual life, which was, however, denied to the Śūdras only for the reason that they were non-Aryans. As regards women, it was pointed out that for them also there was no need for an elaborate course of education, and, if any, it was very inconvenient for girls to leave their homes to live with the teacher for a period of time. The law-giver was of opinion that marriage was the aim or end of the life of a woman. And the best thing for her would be to regard her husband as her teacher and to serve him with devotion. The idea, in short, was that man and woman were different in their nature as well as in their functions. Women were simply to bear children and do domestic work for their menfolk. By comparison, ancient Greece was liberal in her conception of education. Therein education was meant for all citizens, irrespective of class, colour

16 For details *vide* Chapter VIII.

and sex, the idea being that intelligence and other mental capacities were equally distributed in men and women, and in all men.

The tradition of Vedic education continued in the country for a long time till in changed circumstances the curriculum was modified or extended according to the needs of the taught. Later, in some territories studies were centralized or organized on a mass scale under the auspices of Buddhist monasteries; teachers and students assembled at a place and did their teaching and studies under the direction of one academic authority. Thus there arose some universities in India in the fairly remote past. In this connection we can mention the names of three universities, Taxila, Nālandā, and Vikramaśilā. They were the oldest universities of the world.

The University of Taxila was founded in Taxila which was the capital of a province of Gāndhāra. By the 7th century B. C. it became a great centre of learning. It was about 20 miles west of Rawalpindi.[17] It was famous even when Alexander the Great invaded India in the 4th century B.C.

Nālandā was about 55 miles southeast of Pataliputra and about 7 miles north of Rajgir in Bihar.[18] The University of Nālandā was founded in 450 A.D. and was in existence in the time of Harshavardhana (7th century A. D.) and developed under his patronage. Scholars from different countries of Asia came to this university for study and research. About ten thousand students studied different subjects, such as theology, logic, art, literature, mathematics, medicine and chemistry. Fa Hien, a Chinese traveller, visited this university, and another Chinese scholar, Huen Tsang, came and stayed at Nālandā in the 7th century, for several years for the purposes of study and copying some rare manuscripts.

The University of Vikramaśilā was founded by King

17 A. S. Altekar, *Education in Ancient India*, Nand Kishore, Varanasi, 1957, pp. 105-116.

18 Radhakumud Mookerjee, *Ancient Indian Education*, Macmillan And Co. Ltd., London, 1947, pp. 478, 557.

Dharmapāla in the 8th century A.D. in Bihar 24 miles east of Bhagalpur. In the 11th century Sri Jñān Dipankar who is also known as Upādhyāya Atīśa, was a great scholar of this university.

Owing to political vicissitudes in India, the development achieved in the field of education was not maintained. The tradition of Vedic education, however, somehow continued in the form of classical learning imparted in *Tols* or Sanskrit schools. Under Mohammedan rule, Sanskrit schools were paralleled by Islamic schools of sacred studies.

With the establishment of British rule in India in the eighteenth century the educational set-up in the country changed. English education was introduced into British India. Schools, colleges, and universities modelled on British universities, were founded in the major provinces. Addressing those who opposed English education, Raja Ram Mohun Roy said, "If it had been intended to keep the British nation in ignorance of real knowledge the Baconian philosophy would not have been allowed to displace the system of the schoolmen which was the best calculated to perpetuate ignorance. In the same manner the Sanskrit system of education would be the best calculated to keep the country in darkness, if such had been the policy of the British legislature. But as the improvement of the native population is the objective of the Government, it would consequently promote a more liberal and enlightened system of education, embracing Mathematics, Natural Philosophy, Chemistry, Anatomy with other useful sciences, which may be accomplished with the sums proposed by employing a few gentlemen of talent and learning educated in Europe and providing a College furnished with necessary books, instruments and other apparatus."[19]

What English education did for the country is a long story. It is not possible to go into it here. We may, however, note that early in the twentieth century some great Indians became critical of it and others proposed a synthesis of traditional Eastern and modern Western systems of

19 *The English Works of Raja Ram Mohun Roy*, Allahabad, 1906, pp. 471-474.

education. In this connection three names are worthy of mention. They are: Rabindranath Tagore, Sri Aurobindo, and Mahatma Gandhi.

Rabindranath was both critical and constructive in his view of education.[20] He criticized English education, and the points of his criticism are as follows :—

English is a foreign language, and it requires a long time to master it. In schools boys and girls spend much of their time over this language. But they cannot learn it properly, particularly because those who teach in schools and colleges are proficient neither in English nor in their mother tongue. This is a sorry state of things. Power of thought and imagination is essentially necessary for life. Young students only struggle with English and scarcely find time and an opportunity to develop their mental capacities by a free exercise of them. It is easy to pass examination by learning things by heart from books. But that is not the way to have a developed mind.

As regards books, it is true that books are records of knowledge achieved in the past. In the matter of education books are only a means or an aid to both teachers and students. But there are two kinds of books, readable and unreadable. Most of the text-books prescribed in schools and colleges are intellectual dustbins. As we see, the destitutes drag their miserable existence by eating from garbage heaps. Our students likewise intellectually feed on rotten stuff presented to them. They cannot therefore have healthy intellect. Furthermore, mere books, however good, will not do. Students pass and can pass examinations by reading books. But their minds cannot develop that way.

As to the teacher, he seeks students, for he needs them. He, like ancient Sophists, sells education. He is the shopkeeper, the students are his customers and education is his commodity. Teaching indeed means imparting ideas. But the teacher finds it easier to deceive the students than to give them light. The school is a machine and the teacher an im-

20 *Rabindra Rachanāvalī*, Viśvabhāratī, Vol. XII, Sections on *Sikshā*; *Asramer Rup O Vikash*; *The Centre of Indian Culture*.

portant part of it. "To our misfortune we have, in our own country, all the furniture of the European university—except the human teacher."

Tagore's constructive view. Rabindranath suggests an overall change in the system of education of the country. According to him, instruction must be imparted through the mother tongue. That is to say, in schools and colleges, even in the universities the mother tongue must be the medium of instruction. In that case, the minds of the students would be relieved of the strain of learning a foreign language. Children have a natural hold on their mother tongue, and they become increasingly proficient in it as they grow up. An easy flow of language upon thought is possible only if the mother tongue is the medium of instruction.

As Tagore tells us, education means the training of the human spirit. So education is not worth the name if it is devoid of joy. But joy accompanies education if it is imparted in the natural surroundings in which boys and girls are born and brought up. In ancient India, a boy went to a spiritual preceptor for learning, who lived, generally, in his cottage in a forest in a genial natural environment, full of trees, flowers corn fields, rivers and rivulets. But in modern times we cannot have hermitages in place of schools. It is, again, not possible to have a Yājñavalkya to teach our children. We may, however, have well-trained teachers to guide them. There need not be any chair, table or bench. The teachers and students would sit on the ground in the class room, or under a tree if the weather is fair, and the teaching should be done in direct contact with Nature. Students must practise continence and develop mind and body. No moral instruction should be given to them. Such instruction implies that those to whom it is imparted are immoral. The best form of moral teaching is done by example and by creating conditions which make for moral virtue in the youths. If education does not build character in the students, the furniture of the class rooms, however costly, the Committees, Senate and Syndicate are all useless.

By culling the best elements of the system of education of ancient India, Rabindranath established at Santiniketan a school according to his own conception. The aim was to bring about all-round development in the students. As we have seen, he was opposed to English education, and was hypercritical of university education when he said that the universities that were then functioning in the country would collapse with the departure of the British rulers from here. The irony is that for some years now a Central University has been established at Santiniketan with English as the medium of instruction, although the emphasis on Bengali is retained therein.

Mahatma Gandhi, like Tagore, dealt with the problem of education.[21] He developed some fundamental ideas about education, which may be set forth thus:

(1) Real education consists in drawing the best out of the children.

(2) There are three defects in the existing system of education, namely, (a) that it is based on foreign culture, (b) that it is exclusively concerned with the head and ignores the developing of the heart and the hand; and (c) that it is imparted through a foreign language.

(3) The text-books that are taught in schools do not deal with things boys and girls deal with in their homes and are therefore filled with artificial stuff. So, as they proceed with their education, they increasingly become strangers to their homes. Most of the educated youths have not yet renounced or denounced their culture only because it is entrenched in them. The text-books, in any case, must accord with students' home life and their surroundings.

(4) More than 80% of the population of the country live in villages and are agriculturists. In the circumstances, "it is a crime to make education merely literary." Their bookish learning makes boys and girls unfit for manual work. They forget all about the professions to which they were born. And as they grow up they find it difficult to earn a living.

(5) "Character-building is independent of literary education. Boys and girls build their character by imbibing good ideas from their parents and teachers. But who are the

21 Nirmal Kumar Bose, *Selections from Gandhi*, Navajivan Publishing House, Ahmedabad, 1957, pp. 283-85.

teachers in schools? The teachers are those who take up the job of teaching because they do not find any other, and they teach, not because they are fitted for teaching, but because we do not find any other people for the purpose. The poorly educated teachers can neither impart instruction to youngsters nor influence them by any quality of character.

(6) Education must be given to boys and girls, men and women. Women must have education not only for their development, but also for the good of men and for well-planned home life. Apparently, there is no difference between a human being and a lower animal. Both of them eat, sleep and procreate. The former, however, has knowledge or the capacity for knowledge which is developed by education. Education is therefore a privilege of man. If women are not educated, men would proceed in a lopsided manner.

Gandhi takes education in three stages, namely, Basic or Preliminary Education, Primary, and Higher Education.

Basic Education. At the preliminary stage, instruction without books should be given to children of tender age. They need not learn the alphabet, or to read and write. They should be taught orally. It is a false idea that intellect is best trained by book-learning. "The true education of the intellect can come through a proper exercise and training of the bodily organs." The emphasis is to be put upon the proper use of the bodily organs. Education means the drawing out of the best in the child in body, mind and spirit, i.e., the all-round development of the child. And its education should begin with learning a useful handicraft. Every school for education should be self-supporting, and it is one of the functions of the State to establish such schools. Children should be taught handicrafts like spinning and weaving, not mechanically, of course, but intelligently, so that they understand the process of manufacturing a thing. Along with the crafts they should be taught elementary history and geography by word of mouth. They will learn mathematics as they learn handicrafts. This scheme of Basic education is a revolutionary one. This was attempted in Gandhi's āśramas under his direction, but is not nowadays taken seriously by anybody.

Primary Education. According to Gandhi, primary education

is education up to the Matriculation less English. Education imparted today in High Schools is taken to represent secondary education, i.e., the second stage of education under the current system. Gandhi, however, takes primary education in his own way. It is obviously less than what is imparted in High Schools. His scheme is a little advantageous in the sense that it consists of some handicrafts plus liberal education. There would indeed be teaching by books subjects like history, geography and mathematics. But a practical bias would be given to education. Every student would be taught a vocation which he may follow and earn a living when he has finished his education. In this way, we can, on the one hand, prevent the people becoming a nation of clerks, or a mass of unemployed men and, on the other, retain the village crafts for the, people to benefit from. That way there would be established also a wholesome relation between the villages and the cities. There would be no need for people to leave their village homes and crowd in the cramping surroundings in the cities. Gandhi plans primary education with a view to carrying education to all children of the country. This primary education would cover elementary principles of sanitation, hygiene nutrition, helping in the domestic work of the family, and "physical training with musical drill." Primary education must be compulsory.

Modern factory production, we believe, has lessened people's interest in the village crafts. Some of them, nevertheless, are still important and persist. The Government will do well to organize Gandhi's scheme of primary education on a nation-wide scale.

Higher Education. Gandhi wants to revolutionize college education by linking it to national necessities. There would be, according to him, provision for Degree courses in engineering with its different branches. Engineers would be required to fulfil some purposes of the State. They would be attached to different industrial organizations, each of which would have a college to train engineers under the supervision of the State. There would indeed be arts colleges. But they would be run independently without State aid, the idea being, perhaps, that such colleges do not serve any national purpose. There would, of course, be medical colleges. But they would be attached to hospitals. Gandhi, obviously, has no scheme of university education. As regards higher education, his position may be summed up thus. He is not opposed to higher education, but is opposed to expenditure on higher education being met from the national exchequer. Education imparted in arts colleges is all useless, sheer waste of energy, time and money. It leads to unemployment among the so-called educated men and women. Such education, being concerned only with the head, affects the physical health of our boys and girls. Higher education is, again, imparted through a foreign tongue. This is preposterous. The medium of higher education is causing intellectual as well as moral injuries to the nation. It is no use arguing that great thinkers and scientists have been produced by English education. Jagadish Chandra Bose, for example, was a product of English education. Gandhi defends his position by saying that Bose became a great scientist in spite of the handicaps from the foreign language as the medium of instruction. That only shows his intellectual acumen and originality. Every nation, in fact, has the mother tongue as the medium of instruction. This is natural. To cite an example, the Japanese do not feel any inconvenience with their own language.

Religious Education. The question is often asked: Should religious instruction form part of the school curriculum? According to Gandhi, religion is a personal affair and there should be no interference with it from outside. So there is no question of the State sponsoring a religion, and the State cannot take upon itself the task of religious instruction. There are different religions and religious instruction should be left to different religious bodies or associations. It is important that every child be acquainted with the elements of his religion and scriptures.[22] Religious education indeed covers all this. Gandhi, however, makes a distinction between religion and moral life, though religion involves moral life. He, therefore, distinguishes between religious instruction and

22 H. A. Jack, *Wit and Wisdom of Gandhi*, Perennial Press, Bombay, 1961, p. 121.

ethical teaching. There are different ideas of God and different religions. But there are some fundamental ethical conceptions common to the religions. So the State should make provision for ethical teaching which would promote the mutual relationships between the citizens of the State. One should not mix up religious with ethical teaching.

It is now quite clear that Gandhi wants to give a practical bias to education. According to him, the State should sponsor only that sort of education which is useful to it. It seems that in his opinion the State should be concerned with engineering and medical science. But his view regarding the place of the sciences in his scheme of education is not quite clear. He is, however, vehemently opposed to arts colleges. According to him, they are sheer waste, and the State should have nothing to do with them. He repeatedly tells us that character building is the aim of education. We have, then, to consider whether the study of humanities—history, philosophy, politics, etc.—has any relevance to intellectual and moral development. If the present state of liberal or literary education is deplorable for reasons best known to us, Gandhi might suggest a way to improvement. He does not do anything of the kind, however. He instead makes short work of arts colleges. Education is, nevertheless. a complicated problem, and we cannot solve it by oversimplifying it.

Aurobindo's theory of Education. Aurobindo enunciates three principles of education. "The first principle of true teaching", he says, "is that nothing can be taught."[23] All that he means is this, that the teacher is not to fill the mind of his pupil with information from outside, but is to draw the best out of him. The utmost that can be done in teaching is to direct the activity of the pupil's mind. Unlike a sculptor, the teacher deals with human material which he cannot shape in any way he likes. He can only by suggestion help it grow and develop. The teacher is only to be a guide and not a drill-master.

23 Sri Aurobindo, *A System of National Education*, p. 3; *cf.* A. C. Das, *Sri Aurobindo and Some Modern Problems*, General Printers, Calcutta, 1958, p. 124.

There is a second principle of education, according to Aurobindo. It is that "the mind must be consulted in its growth." All minds are not of the same type. Each mind has its peculiar capacities and aptitude. So the teacher must be a trained psychologist and must guide his pupil according to his disposition and tendencies. "The chief aim of education should therefore be to help the growing soul to draw out that in itself which is best and make it perfect for a noble cause."

Aurobindo mentions yet another principle, a third principle of education which is : we have to look into the past and look forward to the future. It is only from the past that we get clues as to the method of moulding the present. The past is the foundation, the present the material and the future our aim. With this end in view he now proceeds to outline a scheme of education, which we analyze below.

An outline of Aurobindo's scheme of education. The sense-organs are the windows of the organism, so to speak. They must be preserved with care and protected against possible diseases. Children should be taught to observe things minutely. Much of our knowledge of the external world comes through the senses. So it is necessary that they mutually confirm each other. The hand and the speech may be brought to the aid of the senses. If the hand can reproduce what the eye sees, the object seen becomes articulate and the image of it is clarified. What is meant is that children should be taught drawing and modelling with clay or any other stuff in order to compel minute observation and to kindle curiosity in them. They should also be trained to speak out their ideas. The effort to express ideas means much activity. They cannot be freely expressed unless they are perfectly formed and systematically arranged in mind.

The yogic discipline must be included in the educational scheme. We should introduce elementary yogic exercises into schools and colleges. By these exercises students will purify the nervous system of the inner obstacles to the healthy functioning of the senses. This process of purification consists in regulating breathing. Once the rhythm of inhaling and exhaling is established, all impediments to the free play of the life force would be removed. Students have to practise

Brahmacharya—continence. They must conserve bodily energy if they want to live a healthy and happy life.

The training of reason. Knowledge gained through the senses is systematized by intellect or reason. The study of reason is therefore very important. Ordinarily, the training of reason which is the logical faculty is done by teaching the science of logic. But book-learning is not important. One may learn by rote a whole book on logic, yet his reasoning faculty may remain undeveloped. Strictly, the reasoning faculty is developed by a proper exercise of it. For this purpose the teacher should give talks to students discussing the relationships between things of everyday experience. The study of logic as a subject should, in any case, be taken up at a higher stage of education. There, again, we have to see how far the study of logic has a bearing upon the development of the intellectual capacity of the students. It will not do to cram their minds with Aristotle, Mill, Jevons and Bain.

The faculty of intuition. Intellect in man is somewhat developed. But intuition in him remains undeveloped. That there is an intuitional fringe of every act of intellection is shown by the powers of the geniuses. The element of genius in the pupil is rather embarrassing to the teacher. But the teacher has to see that the genius in the pupil is not in any way stifled. There should be provision for its nurture and growth.

At what age should children be put to school? Children should be put to school at the age of six years. In their earlier years, they should be given sufficient time and opportunity to develop the body and requisite powers of the brains. Study is a hard discipline. Children should not be switched to it at their tender age, or should be switched to it only through play so that they may not find it to be a drudgery.

The medium of Instruction. The medium of instruction is of paramount importance. It does not need saying that the mother tongue is the proper medium of education. If the mother tongue is the medium in schools, the continuity of children's usual mode of communication in the family with the mode through which they receive instruction in schools is maintained to advantage. So in schools children find much the same surroundings as in the family.

The number of studies. In the beginning, there should be a small number of studies. Subjects for study should not be multiplied until the pupils have made some progress in the acquisition of the vocabulary and other details of their own language. And they should not be introduced to a foreign language unless they have learnt to read and write fairly well in their own.

The load of studies. In the present-day Indian schools, the course of study prescribed for children is definitely heavy. They have to learn two or three languages, including Sanskrit. They, again, have to learn a number of subjects, namely, mathematics, history, geography, elementary science, hygiene, etc. And, what is worse, students are introduced to these subjects when they do not have a grounding even in their own language. This is unnatural. Again, Sanskrit is a difficult language. Students have to devote a good part of their life to mastering the Sanskrit grammar. This is sheer waste of time.

Modern Education. There was much of value in the old Indian system of education. But it is not possible, nor desirable, to introduce the old system into our schools and colleges that have to work under modern conditions. A defence of the modern system of education is possible on psychological grounds. It may be pointed out that students study several subjects to advantage. A frequent change of subjects during the day relieves the monotony of the same study and affords an opportunity of choosing a subject in accordance with their bent of mind and aptitude. But it is difficult to ascertain whether one has a talent for this or that course of study. Students themselves do not know, at least at the primary stage, what subjects are suitable for them. They can make their choice if they are put through an academic experiment which is possible under the present system. By taking the students through some different courses and often alternative courses of study at different stages, we give them an opportunity to exhibit their individual capacities and to choose their lines at the higher stages. All this relates to Aurobindo's second principle of education, namely, that the mind of the student must be consulted in its growth.

Moral and Religious Education. The training of the intellect covers only a part of man's being. The other part still remains to be developed. This is man's moral and religious consciousness. The development of the whole man is the aim of education. Therefore, the educational scheme must include moral and religious instruction. "The lack of moral and religious education tends to corrupt the human race." In the middle of last century, some universities were founded in India, and young graduates, generally speaking, grew sceptical of the spiritual tradition of the country. This in the long run led to laxity in the morals of youths of the country. Such a sorry state of things was obviously the result of over-intellectualism in instruction imparted in the newly-started universities. It is to be noted, however, that a mere study of moral consciousness is all theoretical. Such a study is called ethics. But it can have no influence upon one's way of life. Morality is practical and consists in acting according to the moral law. But the moral law, unlike a natural law, exercises no compulsion upon a man, though a man feels that he ought to follow the moral law. The question of moral education therefore turns out to be the question of helping one to develop one's moral sense, the idea being that the more a man develops his moral sense the more inclined he would be to act morally. But how help one to improve one's moral life ?

Religion, on the other hand, consists in living for God, and involves love of God and love of men. But all this is practical. "While it is easy to arrange some kind of curriculum or syllabus which will do well enough for the training of the mind, it has not yet been possible to provide under modern conditions a suitable moral training for the school and college. The attempt to make boys moral and religious by the teaching of moral and religious text-books is a vanity and a delusion, precisely because the heart is not the mind and to instruct the mind does not necessarily improve the heart."[24]

The only way to train a man morally is to rouse him to the right emotion, to put him in the right association and

24 *Vide* A. C. Das, *Sri Aurobindo and Some Modern Problems*, p, 142.

to stimulate the impulses of his essential nature. For moral training children should be put under a strict discipline by which they would mould their habits for the better and develop some settled notions of right and wrong. It is true to say that in the old Indian system of education the *guru* was a man of vast learning and sterling moral character, and the pupil automatically emulated him. But the old system cannot be restored in modern times, primarily because a man of the ancient teacher's quality and character is nowadays rare. "The ill-paid police-like instructor of the present time borne down by the cares of the world and consumed with envy, jealousy and hatred cannot possibly take the place of the saintly teacher of the olden time." Still, we have to depend upon the teacher of the present time, and he can inspire in his pupils moral feelings and moral fervour by his personal life.

As regards religious teaching, it is absurd to think that we shall be able to make children religious by teaching them the dogmas and doctrines of a religion. That way religion becomes mechanical and leads to bigotry and fanaticism. "Religion is to be lived, not learned as a creed." We may nevertheless attach some value to the study of scriptural texts, though we emphasize meditation, prayer, rites and ceremonies.

Aurobindo maintains that education must be national, i.e., based on the traditions of the nation concerned. An individual is born in a country with its tradition, social, political, and religious, and his natural growth requires that he should be nurtured on the culture of the country.

A comparison of the three views considered above. The thinkers we have considered above broadly agree that education aims at the development of children and young people in body, mind and spirit. They also more or less agree how the education of children of tender age should begin. They tell us that the process of their education should be continuous with spontaneous play and imagination which are natural to them. Tagore, Gandhi and Aurobindo indeed recognized the value of the old Indian system of education but they hold that we cannot introduce the old system wholly under modern conditions. Rabindranath, however, in his way made an experiment with a scheme of education by establishing at Santiniketan a school somewhat on the model of an *asrama* school of ancient India. Gandhi, on the other hand, lays emphasis on vocational and useful education and seems to depreciate literary education. He goes to the length of saying that the latter is sheer waste. Aurobindo, for his part, opposes a scheme of the old Indian system. He makes a psychological approach and works out much that would go to justify the modern system of education in all its aspects. Above all, he insists that education be national. But there is one major problem. It is well known how nationalism in its extreme form led to World Conflicts in the past and is even today a source of unrest in the world. We do not know how on the foundation of nationalism and national education we can build a superstructure of internationalism. Unfortunately, Aurobindo or anybody else does not help us in this matter by suggesting how national education should be reoriented in order that nationalism is synthesized with internationalism.

All three—Tagore, Gandhi and Aurobindo, are all for the mother tongue as the medium of instruction. That the mother tongue should be the medium of instruction needs no arguing. And in the present Indian system the regional language is the medium in schools, while English is the medium in colleges? So there is the problem: how adjust school to college education. On the other hand, if it is possible, it is not yet possible, to replace English by the vernacular at all stages of education, there would be a cultural blackout between the Indian States, between India and the world as well.[25] The mother tongue as the medium of instruction is one of the major problems of India today. It needs hard thinking. None can be complacent about it. The aforesaid three thinkers do not quite discuss the problem of co-education.

However, the basic elements of the schemes of education developed in ancient Greece, ancient India and in mediaeval Europe have their place in the modern system of education.

The Modern System of Education. The modern system of

25 *Cf.* A, C. Das, *Studies in Philosophy*, Firma K. L. Mukhopadhyay, Calcutta, 1962.

education comprises three stages, namely, primary, secondary, and higher education. Primary education is given to children of tender age, of the age of two to six years. At this stage, ideas are imparted to them by suggestion through their play. Education to be imparted at this stage is conceived differently, however, by different educationists. Their conceptions are broadly distinguished as the Nursery School, the Montessori Method, and the Kindergarten system of education.

Kindergarten. Kindergarten is a kind of school founded by Froebel in Germany in 1840 for children of four to six years of age. In this method of education the emphasis was laid upon some play materials. There were six sets of such materials arranged in order of complexity to provide exercises for the child mind. In the Kindergarten school the infants found themselves in the first period of their social life. It was the period in which they met together in one institution and as members of it developed among themselves mutual feelings through their play. The Kindergarten method aims to train children of tender age and teach them how to live harmoniously. Previously, education was given in a mechanical way. Children were at the very beginning introduced to the alphabet and taught to read and write. They learnt their lessons by rote. The Kindergarten method rectified the old way of teaching and brought naturalness and joy to primary education. It arranged for excursions by the pupils and teaching by means of stories, games and hand work. It recognized the fact that children could best learn through play. This system of education devised many useful playthings.[26]

The first Kindergarten school in the United States of America was established in 1855. At the present time there are such schools all over there. At the turn of the twentieth century the aim and method of the Kindergarten were included in those of primary education, and the Kindergarten is now regarded as a grade of primary education, the other grade being the nursery school.

26 *Encyclopaedia of Modern Education*, Ed. by Harry N. Rivlin, Philosophical Library, New York, 1943, pp. 437-38 ; also *Dictionary of Education*, 2nd ed. C. V. Good, McGraw Hill, Book Company, New York, 1959, p. 307.

Nursery school. The nursery school is an educational institution which deals with children of two to four years of age. This kind of school was founded in London in 1907, and was then introduced into America. We are told that the nursery school began in the United States of America as an experiment in New York city in 1917. It then spread over the whole country.[27] Nowadays the Public School System there includes nursery education. The nursery system obviously represents the stage of education prior to that of the Kindergarten. The former is concerned with children of two to four years of age, while the latter with children of four to six years of age. The aim and ideal of the nursery are, however, similar to those of the Kindergarten. The only difference between them is this, that they deal with two different age-groups.

Montessori. Madame Maria Montessori (born in 1870) founded the Montessori method of teaching sub-normal children. Her success with them encouraged her to extend her method to normal children. For them she opened a school in Rome in 1907. She was an Italian psychologist and based her system on the faculty psychology. She believed that the education of children should begin by training one sense at a time. We perceive things with the senses. The senses are, therefore, the basic instruments with which knowledge of things is acquired. It is for this reason that Madame Montessori laid emphasis on the training of the senses. The main features of the Montessori method are the development of the child's power of observation and freedom of action through training, and the creation of social sense in children through their play, excursion, etc.[28]

This method was widely used in Europe, America and some other countries. But it has now been abandoned by most educationists. They prefer the Kindergarten method of teaching.

Higher education. Higher education means college or university education. As we have already seen, the pattern of modern higher education comes from the mediaeval universities, though there is no denying that some features of it have been

27 *Sociological Theory*, Ed. by L. A. Coser and B. Rosenberg, The Macmillan Company, New York, 1957, p. 647.

28 *Columbia Encyclopaedia*, p. 1411 ; also *Encyclopaedia Americana*,, Vol. 19, 1957, p. 404.

newly conceived and worked out. A university is, broadly, an organization of students and teachers for study and research. Some universities are residential in the sense that the teachers and students live in the campus of their institution, while others are affiliating. In the latter case, a number of colleges together with a central authority to guide and control the organization of the colleges constitute a university. However differently the universities may be organized, the courses of study comprised in their curricula are uniform. They are divided into humanities, science and technology. Humanities are the arts subjects, while technology is applied science. These three courses cover or may cover some different faculties such as the Faculty of Arts, the Faculty of Education, the Faculty of Commerce, the Faculty of Law, the Faculties of Science, Medicine, etc. At present education is imparted in Indian universities in three stages, namely, the pre-university, Degree and Post-graduate stages.

These are the days of science, and some think that students should study only science and technology, which are very useful in practical life. But we must remember that according to educationists, ancient and modern, the aim of education is to develop man in body, mind and spirit. Man is not a mere animal. He has indeed his physical needs and must supply these needs. But he is the seat of knowledge as well as moral and spiritual values. So the study of the humanities cannot be neglected, because it has a direct bearing upon his mental and moral development. The study of history, ethics, sociology and philosophy among others gives man an insight into his deeper nature and an understanding of the source of value, which make him so different from a beast or bird. It is therefore legitimate to combine science and the humanities. They together give man an all-round education.

Co-education. The term "co-education" is generally taken to mean that, in spite of the physical differences between the sexes, boys and girls should be taught together in the same institution under the same authority. In ancient times, Plato was a zealous advocate of co-education. He proposed to employ women "at the same tasks as men" and to give them the same education which consisted of music and gymnastic *plus* the art of war. He even proposed that men and women should undergo training in the gymnasium together, women taking exercises naked along with men in the same state.[29] The practice of co-education is modern, however. Early in the nineteenth century girls were admitted neither into schools nor into universities. Even today opinion varies on the principle of co-education.[30] The opponents of co-education press some psychological reasons against it. The most important of them is that during the period of adolescence the sex impulse in boys (between 14 and 25 years of age) and in girls (between 12 and 21 years of age) becomes intense, and that the mixing of boys and girls during this time would aggravate their conditions and lead to irregularities. They, therefore, recommend segregation of girls from boys. We can counter this argument by saying that the sexes have a mutual attraction towards each other, which is indeed increased because of the fact that they are normally kept apart until they are socially related to each other. Generally, either of the sexes has a charm for the other, which is truly enacted by the sex-instinct. If, however, both sides analyze and understand each other, it would mitigate much of the charm with which they view each other. This circumstance would definitely make for judicious sexual selection and a stable family life. But co-education has come into practice not so much because of a principle as by way of an economic necessity. Roman Catholicism, Islam and Orthodox Hinduism are opposed to co-education. But Protestantism and other Progressive cults commend co-education. There is, however, no definite policy or principle behind co-education that prevails in different countries. It came about only by way of convenience.

Into England co-education was introduced at the primary stage of education. In 1945 the Ministry of Education suggested mixed schools if they were found necessary. There was no trouble in so far as the primary stage was concerned because infants are not, if we disbelieve Freud, sexually conscious. Though there was hesitancy about the secondary

29 *Republic*, 451, 452.

30 *Encyclopaedia Britannica*, Vol. 5, p. 928.

stage, yet, as there were not enough resources for establishing separate schools for the sexes and as there was a large number of boys and girls to be accommodated in schools, about half the schools of England became mixed during the nineteenth century. The girls, nevertheless, used to sit on one side of the class room and the boys on the other. Under the Education Act of 1902, many Public High Schools were mixed for reasons of economy and number. The number of mixed high schools was far greater in Wales than in England. The state of affairs was different in Scotland. The population of this country was not dense and the villages were scattered. In consequence, in any area there was not a large number of students to justify separate schools for the sexes. Nevertheless, there has been co-education in Scotland since the 17th century.

In Australia and New Zealand, outside the towns and cities the conditions are such that the schools are bound to be mixed. There are, of course, many single-sex schools at the secondary stage.

In Norway and Sweden co-education is practised on a universal scale. In Netherlands this form of education is partly adopted. The German elementary schools admit both boys and girls but the High Schools are generally single-sex institutions. Germans were comparatively conservatives. In Germany of the nineteenth century it was not possible for girls to get admitted into secondary schools. In Russia of the olden days the schools were single-sex. But under the Soviet regime there has been complete co-education at all stages of education.

In the United States of America, religion and politics have much to do with co-education. The Catholic Schools are opposed to it, while the Protestant ones sponsor it. Previously, the professional schools refused admission to women. But nowadays opposition has broken down. Women are freely admitted into medical colleges, for example.

In the East the idea was that women, being physically different, had their own sphere, i.e., they were to work in the home. So it was taken for granted that women did not require much education. It is true to say that in modern times education was open to women in the East when Christian missionaries established their schools for girls. During the latter half of last century under a system of public education in Japan, separate schools were founded for the sexes. Some time later China adopted co-education. However, in both countries co-education was introduced first at the primary stage. It was around 1920 that universities began to admit women students to their classes. After the Second World War co-education spread all over Japan, and most of its public schools became mixed. According to some, two facts account for the ready adoption of co-education by Japan. One is increasingly close contact with Western culture among the people, and the other is the inability of the Government for economic reasons to establish separate schools for the sexes.

Early in the nineteenth century, Raja Ram Mohun Roy was an ardent advocate of female education. But the question of co-education did not come up to occupy his mind. Afterwards, of course, it worked itself up in India. At first the schools established in India under the system of English education were single-sex. Later indeed some schools became mixed up to the primary level. Secondary High Schools nevertheless remained single-sex. At present, in any case, co-education prevails in most of the Indian universities at the post-graduate level. But only a few Degree colleges are mixed. Generally speaking, there are separate High Schools and separate Colleges for the sexes. In India, policy or principle preponderates against economic reasons. Most of the people do not like that their daughters should mix with boys during their adolescence, although they have confidence in them when they have reached the years of discretion after graduation. Whatever the conservatives may say, co-education has come to stay at the post-graduate stage in India, the chief reason being partly economic and partly academic. It is difficult for lack of resources as well as for want of an adequate number of efficient teachers to have separate universities for the sexes, even though people desire to have them.

Some people point out that in the colleges and universities little is being done to prepare the youths for life.[31]

31 J. K. Folsom, *The Family and Democratic Society*, Routledge And Kegan Paul Ltd., London, 1948, p. 645.

Boys and girls have their different problems such as personality, health, shyness, sex-relation, house-keeping, parent-child relation, etc. It seems that the educationists are not concerned with these problems. All education is more or less a preparation for family life as for vocational and general life. So it is imperative to give sex-education to youths. It would be advantageous to teach them the dangers of illicit sex-relation and the value of complete continence before marriage. An outline knowledge of sex-relation and its responsibility would make co-education more satisfactory than ever.

Religious Education. We have already considered the views Gandhi and Aurobindo held about religious instruction. Here we shall do well to consider some details about it.

As we know, there is an elaborate arrangement for religious instruction in the Christian world. Generally, however, a distinction is made between religious instruction imparted in the Sunday schools and religious education. We are told that there was religious education when there was no Sunday school. Then religious education consisted of going to Church, attending sermons delivered there, praying and meditating. Sunday was a rest day and was meant for religious activities. This spontaneous method of education was supplemented by catechism. The teacher in the early church taught the elements of Christianity by the method of question and answer. The Sunday school is, however, a modern institution which has been organized by some lay people, not by the clergy. The old method of catechism was long neglected by the church. The failure of the church to provide religious instruction to children, in the long run, led to the origin of the Sunday school. In this connection, the name of Robert Raikes, Editor of the *Gloucester Journal*, is worthy of mention.[32] Raikes observed the conditions of the young people employed in the local factories. They worked on week days and had a holiday on Sunday, which they enjoyed in a depraved way. He persuaded a large number of them

32 *Encyclopaedia of Religion and Ethics*, Vol. XII, Ed. by James Hastings, pp. 111-112.

to gather together on Sunday for instruction. He employed four women "at one shilling per day to teach them." This organization, small as it was, came to be set up in 1780 and was known as the Sunday School. It was an enterprise undertaken by some lay Christians. The Sunday School was introduced into the United States of America in the course of time. But from the very beginning the Sunday School was controlled by the Church for the purpose of religious instruction on Sunday. And in no time there arose organizations to uphold and propagate Raikes's institution.

Religious instruction in general. We have briefly considered above how religious instruction in the Christian fold developed. It goes without saying that children should be acquainted with the elements of their own religion. And, as we see, they more or less pick up these from their surroundings, first of all from their families and then, as they grow up, from the sermons delivered and prayers said in the church, mosque, temple, synagogue, as the case may be. This is religious education as distinguished from religious instruction. We are not far wrong when we say that there is arrangement for religious instruction in the form of discourse or discussion in every religion. It is quite good that one thoroughly knows his religion. But there is one great danger about religious instruction in this sense. It tends to make one bigoted and fanatic. The content of a religion consists of some dogmas and doctrines which are formulated so as to make the followers of the religion think that theirs is the only true religion. So a religion which is indeed a way to God becomes a way to hatred and an eventual conflict. Though internationalism has already come upon us, we are still ruled by religious imperialism. Everyone today thinks that his religion is fit to be a world religion. This attitude means that only one religion is true religion and that all the others are trash. But we cannot afford to forget that each of the organized religions has a history and is based on some religious experience or experiences. A religion cannot be made to order, nor can it grow and thrive on falsehood. There is therefore no respite from evil for humanity until the people professing different Faiths come to understand that religion is a way of life and that the religions differ from each other, if ever, only because of topographical and other conditions, they in their essence being one in the sense that they all aim at God. It is here that we must fall back upon the world teachers who teach about all religions and do not extol one religion at the expense of all the others. In this context, we are reminded of Ramakrishna who in the latter half of the nineteenth century demonstrated by practising the major religions and cults that they all led to God. The synthetic teaching of the teachers like Ramakrishna must be broadcast all over the world through educational institutions. Barring this, we do not know how religious instruction can be given to the adults.

CHAPTER XI

SOCIAL MIND

We have already seen that society consists of individual minds. Now a question arises. It is : if society is a whole, is there a social mind over and above the individual minds? Sociologists and social philosophers answer this question differently and in consequence there are different views about the social mind. Let us piscuss them one by one.

I. *The Social Mind as Collective Consciousness.* According to some, the social mind is the collective consciousness of the individual minds. But this view is wrongly ascribed to Hegel.[1] As we know, for him the Absolute is the ultimate reality and the individual minds or selves are only its manifestation. It is, however, a metaphysical category and cannot be clarified with the conception of whole and part. In any case, absolute consciousness cannot be explained as the collective consciousness of the individual minds, for the former far exceeds the latter. So the nature of the social whole cannot be explained by Hegel's metaphysical theory.

One of the British Neo-Hegelians, McTaggart, on the other hand, conceives the relation of the individual selves to the Absolute in terms of society. He maintains that the Absolute in relation to the finite selves is what society is to individuals. Society is a whole which consists of individuals in the sense that society apart from individuals is an abstraction, i.e., no fact. So also is the Absolute apart from the finite selves. It is, in short, the unity which involves the latter. The unity is, indeed, something more than the individual selves which it unifies. But still the Absolute is nothing apart from the selves. The relation between the two sides McTaggart tries to make clear by the help of the concept of society. In direct antithesis to the position that human personality, in Hegel's view, is "only a transient modification of the Absolute, we have the

1 William McDougall, *Group Mind*, Cambridge, 1939, p. 30.

theory that Hegel's Absolute is a *society* of finite but perfect individuals". As McTaggart puts it, "Now Hegel's conception of Absolute Reality is one which might very fitly be called a society. It is a differentiated unity, of which the parts are perfectly individual, and which, for that reason, is a perfect unity."[2] Here the metaphysical theory, far from explaining society, presupposes it. The Absolute itself is conceived as the society of selves, "the most perfect of all societies". Society is a fact of our experience, and we have to analyze its nature and structure.

Espinas holds that society or the social mind is a collective consciousness which arises out of a fusion of the consciousnesses of the individual minds. According to him, individual minds include or embrace each other. In Wündt's words, "It is a sort of creative synthesis resulting in the development of a social mind."[3] As individual consciousness posits an individual mind, so does collective or social consciousness involve a social mind.

Durkheim in his own way makes a distinction between individual and collective representations. The individual consciousness is based on sensations, he says. But the collective consciousness, in his opinion, is the product of the consciousnesses of the individuals. Their mental elements are synthesized and transformed by the "act of fusion." The collective representations exist in the assemblage of individuals in society. As he puts it,

> "In fact, if left to themselves, individual consciousnesses are closed to each other; they can communicate only by means of signs which express their internal states. If the communication established between them is to become a real communion, that is to say, a fusion of all particular sentiments into one common sentiment, the signs expressing them must themselves be fused into one single and unique resultant. It is the appearance of this

2 H. Haldar, *Neo-Hegelianism*, Heath Cranton Ltd., London, 1927, p. 432 ; McTaggart, *Studies in Hegelian Cosmology*, Cambridge, 1901, p. 187.

3 M. Ginsberg, *Psychology of Society*, Methuen And Co., Ltd., London, 1933, p. 51.

> that informs individuals that they are in harmony and makes them conscious of their moral unity. It is by uttering the same cry, pronouncing the same word, or performing the same gesture in regard to the same object that they become and feel themselves to be in unison."[4]

The Individual minds are in fact combined into a collective mind, which is the social mind. According to Durkheim, there are some characteristic features of this collective consciousness or collective mind. First, the collective consciousness is exterior to individual consciousness; the former surpasses the latter. Second, there is a difference in kind between these two forms of consciousness. Society or the social group thinks, feels and acts differently from isolated individuals. Third, the social mind regulates individuals in their thoughts and behaviour and is therefore the highest form of mental life.[5]

II. *The Social mind as a group mind.* McDougall rejects the theory of collective consciousness, and his reason is this: it is true that people often act in a collective way; but it does not follow that they are then fused into one mind. Consider the behaviour of a crowd or mob. A mere concourse of people is not a mob. It becomes one when they confront the same situation, and feel and act in the same way. There are, indeed, some essential conditions of collective action. They are: a common mode of feeling, mutual influence between the individuals and a common interest. To take McDougall's very illustration, let a fire-engine dash through the traffic on the street, and immediately the concourse of people that is there would become a crowd; the individuals would feel and act in the same way. To cite an illustration of our own. One day there was a stir among people on Chowringhee Road near Esplanade at about 7 P.M. when detectives in plain clothes arrested a man and seized from him an unlicensed country-made revolver with four live cartridges. The man struggled with the police but was overpowered. The onlookers nearly caused a traffic jam as they tried to catch a glimpse of him and his weapon. There was something on the road in which

4 Emile Durkheim, *Elementary Forms of the Religious Life*, George Allen and Union, London, p. 230.

5 Ginsberg, p. 56.

the individuals were interested in the same way. But the point is that in the collective feeling and action the people were not combined into one individual. As McDougall points out, there is no spatial contiguity between social individuals to be fused into one consciousness.[6] He further criticizes the theory by saying that it would carry the organic view of society to an extreme, for which there is no justification whatsoever. If there is collective consciousness, there is a collective mind. But there is only the consciousness of the individual mind. McDougall nevertheless speaks of the group mind in the sense of "an organized system of interacting mental or psychical forces." In this sense, certainly there is no mind in a crowd; in it there are only some individual minds without any organization among them.

III. *The Social mind is, again, explained in terms of General Will.* Rousseau and others emphasize the conception of a general will, and seek to explain society as an embodiment of the general will. Broadly, there are five theories of the General Will.[7] They are as follows:

(1) There is general will when every individual in a group or society, or a vast majority of such a group have an idea of the whole they belong to and identify their good with the good of the whole. This is Rousseau's view and appears to be the view also of McDougall when he says that a group mind is a system of interrelations of individual minds.

Society is a complex of individuals with their rights and duties. It does not, however, proceed from Nature, according to Rousseau. A man, in his opinion, has no natural power over another. So right and all it implies rests on a contract. But this contract is not one between ruler and people, but among the people themselves. In the contract by which society is brought into existence every individual surrenders his powers and his goods to the community so as to gain the protection of it. With this act the whole, the body-politic, comes into being and "attains its unity and its

6 McDougall, *Group Mind*, p. 37.

7 Ginsberg, p. 71.

will." The body-politic is the seat of authority—sovereignty. The people are sovereign and law is the general popular will which seeks the common good. As Rousseau puts it,

> "The first, and most important, consequence of the principles so far established is that only the general will can direct the powers of the State in such a way that the purpose for which it has been instituted, which is the good of all, will be achieved.
>
> "I maintain, therefore, that sovereignty being no more than the exercise of the general will, can never be alienated, and that the sovereign, who is a collective being only, can be represented by no one but himself. Power can be transmitted, but not will.
>
> "There is often considerable difference between the will of all and the general will. The latter is concerned only with the common interest, the former with interests that are partial, being itself but the sum of individual wills. But take from the expression of these separate wills the pluses and minuses—which cancel out, the sum of the differences is left, and that is the general will."[8]

These quotations show that according to Rousseau, the general will as the will of the social whole exercising sovereignty is to be distinguished from the individual will. The former is not to be identified with the will of all. The individual will is concerned with private or partial interest, and consequently the sum of individual wills would be concerned with the sum of private or partial interests and as such would fall short of the general will which is concerned with the common interest or common good, i.e., the good of all. Suppose that an individual will has an interest which is p and another has an interest which is q. Now the latter has $-p+q$. If we in this way take a series of wills, we can note the pluses and minuses in relation to each other. Rousseau says that if we take away the pluses and minuses, there is left only the sum of differences between the separate wills, which

8 *Social Contract*, Ed. by E. Barker, Oxford University Press, 1958, pp. 269, 274.

Cf. Bosanquet, *Philosophical Theory of the State*, Macmillan And Co., Ltd., London, 1910, p. 111.

is the general will. But this is only a negative conception of the general will. Positively, however, it is the will of the body-politic which is concerned with the good of all. Nevertheless, the general will is intelligible only in contrast to individual wills and interests. Were there no individual wills, there could be no general will. The idea of a common interest is realized only as against individual or private interests. Individual wills therefore persist and do not merge into the general will.

(2) According to Mackenzie, the general will comes to function in the situation where a decision is reached by way of discussion and a real integration of differences. He tries to make his point clear by the help of an illustration. He takes the instance of a family deciding to go to a place for a holiday.[9] Each member there has his own conception of a holiday. So their conceptions of it are different, though they all agree to go out for a change and they want to go to one place. But how to decide? There are obviously as many possibilities as there are members of the family. The head of the family may, of course, cut short the discussion by forcing his decision upon the other members of the family. But the members may try to come to a decision by discussion, i.e., by overriding their individual interests and by willing the common good of the group. The seeking of the common good of a group brings out the essential feature of the general will. An individual wills a course of activity only after he has arrived at a decision by deliberation. First he faces several alternatives. Then he considers the relative importance and suitability of the alternatives. In the end his point of view prevails and determines the decision. But in the case of the general will an individual feels that there is an urge in him which is external to his personal point of view and impels him to pursue a course in harmony with others.

(3) According to some, the general will is in evidence when society or the social good is the common content of consciousness. It appears that there is no distinct line between

9 J. S. Mackenzie, *Outlines of Social Philosophy*, George Allen And Unwin, London, 1918, p. 54.

the individual and general will. An individual will becomes general when a general interest or general good is its content. Generality and particularity are only two aspects of a will. In this way, perhaps, Spinoza speaks of a common will and a common good.

(4) Wündt bases his theory of the general will on an analysis of the mutual implications of presentation and will. According to him, will is no activity which occurs in a vacuum. It implies presentation, which in its turn presupposes a presentative activity which results from the action of one will upon another. It is clear that one will posits other wills. Wündt thus develops the position that there is nothing like a will in isolation and that there is only a series of wills in mutual relationships. This implies that the individual will is the general will.

(5) B. Bosanquet in his own way identifies the real will with the general will. He makes a distinction between the acts of the will of an individual and the volitional dispositions. He says,

> "Every individual mind, in so far as it thinks and acts in definite schemes or contexts, is a structure of appercipient systems or organized dispositions."[10]

The system of volitional dispositions constitutes the character of an individual. As the character of an individual determines his volitional acts, the former is regarded as the real will of the self. According to Bosanquet, this real will is social in nature and is the same in all individuals. The real will is therefore one will as against the individual wills and is the general will.

It may seem, Bosanquet tells us, that the general will as Rousseau conceives it, has no actual existence, and we might say that it is the will of the whole society as such, or "the wills of all individuals in so far as they aim at the common good. The general will is expressed in law in so far as law is what ought to be; and sovereignty as such...acting for the common interest is the exercise of the General will."[11]

10 *The Philosophical Theory of the State*, Macmillan And Co., Ltd London, 1910, p. 173.
11 *Op. cit.*, p. 107.

Social life, in short, postulates "a will which in some sense transcends the individuals whose will it is and is directed upon an object of wider concern."

Bosanquet makes an approach to Rousseau's thought by analyzing what is implied in "the nature of will as a characteristic of an intelligent being." Bosanquet says that what Rousseau means by the general will is the will in itself or the will as it would be if it carries out what its nature implies. The general will, in Bosanquet's opinion, is the impulse of an intelligent being to a common good. And a true interest is never a private interest. A true interest as opposed to an apparent interest, has the character of a universal as against the sum of particulars. So if everyone pursues his true interest, he would pursue the common interest. In that case, the Will of All will be identical with the General Will. This analysis leads us to the contrast between the real will and the actual will. And we reach out to the real will only through an interpretation of the functioning of an individual will. Bosanquet means to say that the real will is a constant disposition or a system of dispositions which often determines the actual will. The system of dispositions is really "the meeting point of the individual minds which is the social mind."[12]

Criticism. Morris Ginsberg brings some criticisms against the theories of the general will. We shall do well to analyze them. In Bosanquet's theory, the real will is distinguished from the actual will. If the real will is the ideal will and is rational, it is determined by the idea of perfection. In that case, there is scarcely a distinction between the real and the actual will, particularly in view of the fact that the actual will as such is determined by the ideal of perfection. Otherwise, there would be no significance in human life. Will is a deliberate and conscious process and must involve the idea of the good or the ultimate good. There is indeed the sense of the ultimate good in us. But it itself cannot be conceived as the real will as contrasted with the actual will, for what determines the actual will cannot itself be a will.

12 *Op. cit.*, p. 298.

It may be contended that the general will as the real will is rational and is just good will, and that such a will is identical in all individuals. According to Kant, a will is rational when it is determined by the moral law, and individuals act morally when their will conforms to the moral law. But it does not mean that the moral will of one individual is identical with that of another individual. It is no doubt true to say that they will the same principle or content. As Ginsberg points out, the identity of the content of the individual wills does not and cannot establish "the identity of their substantive unity." That is to say, from the fact that individuals seek to realize the same ideal, it does not follow that there is one self-identical will besides or over and above the individual wills.

As regards Wündt's position that the individual will is really a general will, there are two alternatives for us to accept, either there is no real distinction between the individual and general will, or the individual and general will are combined in one entity, though we cannot understand how opposition between them is overcome. One definite point is, nevertheless, urged against those who posit a general will as against the individual wills. It is this: in the case of a volition we have to make a distinction between the act and the object. And there are ideas, ideals and acts of will. Ideas and ideals are entertained by individual minds, and they have much in common. Still, corresponding to the community of them we cannot posit a general mind. The community itself is a content for individual minds. Similarly the individual wills desire different things and act differently. Even if there be a common interest, it is willed by the individual wills, and is a common content for them all. But on the basis of a common content for the individual wills we cannot posit anything like a general will. It is only an individual that wills, and there is no will of the body-politic, for it is only a whole which consists of individuals and is not itself a conscious individual. If there be, then, no general will, it is futile to conceive of the social mind in terms of the general will.

IV. *Social mind as social harmony.* This view has been developed by L.T. Hobhouse. He seems to depreciate the conception that society is an organism when he says,

> "To speak of society as if it were a physical organism is a piece of mysticism, if indeed it is not quite meaningless."[13]

He, however, agrees that the term "organic" applies to the life of society in the sense that it consists of interdependent parts. And the social life of a man is a harmony. The word "harmony" has many applications. There is a harmony in the life of an individual, and also the harmony of the individual and his geographical conditions. There is, again, "the harmony of man in society." However, harmony in its different senses is not spontaneous, but is achieved by efforts, intelligence and will. So to understand harmony is to understand the psychology of man, and harmony, especially harmony in society, we can analyze only in terms of psychical facts.

The important fact we have to recognize is that the social *milieu*, to a great extent, determines the thought and will of the child from his birth. The social *milieu* consists of the physical environment and settled ideas, thoughts and habits of the generations which precede him. It is indeed true that thought exists only in the mind of an individual. But a man does not think in an isolated context. The thought of a generation, even of an individual, is a social product. An individual has thought and will only in relation to other individuals. Furthermore, there is the sum of thought at any time. But this sum does not exist in the mind of an individual; it is something which is brought about by many minds in their mutual relationships. If we consider an advanced complex science, we find that it cannot be reduced to the thoughts of a single individual mind. But the science as a body of knowledge is used for social and individual purposes. It is, again, embodied in a book. The science is social knowledge or thought. But it is not that this thought exists in the mind of a mysterious unit called society. Nor is it the common property of all individual minds, but is the product of many minds in their relationships. Individuals start from this thought and are brought up in it.

13 *Social Evolution and Political Theory*, The World Press Private Ltd., Calcutta, 1962, p. 87.

There is also a social will. It is more pervasive and permanent than an individual will. The social will gets embodied in institutions and customs and through its embodiment determines "all modes of action that the existing constitution of society dictates."

It is now sufficiently clear that when Hobhouse speaks of social thought, social will, or rather of social mind he does not refer to any mystical psychological entity. The term "social mind" he employs only as an expression for a mass of ideas which serves to direct or guide the thoughts and actions of individuals. The function of an individual mind is to organize the life of the individual, while the function of the social mind is to organize the life of society, to exercise control over the environment and the relations of individuals to one another and of one community to other communities.

Hobhouse's theory that the social mind is social harmony clarifies some of the theories of the social mind, especially the theory developed by McDougall, that there is a group mind besides the individual minds, which is "constituted by the system of relations between the individual minds which are its units."

Ginsberg criticizes this view by saying that society is not a mind any more than a house is a brick, consisting as it does of bricks. The fact, however, remains that the nature of the house is to be understood in the light of the nature of the bricks. This point Hobhouse emphasizes. The problem of a social mind is, then, the problem: what kind of reality is the social whole? Ginsberg means to say that it is a mistake to conceive community as a mind.[14] But we cannot deny that group life is based on ideas, interests and values which constitute a coherent system. But this system is not a product of any individual mind. On the other hand, every individual is born to it and is sustained by it. The question is whether we can legitimately speak of this system as the social mind as distinct from the individual minds. We are thus led on to consider a very important theory, the theory developed by F.H. Giddings.

14 *The Psychology of Society*, 1933, p. 66.

V. *Giddings's theory of the Social Mind.* According to Giddings, the consciousness of kind is the basic social fact in the sense that society or social life developed out of it. This consciousness is the innate sense of kinship in conscious beings. It was because of this sense, says Giddings, that primitive men came together and lived together. They thus formed an association through which there evolved first the individual minds and then the social mind. In his opinion, society is a large number of people living together in a territory, speaking a common language, and following a common way of behaviour, common customs and beliefs. He maintains that when an association of men in an area continues for a long time, it comes to have a stock of ideas, ideals, beliefs, values, etc., in which all individuals share and to which they contribute and which they even modify from time to time. Such a system of psychical forces is, of course, not a product of a particular individual mind and is not dependent upon the individual minds of any time. The system is there and is objective in the sense that it is embodied in the customs and institutions of society. It in its embodiment guides and regulates the behaviour of the social individuals.[15]

Like Aurobindo, Giddings suggests that human evolution starts at an infrarational stage in which men have not yet learned to determine their actions by intelligence. But he does not agree with Aurobindo when he says, "For they still act principally out of instincts, impulses, spontaneous ideas, vital intuitions or else obey a customary response to desire, need and circumstance—it is these things that are canalised or crystallised in their social institutions."[16]

The common stock of ideas, embodied in social institutions is the work of intelligence. That is why he refers to it as the social mind.

This common stock we can understand if we have understood what is called tradition. It is, as we know, a body of knowledge which is transmitted from generation to generation, and is ultimately based on public opinion.

15 F. H. Giddings, *The Principles of Sociology*, The Macmillan Company, New York, 1920, pp. 132-152.

16 *The Human Cycle*, Pondicherry, 1949, p. 228.

Public opinion. Public opinion means the opinion of the public. But who is the public? The phrase "the public" is taken to be opposed to "a single individual." The former in fact means all individuals of society, or a majority of them. There is public opinion about a matter when all or a majority of social individuals share an opinion about it. Generally, an individual forms his opinion about anything after having considered the pros and cons, i.e., after he has had much relevant experience and done a lot of thinking. Opinion is, therefore, a product of reason or intelligence. For instance, there is at present much talk about the devaluation of the rupee. One forms his opinion for or against it on his own grounds. But public opinion does not come about as the sum of such independent opinions similar to each other. It is not that everyone in the majority in question reasons and forms his opinion by deliberation. If we look into the origin and development of public opinion, we shall find that most people do not quite form the opinion they have, that they simply pick it up from the surroundings. It is true to say that public opinion is, in the ultimate analysis, the opinion of one influential man in society, or of a group of such men. As sociologists point out, behind public opinion there are certain agencies like the Press, Platform, and the Pulpit. In former times when religion held a sway over the people, sermons delivered from the Pulpit in the churches greatly moulded the minds of men. When Ram Mohun Roy, for example, wanted to abolish the barbarous custom called the *Suttee* the whole country was against him, and public opinion regarding the *Suttee*, as we should call it. was really the opinion of some religious leaders, the priests. But the influence of religion upon the popular mind waned long since. The Press and Platform, however, continued to play a vital role in the formation of public opinion.

The newspaper is a great innovation of modern times. It is so important that it seems that we can go without food but we cannot go without newspaper. It is the magic of a human organisation that news of the world reach us every morning through newspapers. There is, indeed, a double function of the Press. It supplies news from all sides and also makes comments on current events. It is this latter function which has a direct bearing upon public opinion. The common run of men have a great regard for news-editors and allowed themselves to be influenced by the ideas expressed in their editorials. There they find a ready-made opinion to accept, and they accept it forthwith. So editors have a great responsibility. They should therefore work out their ideas very carefully.

There is another side to the picture, however. Though the Press helps form public opinion, it is not true to say that it is formed by the Press alone. It may be that some people in society form their opinion after due deliberation, which spreads far as it is picked up by the people from one another. It is no doubt a long process, and public opinion takes a long time to form by this process. This was the inevitable one before the innovation of printing. Nowadays people express their ideas when they do so through books and journals. In any case, if there is public opinion, it is the duty of editors of journals to give an effective expression to it. Such a role is a worthy one they are to perform.

The platform also is important in so far as the formation of public opinion is concerned. In normal circumstances speakers address large audiences on issues—social, political and others, and try to persuade them to their way of thinking. Platform speakers are at an advantage especially in time of unrest or in an election in the country. By word of mouth they cover a large number of people in a comparatively short time. They also choose a short-cut to the fulfilment of their end. They in their speeches play upon the feelings and impulses of the audience and attempt an easy conversion of them to their doctrines. This is obviously a mischievous way of approach to the public and is the best way to mislead them. That way, surely, one man or a few men can manage to mould the views of a large number of people.

Nowadays the radio and television surpass the press and platform in propagating ideas. They cover a far wider range in a far shorter time. Through them speeches are broadcast. There is difference between the radio and television, however. In the case of the radio we only listen in, while we both listen and see in the television set. In the latter we see and hear at the same time the man who speaks at the Air Station. Television is communication both of the word of mouth and of the picture of the man who broadcasts.

Public opinion and tradition. Whatever be the conditions under which public opinion is formed, we may say that it exists as opposed to individual opinions. But, generally, public opinion is temporary; it comes and goes. Sometimes, however, the public opinion of this or that generation persists and settles down in society. The public opinions of many generations thus remain and combine to constitute what is called tradition. A tradition needs a fairly long time to take shape. Tradition is to society what memory is to an individual mind. An individual mind has at different moments experiences of different things. Some of these no doubt drop out but some remain in the mind. The faculty of retention is called memory, which is indeed aided by attention and interest. Public opinion, when formed, becomes in a way independent of the individual minds which nevertheless share in it. If public opinion proves socially useful, it persists in the social whole. Its persistence is conceived to be social memory, i.e., tradition.

Three kinds of tradition. Some sociologists distinguish between three kinds of tradition, primary, secondary, and tertiary. The primary tradition consists of the economic, juridical and political traditions. The secondary tradition is the record of the experiences of the invisible world, while the tertiary tradition covers cultural traditions.[17]

The primary tradition. (a) The economic tradition. As we have considered above, primitive men in the remote past gathered their daily food supply from their surroundings. Individuals went about in search of food, and their whole energy was expended in acquiring it. So there was no surplus energy left in them to play in any new direction. Later, however, they learnt to deposit food and provide against future. The daily acquisition of food is called the primary means of subsistence, while the saving of food for days ahead is called

17 Giddings, *The Principles of Sociology*, pp. 140-142.

the secondary means of subsistence. The development of the latter means of subsistence was very important as it made for much surplus energy which was in fact the cause of varied social development. But the secondary means of subsistence was based on the primary. If we reflect a little, we shall find that the primary means of subsistence presupposed much experience and labour concerning different things. Primitive men could know through elaborate experiences and experiments what things were, and what things were not, edible. Only through such a process they could develop a set of ideas about the eatable. These ideas were the basic economic ideas as they proved useful to the sustenance of life. As such ideas settled down in the individual minds, they became their common possession and were later transmitted from generation to generation. These in their settled form became a basic tradition. As the needs of the body were primary and pressing needs and as primitive men had to attend to them, the body of knowledge that was developed about things which satisfied the needs constituted the economic tradition. The economic is therefore a primary tradition. This tradition, indeed, developed as society developed and as individuals experienced new physical needs—housing, clothing, transport, etc., and discovered new utilities. But the root of the tradition lies in primitive society.

(b) *The juridical tradition* or *the tradition of toleration.* Society could not come into existence if individuals did not recognize their mutual rights. The minimum that was needed for society to exist was a set of norms of conduct, which would regulate the mutual relationships among individuals. They in fact followed the principle, "Live and let live." The norms were, of course, inarticulate at first and were in the form of customs. Primitive men adjusted themselves to one another through their customs and cultivated toleration under the customs. They recognized the fact that they could enjoy their right to live only by allowing others to do so. The customs of primitive society were later crystallized into laws which prescribed in articulate terms the modes of behaviour individuals were to adopt in relation to each other. Thus a fund of legalistic ideas was gradually developed by a progressive formulation of the modes of social conduct.

(c) *The political tradition.* Political life means life lived by a citizen of the State. There was a time when there was society but no State. The State, as a matter of fact, came into existence as an instrument of society. It came up to deal with the problem of law and order. The social laws were more or less prescriptive. If an individual defied them, there was no effective means of bringing him to book. It was primarily with the object of dealing with anti-socials that the State was brought into existence. It was given the sole authority to deal with those whose activities were disruptive of ordered life. Under the State the people learnt to obey and to do homage to the sovereign, how to fulfil their obligations and duties to their fellow-citizens. They also developed ideas regarding internal peace and defence of the State against external aggression. All these ideas gradually became permanent and settled down in society. These, later handed down from generation to generation and enhanced by new experiences, formed the political tradition of the people.

The Secondary tradition. The secondary tradition is divided into (a) the animistic, (b) aesthetic, and (c) religious traditions.

The animistic tradition. It is based on the idea that nothing in the world is lifeless and inert, that everything has a soul in it. Primitive people believed that there was a spirit in every phenomenon in the world. This belief was greatly responsible for a form of primitive religion which was worship of a multitude of gods and goddesses. The idea was that activity was an effect or expression of a spirit or conscious being. A primitive man was in some way aware of himself as a self and as he felt that all his activities proceeded from within of himself, he conceived all things and beings, even physical things, on the analogy of his own being. Such ideas settled down in primitive minds but were later liquidated at the advent of civilization, especially at the dawn of science.

The aesthetic and religious traditions. These two traditions relate to the invisible world that lies behind the visible one. They are based on experiences on the part of artists and religious teachers. A painter and a sculptor experience and enjoy beauty and give expression to their experiences and ideas through their creations—pictures and statues. There is indeed difference between art perception and ordinary perception. In the latter we perceive physical things that are there. It is true that the creations of an artist are physical. But their physicality does not reveal their artistic nature. So from the ordinary point of view there is no difference between any physical thing and an artistic creation. But as we come to recognize and appreciate an artistic piece, we understand that artistic perception and appreciation imply a level of experience different from that of ordinary perception. In the former there is a penetration into a realm beyond the physical, though whatever is grasped thereof is presented and preserved in sensuous garb. So an artistic creation only serves as a symbol for a non-sensuous truth received through a sensuous medium. It is for this reason that when we stand before an artistic creation and appreciate its beauty we are led away from the visible or the physical and are lost in contemplation. There is no denying that artistic creation, art perception and art appreciation presuppose some amount of culture in the percipient. But nevertheless artistic experiences and creations were there in primitive society. As art has an appeal to feeling and the heart rather than to reason, primitive men were presumably fitted for artistic creation and art appreciation. It is true that artistic ideas originated with some individuals. But they were shared by social individuals when they settled down in society. The accumulated artistic ideas of primitive men were transmitted from generation to generation and became the aesthetic tradition.

God is admittedly the object of religion. But religion has two sides, the inner and the outer. Ideas and beliefs constitute the inner side of religion, whereas the outer side of it is the expression of the ideas and beliefs. The outer side of religion is just what is called worship, which is practice and is visible to an observer as it consists of some rites, rituals and ceremonies. And ideas, beliefs and practices together constitute the content of a religion.

Generally speaking, a religion is based on the spiritual experiences of its founder. These experiences, though personal, are communicated to social individuals. And dogmas and doctrines come about by way of the formulation of the content of a religion in articulate terms. These become the articles of faith for those who accept the religious teacher as the guiding light in their lives. They, therefore, become a common possession of society, even though they originate from a definite individual. This point may be clarified by reference to the origin of any religion like Buddhism, Christianity, Hinduism, and Islam.

The Tertiary tradition. This is a third kind of tradition which is constituted by funded ideas based on speculation. There are three forms of it, namely, theology, metaphysics, and science.

Theology. There is an ambiguity about the word "theology". Some take it to mean the philosophy of religion. We may, however, make a distinction between theology and the philosophy of religion. The latter may be taken to be the speculative study of religion as such or of religion in its universal aspect, while the former may be regarded as the study of religion in its particularity, i.e., as an exposition or interpretation of a particular religion. Every religion has more or less a theology of its own and must have it because every religion carries about itself an explanation of its content. Theology as an exposition of the articles of faith involves some settled ideas about the world, including finite selves, and God, the Supreme Being. Such ideas nevertheless are not necessarily present in the consciousness of every individual who professes the faith. They are indeed recorded in books upon which social individuals draw as they feel the need to do so. Such ideas, though produced by an individual mind or some individual minds, are shared or are capable of being shared by individuals in society.

Metaphysics. Metaphysics is the speculative study of the world as a whole. It considers whether there is any ultimate reality behind the visible world, or whether the world as it exists is real. Metaphysics is, then, the body of knowledge that consists of some settled ideas regarding the nature of the world, the nature and status of the human beings, their ideals and aspirations. Such ideas are propounded by a man or some men and are recorded in books. But they do not necessarily enter into the consciousness of every individual in society. This recorded body of knowledge becomes a possession of society, however. It persists for the coming generations who may modify or enhance it, as the case may be. It ought to be clear nevertheless that every individual is not metaphysician and that every individual does not contribute to the metaphysical tradition. He in any case takes advantage of it, if he wishes to, or if he is capable of doing so. One fact stands out clear. It is that metaphysical ideas in their sum often percolate into the popular mind and determine to some extent the outlook on life.

Science. Science, on the other hand, is the study of empirical facts. It accepts them as real and then investigates their structure, relationships, laws, etc. Human beings live in their environment which comprises empirical things in their reciprocal relationships. So the body of knowledge called science has a direct bearing upon our practical life. This kind of knowledge is utilized for the purpose of life. Scientists being specialists, though everybody is not a scientist, yet most of the social individuals pick up scientific ideas and conceptions from the surronudings. It is nowadays common knowledge that a body cannot remain unsupported in the air, that one should not touch a live wire, that a machine is not moved by a ghost when it moves, but by power, that this or that disease is cured by a proper medicine, and so on. In short, the conception that every event has a cause comes from science and is part of the scientific tradition. This tradition obviously plays a very important role in moulding the minds and behaviour of the social individuals.

We should, however, bear in mind the fact that the tertiary traditions develop only in civilization. It is only when society has reached a fairly developed stage that the human pursuit of knowledge ramifies and that thinkers come up to develop their ideas or conceptions regarding life, religion and the rest.

Is the common stock of ideas, beliefs, etc., the social mind? We should now consider whether the common stock of ideas, ideals, beliefs, etc., is to be called the social mind. According to Giddings, it is to be so called. But he does not mean to say that society as against the individuals has a mind of its own. He is definitely of the opinion that society is "an association of minds." So there is or can be no mind as apart from an individual. Nonetheless, the social mind is not an abstraction from individual minds. It is not that we exclude the differences of the individual minds and sift out their common features. There are indeed some characteristics common to them all. But there is no justification for calling these common characteristics the social mind, for a mind cannot float about, but must have a locus. Giddings lays emphasis on the common stock of ideas, etc., which is not dependent upon any single individual Individuals no doubt contribute to this stock. But once the stock is created, it becomes independent of the individuals, in the sense that it is external to them and that it regulates their activities from outside. Individuals come and go. But the stock remains and even grows and develops. There is therefore some justification for calling this stock the social mind. This stock, to be sure, exists in individual minds, but not as ideas of individual minds. If this be so, the stock can be taken to represent one peculiar aspect, i.e., the super-individual aspect of the individual minds, that aspect which determines them in relation to each other. Psycho-analysts speak of three layers or levels of the individual mind—the conscious, the subconscious, and the unconscious. Jung speaks also of the collective unconscious. He means to say that the collective unconscious is the source of links between individual minds. We, of course, cannot say that the social mind belongs to the unconscious. Still, it is the general background against which the individual minds work.

INDEX

A

Africa, 7
Agnatic relation, 88
America, 7
Animal Society, 3
Anthropology, 11
Archaeology, 11
Aristotle, 20, 76, 163, 173, 174
Arranged marriage, 136
Aspects of marriage, 115
Association, 31, 33
Atomistic conception of society, 159
Auguste Comte, 5, 14
Aurobindo, 50
Aurobindo's theory of education, 193

B

Baccalaureate, 177
Basic education, 190
Basis of the family, 95
Behaviour of organism, 15
Birth control, 97
Book-learning, 179
Bosanquet, 2, 215

C

Cathedral schools, 177
Caste, 28
Charlemagne, 176, 177
Child as the basis of the family, 97
City-State, 12
Co-education, 202
Classificatory system, 86
Cole, 26, 57
Community, 25, 145
Comparative Philology, 4
Conception of Society, 161
Consciousness of Kind, 63, 78
Contract theories of society, 69
Cross-cousin marriage, 41
Custom, 34, 35, 36

D

Deliberate actions, 19
Departmental study, 21
Dipankar, 186
Disciplines for four Classes, 141
Durkheim, 210
Divine law, 37
Division of labour, 144
Divorce, 99
Dogmas, 227
Dynamic forces, 16

E

Earliest form of the family, 82
Education, 170
Education of ancient India, 183
Engels, 100
English education, 186
Endogamy, 126
Environment, 49
Epicurus, 66
Exogamy, 126
Experiment, 44
Explanation of the whole, 18
Evolution of marriage, 119

F

Fa Hien, 185
Faculty of intuition, 195
Family, 80
Forms of family, 84
Forms of Hindu marriage, 136
Four Castes, 139
Fourfold organization of society, 66
Freedom, 180, 181

G

Gāndharva, 132, 133
General will 216
Geographical area, 11, 16
Geology, 11, 82
Giddings, 4, 6, 9, 74, 76, 228
Ginsberg, 25, 59, 216
Gotra, 128
God, 174, 193, 226, 227
Grammar, 179
Greece, 13, 171
Group mind, 211
Gymnastic, 171

H

Head of the family, 65
Hegel, 137
Herbert Spencer, 4, 5, 163
Herding instinct, 22, 65
History of society, 10
Historical method, 50, 51
Hitler, 99

Hobbes, 67
Hobhouse, 217
Householder, 150
Human infants, 163
Huen Tsang, 185

I

Ideal form of marriage, 136
Ideal system of education, 180
Imitation, 73
Instinct, 3
Institution, 32
Involuntary actions, 18
Individual minds, 3, 7, 16
Individuals, 161, 162, 163
Individual and society, 165

J

Jesus Christ, 38, 77
Juridical tradition, 224
Jurisprudence, 37, 39
Justification of the social mind, 229

K

Khasia Hills, 92
Kindergarten, 200
Kinds of tradition, 223
Kurukṣetra, 93

L

Late marriage, 107
Law and order, 225
Learned language, 179
Levirate, 85
Locke, 68, 177
Love and sex, 116

M

MacIver and Page, 26
Mahatma Gandhi, 189
McTaggart, 209
McDougall, 15, 211
Manu, 149
Marriage, by capture, 138
Marriage and domestic work , 114
Marriage relation, 138
Marx, 101
Mechanical explanation, 52, 160
Mechanical whole, 161
Mechanisation of man, 99
Medicine, 162, 170
Medium of instruction, 195
Mental phenomena, 16
Mill, 36
Modern education, 196
Modern family, 103
Monogamy, 101, 120, 123
Montesquieu, 77
Morgan, 84
Music 172
Mussolini, 99
Mutual aid, 75

N

Nālandā, 185
Norm, 19
Normative science, 19

O

Objective method, 45
Obligations, 225
Observation, 44
Old Testament, 118
Organism, 5, 162
Organistic conception of society, 161
Origin of the State, 72
Origin of the four castes, 142

P

Parental instinct, 57
Patriarchal family, 89
Patria potestas, 88, 103, 109
Perception of utility, 66
Philology, 9
Philosophy of history, 21
Plan of Nature, 53
Plato, 65, 66, 98, 144, 145, 163, 170, 172, 174, 179
Primary tradition, 223
Primitive society, 65
Property, 33
Psychology, 15
Public opinion, 221
Purdah, 103

R

Rabindranath, 187
Ram Mohun Roy, 203
Relation between philosophy and science, 1
Religious education, 190, 206
Relation between sociology and some sciences, 11
Republic, 170, 173, 179
Rights of women, 105
Roman Code, 39
Roman Empire, 189
Roman Law, 39
Ross, 45
Rousseau, 69, 71, 177, 212
Rousseau's theory of education, 179

S

Sacred dishes, 41
Saptapadī, 155
Science of medicine, 162
Sex, 57
Sex life, 1, 12

Scientific civilization, 11, 16
Social adaptation, 48
Social composition, 42
Social constitution, 43
Social function, 156
Social nature, 56, 66, 78
Social recognition, 119
Social harmony, 217
Social Mind, 209
Social sanction, 81
Social science, 1
Society, 2, 3, 11, 16, 17, 35, 50, 65
Sociology, 5, 6, 10
Statisical method, 51, 53
Status of women in ancient India, 102
Student life, 184
Śūdras, 184
Superorganic development, 22
Supreme Court, 40
Svayaṁvarma, 135

T

Tables of Rome, 39, 40, 41
Taboo, 40, 41
Teleological method, 53
Tertiary tradition, 227, 228
The State, 7
The social philosopher, 16
The state of Nature, 69
Theology, 227
Totemism, 127

U

Unconscious, 229
University education, 177
University of Paris, 177
University of Taxila, 185
Utility, 64
Upanayana, 149

V

Varṇa, 140
Varṇāśrama-Dharma, 148
Vedic education, 183, 184
Vedic people, 65, 185

W

Weber, 52
Westermarck, 92
Widowed woman, 35
World Community, 37
Wündt, 217